T0212638

Lecture Notes in Computer Science 13139

More information about this subseries at https://link.springer.com/bookseries/7410

Dimitri Percia David · Alain Mermoud ·
Thomas Maillart (Eds.)

Critical Information Infrastructures Security

16th International Conference, CRITIS 2021
Lausanne, Switzerland, September 27–29, 2021
Revised Selected Papers

 Springer

Editors
Dimitri Percia David ⓘ
University of Geneva
Geneva, Switzerland

Alain Mermoud ⓘ
armasuisse Science and Technology S+T
Thun, Switzerland

Thomas Maillart ⓘ
University of Geneva
Geneva, Switzerland

ISSN 0302-9743   ISSN 1611-3349 (electronic)
Lecture Notes in Computer Science
ISBN 978-3-030-93199-5   ISBN 978-3-030-93200-8 (eBook)
https://doi.org/10.1007/978-3-030-93200-8

LNCS Sublibrary: SL4 – Security and Cryptology

This Springer imprint is published by the registered company Springer Nature Switzerland AG
The registered company address is: Gewerbestrasse 11, 6330 Cham, Switzerland

Preface

This volume contains the proceedings of the 16th International Conference on Critical Information Infrastructures Security (CRITIS 2021). The conference was held during September 27–29, 2021, at the EPFL SwissTech Convention Center (STCC) in Lausanne, Switzerland. The CRITIS community was delighted to be back in Switzerland, as the 6th edition of the conference (CRITIS 2011) was held in Lucerne exactly 10 years ago.

CRITIS 2021 was hosted in hybrid mode at EPFL by Trust Valley, the University of Geneva, and the Cyber-Defence Campus of armasuisse S+T, the Swiss Federal Office for Defence Procurement. Despite the pandemic, over 130 participants registered for the onsite conference and about 100 participants registered for the online option. Overall, the conference enabled the connection of different continents and time zones, audiences, and scientific disciplines, as well as generations of researchers.

On the second day, the conference was held in conjunction with a Cyber-Defence (CYD) Campus conference. Indeed, the CYD Campus and CRITIS share an important goal: to provide a platform to bring together different audiences from academia, industry, and government. Ongoing discussions between these audiences can be found on social media with the hashtags #CRITIS2021 and/or #CYDCAMPUS, as well as on the conference Twitter account: @critis21.

The final conference program is available on the conference website. The 40 conference podcasts are available for download (HD, 1080p) here. As a thank you to the attendants, pre-proceedings, video recordings, slides and conference pictures are available in the following shared drive, password: *SwissTech2021*. The conference program and podcasts, as well as conference pictures and slides are available on the conference website: critis2021.org

In total, 42 papers (full and short) were submitted on EasyChair, the scientific conference management platform used for CRITIS 2021. Each paper received a minimum of three double-blind reviews thanks to the thorough and generous work of the Technical Program Committee, which welcomed over 10 new active members this year.

As a result of this double-blind peer-review process, 12 full papers were accepted (one with shepherding) along with one short paper, which brings the overall acceptance rate to about 30%, thus maintaining the scientific quality of the conference. Additionally, eight keynotes, two testbeds, three demonstrations and five posters were accepted for presentation at the conference. Accepted papers were presented in four scientific sessions (reflected in the structure of this volume) organized around the following topics:

1. Protection of Cyber-Physical Systems and Industrial Control Systems (ICS)
2. C(I)IP Organisation, (Strategic) Management and Legal Aspects
3. Human Factor, Security Awareness and Crisis Management for C(I)IP and Critical Services
4. Future, TechWatch and Forecast for C(I)IP and Critical Services

Three industrial sessions (one per day) were chaired by David Baschung to allow major players from industry to present current challenges and solutions to better protect critical infrastructures and critical services. The panel discussions were particularly interesting for building bridges between the academic world and industry.

On September 28, the CYD Campus hosted its start-up challenge organized around the topic 'Boost your Information Sharing and Analysis Center (ISAC)'. The three finalists were the following:

1. Decentriq
2. Constella Intelligence
3. Pandora Intelligence

Following in the footsteps of the previous years, CRITIS 2021 awarded prizes to the best young researchers:

1. Siddhant Shrivastava, Singapore University of Technology and Design
2. Santiago Anton Moreno, EPFL
3. Stéphanie Lebrun, CYD Campus

We thank the Master of Advanced Studies in Information Security of the University of Geneva for sponsoring the award, thus helping the event carry on through the years.

In summary, CRITIS 2021 continued the well-established series of successful CRITIS conferences. We hope it will remain a memorable edition that also tried to bring new features to the community: hybrid mode and podcasts, paper shepherding, a rump session, and a scientific session on technology market monitoring and forecasting.

Organizing a conference in the middle of a pandemic is a tough challenge. A big thank you goes to all our stakeholders for their trust and to all our sponsors for their precious support: Fortinet, ELCA, AWK Group, Monti Stampa Furrer & Partners AG, AdNovum, Kudelski Security, and the University of Geneva.

We wish Stefan Pickl every success as he takes over the role of general chair for CRITIS 2022, which will take place in Germany at the Bundeswehr University Munich. The CRITIS franchise is thus in good hands and its future is fully assured, thanks also to the good advice of Bernhard Hämmerli, head of the CRITIS Steering Committee.

October 2021

Alain Mermoud
Dimitri Percia David
Thomas Maillart

Organization

General Co-chairs

Alain Mermoud   Cyber-Defence Campus armasuisse S+T, Switzerland
Thomas Maillart   University of Geneva, Switzerland

Program Committee Co-chairs

Dimitri Percia David   University of Geneva, Switzerland
Alain Mermoud   Cyber-Defence Campus armasuisse S+T, Switzerland

Steering Committee

Bernhard Hämmerli (Chair)   Lucerne University of Applied Sciences, Switzerland
Javier Lopez (Chair)   University of Malaga, Spain
Stephen Wolthusen (Chair)   Royal Holloway, University of London, UK
Robin Bloomfield   City University London, UK
Sandro Bologna   AIIC, Italy
Gregorio D'Agostino   ENEA, Italy
Grigore Havarneanu   International Union of Railways (UIC), France
Sokratis Katsikas   Norwegian University of Science and Technology, Norway
Eric Luiijf   TNO (retired), The Netherlands
Alain Mermoud   Cyber-Defence Campus armasuisse S+T, Switzerland
Marios Polycarpou   University of Cyprus, Cyprus
Reinhard Posch   Technical University Graz, Austria
Erich Rome   Fraunhofer IAIS, Germany
Antonio Scala   IMT-CNR, Italy
Inga Šarūnienė   Lithuanian Energy Institute, Lithuania
Roberto Setola   Università Campus Bio-Medico di Roma, Italy
Nils Kalstad Svendsen   Gjovik University College, Norway
Marianthi Theocharidou   European Commission Joint Research Centre, Italy

Technical Program Committee

Cristina Alcaraz   University of Malaga, Spain
Magnus Almgren   Chalmers University of Technology, Sweden
Fabrizio Baiardi   University of Pisa, Italy
Sandro Bologna   Association of Critical Infrastructure Experts, Italy
Tom Chothia   University of Birmingham, UK

Gregorio D'Agostino	Italian National Agency for New Technologies, Italy
Geert Deconinck	KU Leuven, Belgium
Steven Furnell	University of Nottingham, UK
Jairo Giraldo	University of Utah, USA
Dimitris Gritzalis	Athens University of Economics and Business, Greece
Bernhard Hämmerli	Lucerne University of Applied Sciences, Switzerland
Chris Hankin	Imperial College London, UK
Grigore Havarneanu	International Union of Railways (UIC), France
Chad Heitzenrater	US Air Force Research Laboratory, USA
Kévin Huguenin	University of Lausanne, Switzerland
Mathias Humbert	Cyber-Defence Campus armasuisse S+T, Switzerland
Mikel Iturbe	Mondragon Unibertsitatea, Spain
Zbigniew Kalbarczyk	University of Illinois, USA
Sokratis Katsikas	Norwegian University of Science and Technology, Norway
Marieke Klaver	TNO, The Netherlands
Vytis Kopustinskas	European Commission Joint Research Centre, Italy
Panayiotis Kotzanikolaou	University of Piraeus, Greece
Marina Krotofil	Hamburg University of Technology, Germany
Jean-Yves Le Boudec	EPFL, Switzerland
Vincent Lenders	Cyber-Defence Campus armasuisse S+T, Switzerland
Javier Lopez	University of Malaga, Spain
Thomas Maillart	University of Geneva, Switzerland
Linas Martišauskas	Lithuanian Energy Institute, Lithuania
Marcelo Masera	European Commission Joint Research Centre, Italy
Kieran Mclaughlin	Queen's University Belfast, UK
Alain Mermoud	Cyber-Defence Campus armasuisse S+T, Switzerland
Simin Nadjm-Tehrani	Linköping University, Sweden
Sebastian Obermeier	Lucerne University of Applied Sciences, Switzerland
Diego Ortiz Yepes	Lucerne University of Applied Sciences, Switzerland
Stefano Panzieri	Roma Tre University, Italy
Mario Paolone	EPFL, Switzerland
Dimitri Percia David	University of Geneva, Switzerland
Adrian Perrig	ETH Zurich, Switzerland
Stefan Pickl	Universität der Bundeswehr München, Germany
Ludovic Pietre-Cambacedes	Électricité de France (EDF), France
Peter Popov	City University London, UK
Awais Rashid	University of Bristol, UK
Anne Remke	University of Münster, Germany
Brian Sadler	US Army Research Laboratory, USA
Andre Samberg	European Commission, Belgium
Henrik Sandberg	KTH Royal Institute of Technology, Sweden
Patrick Schaller	ETH Zurich, Switzerland
Roberto Setola	Università Campus Bio-Medico di Roma, Italy
Florian Skopik	Austrian Institute of Technology, Austria
Vladimir Stankovic	City University London, UK

Martin Strohmeier   Cyber-Defence Campus armasuisse S+T, Switzerland
Nils Ole Tippenhauer   Helmholtz Center for Information Security, Germany
Alberto Tofani   Italian National Agency for New Technologies, Italy
Claire Vishik   Intel Corporation, UK
Florian Wamser   University of Würzburg, Germany
Jianying Zhou   Singapore University of Technology and Design,
                           Singapore
Inga Žutautaitė   Lithuanian Energy Institute, Lithuania

Industrial/Practical Experience Reports Chair

David Baschung   Military Academy at ETH Zurich, Switzerland

Young CRITIS Award Chairs

Thomas Maillart   University of Geneva, Switzerland
Bernhard Hämmerli   Lucerne University of Applied Sciences, Switzerland

Local Organizing Chair

Lena Perrenoud   EPFL SwissTech Convention Center, Switzerland

Publicity, Communication, and Sponsorship Chair

Kilian Cuche   Armed Forces Command Support Organisation of
                           DDPS, Switzerland

Registration, Merchandising, and Social Events Chairs

Monia Khelifi   Cyber-Defence Campus armasuisse S+T, Switzerland
Sarah Frei   Cyber-Defence Campus armasuisse S+T, Switzerland

Sponsors

Contents

Protection of Cyber-Physical Systems and Industrial Control Systems (ICS)

Bank of Models: Sensor Attack Detection and Isolation in Industrial Control Systems

Chuadhry Mujeeb Ahmed[1][(✉)] and Jianying Zhou[2]

[1] Computer and Information Sciences, University of Strathclyde, Glasgow, Scotland
`mujeeb.ahmed@strath.ac.uk`
[2] Singapore University of Technology and Design, Singapore, Singapore
`jianying_zhou@sutd.edu.sg`

Abstract. Attacks on sensor measurements can take the system to an unwanted state. The disadvantage of using a system model-based approach for attack detection is that it could not isolate which sensor was under attack. For example, if one of two sensors that are physically coupled is under attack, the attack would reflect in both. In this work, we propose an attack detection and isolation technique using a multi-model framework named *Bank of Models* (BoM) in which the same process will be represented by multiple system models. This technique can achieve higher accuracy for attack detection with low false alarm rates. We make extensive empirical performance evaluation on a realistic ICS testbed to demonstrate the viability of this technique.

Keywords: Sensor security · Attack detection · Industrial control systems

1 Introduction

An Industrial Control System (ICS) is a combination of computing elements and physical phenomenon [37]. In particular, we will consider examples of a water treatment plant in this paper. An ICS consists of cyber components such as Programmable Logic Controllers (PLCs), sensors, actuators, Supervisory Control and Data Acquisition (SCADA) workstation, and Human Machine Interface (HMI) elements interconnected via a communications network. The advances in communication technologies resulted in the widespread of such systems to better monitor and operate ICS, but this connectivity also exposes physical processes to malicious entities on the cyber domain [8,30]. Recent incidents of sabotage on these systems [9,16], have raised concerns on the security of ICS.

Challenges in ICS security are different as compared with conventional IT systems, especially in terms of consequences in case of a security lapse [5]. Attacks on ICS might result in damage to the physical property [12,48] or severely affecting people who depend on critical infrastructure as was the case of the recent

© Springer Nature Switzerland AG 2021
D. Percia David et al. (Eds.): CRITIS 2021, LNCS 13139, pp. 3–23, 2021.
https://doi.org/10.1007/978-3-030-93200-8_1

power cutoff in Ukraine [9]. Data integrity is an important security requirement for ICS [22] therefore, the integrity of sensor data should be ensured. Sensor data can either be spoofed in cyber (digital) domain [44] or in physical (analog) domain [42]. Sensors are a bridge between the physical and cyber domains in an ICS. Traditionally, an intrusion detection system (IDS) monitors a communication network or a computing host to detect attacks. However, physical tampering with sensors or sensor spoofing in the physical/analog domain may go undetected by IDS based only on network traffic [42]. Recently, a live-fire cyber attack-defense exercise on ICS, evaluated commercially available network layer attack detection products with the process-aware research prototypes and concluded that the network-only products do not succeed in detecting process layer attacks [25].

Data integrity attacks on sensor measurement and the impact of such attacks have been studied in theory, including false data injection [35], replay attacks [34], DoS attacks [28] and stealthy attacks [13]. These previous studies proposed attack detection methods based on the system model and statistical fault detectors [1,3,7] and also point out the limitations of such fault detectors against an adversarial manipulation of the sensor data. A major limitation of these model based attack detection methods, is that it is difficult to isolate the attacks.

The Attack Isolation Problem: The attack isolation problem also known as determining the source of an attack is important in the context of ICS [49]. Anomaly detection research suffers from this issue, especially methods rooted in machine learning [2,43]. Using machine learning methods with the available data might be able to raise an alarm but are not able to find the source of the anomaly. In the context of ICS, if a model is created for the whole process it is not clear where does an anomaly is coming from?

Motivating Example: To understand the idea, we need to consider an example from the SWaT testbed [33]. SWaT is a six-stage water treatment plant. Figure 1 shows stage 1 of the SWaT testbed. This stage holds the raw water that is to be processed. The central entity is a water storage tank with a level sensor (LIT-101). For this example, we shall focus on another sensor that is the flow sensor (FIT-201) at the outlet of the tank to measure the outflow of the water from the tank. LIT-101 and FIT-101 are coupled physically, meaning when FIT shows outflow level shall go down in LIT-101. In the following, this explanation will help us understand the problem.

Figures 2 and 3 show an example of such a problem in a real water treatment process in which both sensor measurements and estimates are obtained through process models. Figure 2 depicts a flow meter at the outlet of the raw water storage tank labeled as FIT-201. A joint physical system model for the stage 1 is created using a Kalman filter (more details on this in Sect. 2). Such a system model captures the dynamics of the physical process. In our case, the physical process is an example of a water storage tank, which collects a limited amount of water to be used by the subsequent stages of the water treatment testbed. It is intuitive to understand that there is a physical relationship between the physical

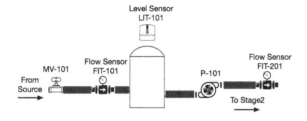

Fig. 1. Stage 1 of the SWaT Testbed.

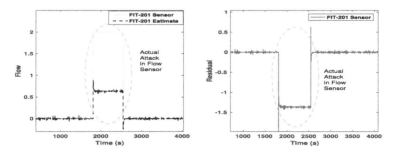

Fig. 2. Flow sensor, FIT-201 is under attack. Flow is simulated to be $2 \, \mathrm{m}^3/\mathrm{hr}$ while in reality it is zero. From the residual signal it could be detected. However, we will see this attack affecting system model for LIT-101 as well in Fig. 3.

quantities, for example, consider that when water flows out of the tank through the outlet pipe then the level of the water should fall in the tank. Hence, water level sensor LIT-101 and outlet flow sensor FIT-201 are physically coupled with each other. In the example attack, an attacker spoofs the flow sensor FIT-201 by spoofing the real sensor measurements of zero flow to $2 \, \mathrm{m}^3/\mathrm{hr}$ volumetric flow level. In the left-hand part of the Fig. 2, sensor measurements and estimates are shown before, during and after the attack. The difference between the sensor measurements and estimates is given as residual on the right-hand plot. It can be seen that the attack would be detected using a model-based detector [3] on FIT-201 residual. However, from Fig. 3 it can be seen that the same attack is detected using the detector for the LIT-101 sensor. For the Fig. 3 it could be seen that using the system model the estimate for the level tends to decrease, for the reason that if there is outflow the level should be decreased, but since there is an attack going on, it could be seen that the estimate deviates from the real sensor measurements. The model-based detectors defined for both level sensor and flow sensor would raise an alarm. It is not possible to figure out where is the actual attack unless manually checked. The problem of attack isolation is important considering the scale and complexity of an ICS. Attack detection and isolating the devices that are under attack is critical for response and recovery.

Proposed Solution: We propose a multi-model framework named Bank of Models (BoM) to detect and isolate attacks on the sensors in an ICS. The proposed attack detection framework improves on the limitations of model-based

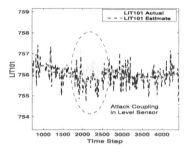 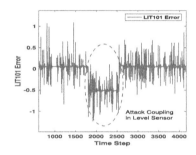

Fig. 3. The attack in flow sensor seen in Fig. 2, can be observed in LIT-101 as well. This is precisely the attack isolation problem, meaning an attack originating in one component can appear in multiple devices.

attack detection schemes [4,44]. BoM uses the estimates for each sensor obtained from the multiple system models. It then creates a profile for each sensor based on a set of time domain and frequency domain features that are extracted from the residual vector (difference between sensor measurement and sensor estimate). A one-class Support Vector Machine (SVM) is used to detect attacks for a multitude of industrial sensors. Experiments are performed on an operational water treatment facility accessible for research [33]. A class of attacks as explained in the threat model are launched on a real water treatment testbed. The major contributions of this work are thus:

- A novel BoM framework to detect and isolate sensor attacks.
- A detailed evaluation of the proposed technique as an attack detection method, for a class of sensor spoofing attacks.
- Extensive empirical performance evaluation on a realistic ICS testbed.
- An ensemble of models based algorithm to increase the attack detection rate and reduction in the false alarm rate.

2   System and Threat Model

2.1   System Dynamics

A system model represents the system dynamics in a mathematical form. A linear time invariant system model is obtained using either first principles (laws of Physics) or subspace system identification techniques. Then, we construct a Kalman filter which is used to obtain estimates for the system states and to find the residual vector. We studied the system design and functionality of the water treatment (SWaT) testbed [33] to obtain the system model. We used data collected under regular operation (no attacks) and subspace system identification techniques [38] to obtain a system model. For SWaT testbed, resulting system model is a Linear Time Invariant (LTI) discrete time state space model of the form:

$$\begin{cases} x_{k+1} = Ax_k + Bu_k + v_k, \\ y_k = Cx_k + \eta_k. \end{cases} \tag{1}$$

where $k \in \mathbb{N}$ is the discrete time index, $x_k \in \mathbb{R}^n$ is the state of the approximated model (its dimension depends on the order of the approximated model), $y \in \mathbb{R}^m$ are the measured outputs, and $u \in \mathbb{R}^p$ denote the control actions. A, B, C are the state space matrices, capturing the system dynamics. η_k is the sensor measurement noise and v_k is the process noise.

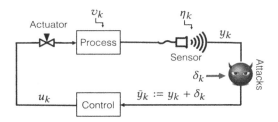

Fig. 4. A general CPS under sensor attacks.

2.2 Threat Model

At the time-instants $k \in \mathbb{N}$, the output of the process y_k is sampled and transmitted over a communication channel as shown in Fig. 4. The control action u_k is computed based on the received sensor measurement $\bar{y}_k$. Data is exchanged between different entities of this control loop and it is transmitted via communication channels. There are many potential points where an attacker can compromise the system. For instance, through the *Man-in-The-Middle (MiTM)* attack at the communication channels and physical attacks directly on the infrastructure. In this paper, we focus on sensor spoofing attacks, which could be accomplished through a *Man-in-The-Middle (MiTM)* scheme [44] or a replacement of on board PLC software [20]. After each transmission and reception, the attacked output $\bar{y}_k$ takes the form:

$$\bar{y}_k := y_k + \delta_k = Cx_k + \eta_k + \delta_k, \tag{2}$$

where $\delta_k \in \mathbb{R}^m$ denotes sensor attacks.

Assumptions on Attacker: It is assumed that the attacker has access to $y_{k,i} = C_i x_k + \eta_{k,i}$ (i.e., the opponent has access to i^{th} sensor measurements). Also, the attacker knows the system dynamics, the state space matrices, the control inputs and outputs, and the implemented detection procedure. All the attacks taken from reference work [21] are executed by compromising the Supervisory Control and Data Acquisition (SCADA) system. An attack toolbox was used to inject an arbitrary value for real sensor measurement.

3   Attack Detection and Isolation

The Problem of State Estimation: State estimation is to estimate the physical state variable of a system given the previous state measurement. A general state estimation problem can be formulated as,

$$\hat{X}_{k+1} = A\hat{X}_k + BU_k + L(\bar{Y}_k - \hat{Y}_k), \tag{3}$$

Equation (3) presents a general estimator design, where L is a gain matrix calculated to minimize the estimation error. $\hat{Y}$ and $\hat{X}$ are estimated system output and system state, respectively. Let's consider an example of a system model with two outputs and one control input and Eq. (3) becomes,

$$\begin{bmatrix} \hat{x}^1_{k+1} \\ \hat{x}^2_{k+1} \end{bmatrix} = \begin{bmatrix} a_{11} \, a_{12} \\ a_{21} \, a_{22} \end{bmatrix} \begin{bmatrix} \hat{x}^1_k \\ \hat{x}^2_k \end{bmatrix} + \begin{bmatrix} b_{11} \\ b_{21} \end{bmatrix} U_k + \begin{bmatrix} l_{11} \, l_{12} \\ l_{21} \, l_{22} \end{bmatrix} \begin{bmatrix} e(y^1_k) \\ e(y^2_k) \end{bmatrix} \tag{4}$$

$$\begin{matrix} \hat{x}^1_{k+1} \\ \hat{x}^2_{k+1} \end{matrix} = \begin{matrix} a_{11}\hat{x}^1_k + a_{12}\,\hat{x}^2_k + b_{11}u_k \\ a_{21}\hat{x}^1_k + a_{22}\,\hat{x}^2_k + b_{21}u_k \end{matrix} + \begin{matrix} l_{11}e(y^1_k) + l_{12}\,e(y^2_k) \\ l_{21}e(y^1_k) + l_{22}\,e(y^2_k) \end{matrix} \tag{5}$$

The two system state estimates are labeled as $\hat{x}^1_k$ and $\hat{x}^2_k$. It can be observed from (5) that the state estimate $\hat{x}^1_{k+1}$ at $k + 1^{th}$ time instance depends on error from both the outputs, i.e., $e(y^1_k)$ and $e(y^2_k)$ since the estimator is designed for both the sensors as a joint model. In this study, we have used Kalman filter to estimate the state of the system based on the available output y_k,

$$\hat{x}_{k+1} = A\hat{x}_k + Bu_k + L_k(\bar{y}_k - C\hat{x}_k), \tag{6}$$

with estimated state $\hat{x}_k \in \mathbb{R}^n$, $\hat{x}_1 = E[x(t_1)]$, where $E[\cdot]$ denotes expectation, and gain matrix $L_k \in \mathbb{R}^{n \times m}$. Define the estimation error $e_k := x_k - \hat{x}_k$. In the Kalman filter, the matrix L_k is designed to minimize the covariance matrix $P_k := E[e_k e_k^T]$ (in the absence of attacks). Given the system model (1) and the estimator (6), the estimation error is governed by the following difference equation

$$e_{k+1} = (A - L_kC)e_k - L_k\eta_k - L_k\delta_k + v_k. \tag{7}$$

If the pair (A, C) is detectable, the covariance matrix converges to steady state in the sense that $\lim_{k \to \infty} P_k = P$ exists [6]. We assume that the system has reached steady state before an attack occurs. Then, the estimation of the random sequence $x_k, k \in \mathbb{N}$ can be obtained by the estimator (6) with P_k and L_k in steady state. It can be verified that, if $R_2 + CPC^T$ is positive definite, the following estimator gain

$$L_k = L := (APC^T)(R_2 + CPC^T)^{-1}, \tag{8}$$

leads to the minimal steady state covariance matrix P, with P given by the solution of the algebraic Riccati equation:

$$APA^T - P + R_1 = APC^T(R_2 + CPC^T)^{-1}CPA^T. \tag{9}$$

The reconstruction method given by (6)–(9) is referred to as the steady state Kalman Filter, cf. [6].

3.1   Attack Detection Framework

In this section, we explain the details of the proposed attack detection scheme. First, we use the Kalman filter based state estimation to generate residual (difference between sensor measurement and estimate). Then, we present the design of our residual-based attack detection method.

Proposition 1. In steady state [6], residual vector is a function of sensor and process noise. Consider the process (1), the Kalman filter (6)–(9). The residual vector is given as, $r_k = Ce_k + \eta_k$ and $e_k = \sum_{i=0}^{k-2}(A - LC)^i(v_{k-i-1} - L\eta_{k-i-1})$, where $v_k \in \mathbb{R}^n$ is the process noise and $\eta_k \in \mathbb{R}^m$ is the sensor noise.

Proof: The state estimation error is the difference between real system state and estimated system state and can be presented as,

$$e_{k+1} = x_{k+1} - \hat{x}_{k+1} \qquad (10)$$

From system state Eq. (1) and state estimation Eq. (6), by substituting the equations for x_{k+1} and $\hat{x}_{k+1}$ we get,

$$e_{k+1} = Ax_k + Bu_k + v_k - A\hat{x}_k - Bu_k - L(y_k - \hat{y}_k) \qquad (11)$$

For $y_k = Cx_k + \eta_k$ and $\hat{y}_k = C\hat{x}_k$ we get,

$$e_{k+1} = A(x_k - \hat{x}_k) + v_k - L(Cx_k + \eta_k - C\hat{x}_k) \qquad (12)$$

As $e_k = x_k - \hat{x}_k$ we get,

$$e_{k+1} = Ae_k + v_k - LCe_k - L\eta_k \qquad (13)$$

$$e_{k+1} = (A - LC)e_k + v_k - L\eta_k \qquad (14)$$

■

Using system model and system state estimates it is possible to extract the residual as defined above. Once we have obtained these residual vectors capturing the modeled behaviour of the given ICS, we can proceed with pattern recognition techniques (e.g. machine learning) to detect anomalies.

Design of the Proposed Framework The proposed scheme begins with data collection and then divides data into smaller chunks to extract a set of time domain and frequency domain features. Features are combined and labeled with a sensor ID. A machine learning algorithm is used for sensor classification under normal operation.

Residual Collection: The next step after obtaining a system model for an ICS is to calculate the residual vector as explained in previous section. Residual is collected for different types of industrial sensors present in SWaT testbed. The objective of residual collection step is to extract a set of features by analyzing the residual vector. When the plant is running, an error in sensor reading is a combination of sensor noise and process noise (water sloshing etc.). The collected residual is analyzed, in time and frequency domains. Each sensor is profiled using variance and other statistical features in the residual vector as shown in the Table 1. A machine learning algorithm is used to profile sensors from fresh readings (test-data).

Table 1. List of features used. Vector x is time domain data from the sensor for N elements in the data chunk. Vector y is the frequency domain feature of sensor data. y_f is the vector of bin frequencies and y_m is the magnitude of the frequency coefficients.

Feature	Description
Mean	$\bar{x} = \frac{1}{N} \sum_{i=1}^{N} x_i$
Std-Dev	$\sigma = \sqrt{\frac{1}{N-1} \sum_{i=1}^{N} (x_i - \bar{x}_i)^2}$
Mean Avg. Dev	$D_{\bar{x}} = \frac{1}{N} \sum_{i=1}^{N} |x_i - \bar{x}|$
Skewness	$\gamma = \frac{1}{N} \sum_{i=1}^{N} \left(\frac{x_i - \bar{x}}{\sigma}\right)^3$
Kurtosis	$\beta = \frac{1}{N} \sum_{i=1}^{N} \left(\frac{x_i - \bar{x}}{\sigma}\right)^4 - 3$
Spec. Std-Dev	$\sigma_s = \sqrt{\frac{\sum_{i=1}^{N} (y_f(i)^2) * y_m(i)}{\sum_{i=1}^{N} y_m(i)}}$
Spec. Centroid	$C_s = \frac{\sum_{i=1}^{N} (y_f(i)) * y_m(i)}{\sum_{i=1}^{N} y_m(i)}$
DC Component	$y_m(0)$

Feature Extraction: Data is collected from sensors at a sampling rate of one second. Since data is collected over time, we can use raw data to extract time domain features. We used the Fast Fourier Transform (FFT) algorithm [47] to convert data to frequency domain and extract the spectral features. In total, as in Table 1, eight features are used to construct the fingerprint.

Data Chunking: After residual collection, the next step is to create chunks of dataset. We have performed experiments on a dataset collected over 7 days in SWaT testbed. An important purpose of data chunking is to find out, *how much is the sample size to train a well-performing machine learning model? and How much data is required to make a decision about presence or absence of an attacker?* The whole residual dataset (total of N readings) is divided into m chunks (each chunk of $\lfloor \frac{N}{m} \rfloor$), we calculate the feature set $< F(C_i) >$ for each data chunk i. For each sensor, we have m sets of features $< F(C_i) >_{i \in [1,m]}$. We have used a one-class SVM algorithm for attack detection. It is found out empirically that a sample size of 120 readings, i.e., $m = 120$ gave the best results. Most of the machine learning algorithms need a chunk of data to operate on and it is common to find an appropriate chunk size through experimentation [11,31].

Size of Training and Testing Dataset: For a total of FS feature sets for each sensor, at first we used half ($\frac{FS}{2}$) for training and half ($\frac{FS}{2}$) for testing. To analyze the accuracy of the classifier for smaller feature sets during training phase, we began to reduce number of feature sets starting with $\frac{FS}{2}$. Classification is then

carried out for the following corresponding range of feature sets for Training :
$\{\frac{FS}{2}, \frac{FS}{3}, \frac{FS}{4}, \frac{FS}{5}, \frac{FS}{10}\}$, and for Testing : $\{\frac{FS}{2}, \frac{2FS}{3}, \frac{3FS}{4}, \frac{4FS}{5}, \frac{9FS}{10}\}$, respectively.
For the classifier we have used a one-class SVM library [10] and it turns out that
the amount of data does not affect the performance. Moreover since we are not
using supervised learning for attack detection, therefore, training is only done
on the normal data obtained from a particular sensor.

3.2   Attack Isolation

A well known idea in fault isolation literature is to use multiple observers [14,
15, 45, 46]. Consider the dynamic system as expressed by (1) with p outputs,

$$y_k = [y_k^1, y_k^2, ..., y_k^p]^T = C x_k \tag{15}$$

For the case of an attack on one sensor i, attack vector $\delta_k^i \neq 0$ and $y_k^i = C_i \hat{x}_k + \delta_k^i$.
Again consider the example of two sensors in the water tank example we have
considered earlier. To use the idea of bank of observers we would drop one sensor
at first and design an observer just using the first sensor, i.e., the flow sensor
FIT-101 and then we will design another observer by using the second sensor,
i.e., the level sensor LIT-101. Let's consider both the cases one by one:
Case 1:

$$\hat{x}_{k+1} = A\hat{x}_k + Bu_k + L_i(y_k^i - C_i\hat{x}_k), \tag{16}$$

$$r_k = C\hat{x}_k - y_k \tag{17}$$

Using the first observer designed for FIT-101 gives the output as,

$$\begin{bmatrix} \hat{y}_{k+1}^1 \\ \hat{y}_{k+1}^2 \end{bmatrix} = C \left(\begin{bmatrix} a_{11} & a_{12} \\ a_{21} & a_{22} \end{bmatrix} \begin{bmatrix} \hat{x}_k^1 \\ \hat{x}_k^2 \end{bmatrix} + \begin{bmatrix} b_{11} \\ b_{21} \end{bmatrix} U + \begin{bmatrix} l_{11} \\ l_{21} \end{bmatrix} \begin{bmatrix} e(y_k^1) + \delta_k^1 \\ e(y_k^1) + \delta_k^1 \end{bmatrix} \right) \tag{18}$$

Case 2: Using the second observer designed for LIT-101 gives the output as,

$$\begin{bmatrix} \hat{y}_{k+1}^1 \\ \hat{y}_{k+1}^2 \end{bmatrix} = C \left(\begin{bmatrix} a_{11} & a_{12} \\ a_{21} & a_{22} \end{bmatrix} \begin{bmatrix} \hat{x}_k^1 \\ \hat{x}_k^2 \end{bmatrix} + \begin{bmatrix} b_{11} \\ b_{21} \end{bmatrix} U + \begin{bmatrix} l_{21} \\ l_{22} \end{bmatrix} \begin{bmatrix} e(y_k^2) + \delta_k^2 \\ e(y_k^2) + \delta_k^2 \end{bmatrix} \right) \tag{19}$$

where δ_k^1 and δ_k^2 are the attack vectors in sensor-1 and sensor-2 respectively. To
isolate the attack using a bank of observers, following conditions are considered
for p sensors,

Condition 1: if $r_k^j \neq 0$ for one $j \in \{1, 2, ..., i-1, i+1, ..., p\}$, then sensor j
is under attack, while sensor i is the one used to design an observer.

Condition 2: if $r_k^j \neq 0$ for all $j \in \{1, 2, ..., i-1, i+1, ..., p\}$ then sensor i
is under attack while sensor i is used to design the observer.

For a simple example, let's consider two observers as designed in (18) and
(19). In the first case we had used FIT-101 sensor measurements to design an
observer and also keep in mind that FIT-101 was free of any attacks. This means

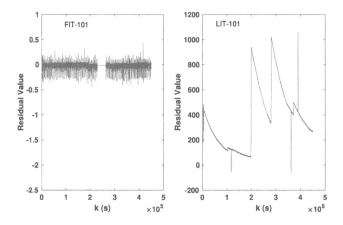

Fig. 5. Sensor-1 FIT-101 is used for observer design but the attack was in sensor-2 LIT-101. Therefore attack can be isolated in residual of LIT-101.

according to the condition 1 above FIT-101 residual mean should go to zero but for LIT-101, it does not. Figure 5 shows the results for the case 1. It can be seen that the sensor-1 (FIT-101) residual does not deviate form the normal residual, while the sensor-2 (LIT-101) residual deviates from the normal operation, hence detecting and isolating the source of attack. For the case 2, the observer is designed using the sensor-2 (LIT-101) and also remember that the attack is also present in the LIT-101. Figure 6 shows the results for this case. This case satisfies the condition 2 as stated above and then we see that the attack is present in both the sensors as the observer used is the one which has the attack. This means δ_k^1 was 0 and δ_k^2 was not zero in (18) and (19) respectively.

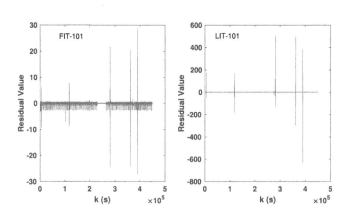

Fig. 6. Sensor-2 LIT-101 used for observer design and the attack was also in sensor-2 LIT-101. Therefore, both the sensor residuals deviate from the normal pattern.

Algorithm 1: Attack Isolation Method

Result: Output the sensor ID under attack

initialization;

θ_s: {Set of Sensors} ;

$r^i_{joint} = 0$, $r^i_{BoM}=0$, i $\in \theta_s$;

$sensor^i_m.Attack = False$ #Flag i^{th} sensor Attack;

while *Sensor Signal* **do**

    for *i in θ_s* **do**

        $r^i_{joint} = y^i_{joint} - \hat{y}^i_{joint}$, $r^i_{BoM}=y^i_{BoM} - \hat{y}^i_{BoM}$;

        if $r^i_{BoM}.Attack = =True$ && $r^i_{Joint}.Attack = =True$ **then**

           | $Sensor^i.Attack = True$;

        else

           | $Sensor^i.Attack = False$;

        end

    end

end

However from the results above it could be noticed that the sensor attacks could be isolated using the idea of bank of observers but it would not detect the case when the attack is in multiple sensors at the same time, e.g., multi-point single-stage attacks in an ICS [21]. Towards this end we are proposing the idea of using a Bank of Models (BoM) to isolate and detect attacks on multiple sensors at the same time in an ICS.

Bank of Models (BoM): The idea is to create multiple models of the physical process rather than the multiple observers. For example if you have two sensors which are physically coupled as in the case of FIT-101 and LIT-101, then we will create three models, 1) with both the sensors as output, 2) with FIT-101 only as the output and 3) with LIT-101 only as the output. We call the first method as *Joint* model and the rest two models as *BoM*. We can use these models in conjunction with each other to isolate the attacks and call that model as *Ensemble* of models. By having a separate model the sensors are no longer coupled to each other. These separate models could be used to detect attacks but accuracy of detection might be low as we will see in the results. Therefore, we propose a method called Ensemble of models combining the joint and separate models to make an attack detection decision as well as isolate the attack.

Fig. 7. Experiments conducted at SWaT Testbed.

4   Evaluation

4.1   Experimentation Setup

Industrial Control Systems have a broad domain. In this work, a Secure Water Treatment testbed (SWaT) [33] shown in Fig. 7 at the Singapore University of Technology and Design is used as a case study. SWaT is a fully functional testbed and is open for researchers to use. A brief introduction is provided in the following to understand the context of the problem.

The SWaT testbed produces the purified water and it is a scaled-down version of a real water treatment process. There are six stages in the SWaT testbed. Each stage is equipped with a set of sensors and actuators. Sensors include water quantity measures such as level, flow, and pressure and water quality measures such as pH, ORP and conductivity. Actuators include motorized valves and electric pumps. Stage 1 is the raw water stage to hold the raw water for the treatment and stage 2 is the chemical dosing stage to treat the water depending on the measurements from the water quality sensors. Stage 3 is the ultra-filtration stage. Stage 4 is composed of de-chlorinator and stage 5 is equipped with reverse osmosis filters. Stage 6 holds the treated water for distribution. Multiple stages from SWaT are used in this study. Actuator signals are input to the system model and sensor measurements are outputs. Level sensors labelled as LIT-s0q, where LIT stands for level transmitter, s for the stage and q for the specific number, e.g., LIT-101 means level sensor in stage1 and sensor 1. FIT-301 is the flow sensor in stage3 and sensor number 1. The performance is evaluated in three areas, namely, attack detection, attack isolation and the improvement in attack detection rate.

4.2   Attack Detection

To show the performance of attack detector we use True Positive Rate (TPR: meaning attack data declared as attack), True Negative Rate (TNR: normal data declared as normal). Attack detection results are shown in Table 2. For each sensor in SWaT testbed attack sequences are shown. These attack sequences and attacked dataset is obtained from already published benchmark attacks [11,21]. We can see a high TPR and TNR indicating the effectiveness of our proposed scheme. There is an interesting observation to make here, as discussed earlier the proposed technique is based on the system model, it exhibits a strong coupling between inputs and outputs of a system. If attacks are executed on level sensors we could see the effect on associated flow meter and vice versa. This indicates the coupling due to the laws of Physics even though the sensors were of different types. Column 3 and 4 indicates this result in form of TNR-Joint and TPR-Joint respectively. For LIT-101 it could be seen that the TPR is 100%, however, we observe attack detection TPR for FIT-101 to be 88.88% while there were no attacks carried on FIT-101. Column 5 and 6 depict results for the case when we have a separate system model for each sensor labeled as TNR-BoM and TPR-BoM respectively. These two single models can help in detecting attacks just in LIT-101 and none in FIT-101 as expected.

Table 2. Attack detection performance. TPR: Attack detected successfully, TNR: Normal data classified successfully. LIT: level sensor, FIT: flow sensor, DPIT: differential pressure sensor.

Sensor	Atk. seq.[a]	TNR-Joint	TPR-Joint	TNR-BoM	TPR-BoM	TNR-Ensemble	TPR-Ensemble
DPIT-301	8	84.66%	100%	83.14%	100%	88.66%	100%
LIT-101	3,21,30,33,36	83.37%	100%	94.55%	85.18%	96.50%	85.18%
FIT-101	None	91.96%	88.88	71.00%	No Attacks	96.07%	No Attacks
LIT-301	7,16,26,32,41	86.28%	78.37%	92.31%	100%	96.82%	78.37%
FIT-301	None	86.41%	83.78%	86.23%	No Attacks	89.89%	No Attacks
LIT-401	25,27,31	87.12%	74.28%	86.66%	65.21%	90.18%	60.86%
FIT-401	10,11,39,40	87.50%	51.42%	87.40%	100%	91.70%	100%

[a] Attack Sequences [21]

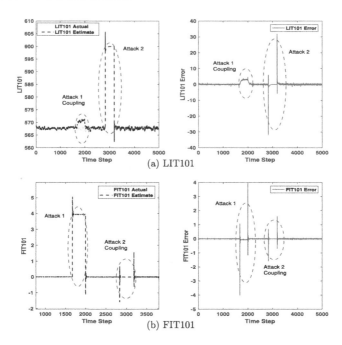

Fig. 8. This shows how two different attacks on two different sensors are reflected in residuals of both the sensors due to the physical coupling.

4.3 Attack Isolation

We have seen the attack isolation performance in Table 2 using the separate model for each sensor. To visually present the idea Fig. 8 shows two example attacks and the coupling effects. Attack 1 is carried out on the flow meter FIT-101 by spoofing the flow value to $4m^3/hr$ as shown in Figure(b) and this attack can be observed in the residual value on the right-hand side. However, attack 1 could be seen in Figure(a) in the level sensor LIT-101 as well. The Attack 2 is carried out on the level sensor by spoofing the water level value as shown in Fig. 8(a). This attack could be seen in the residual of the level sensor LIT-101 and also on the right-hand side in the flow sensor FIT-101 residual.

In Fig. 9 it can be seen that separate system models for both the sensors were able to isolate both the attacks. Attack 1 only appears in the residual of FIT-101 and Attack 2 is detected only by LIT-101.

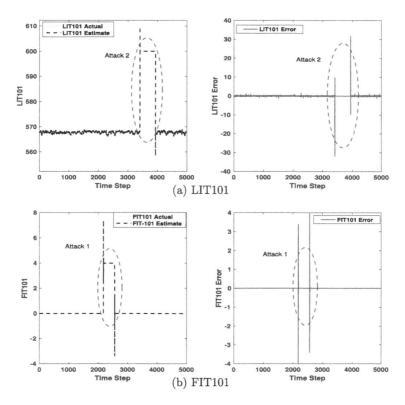

Fig. 9. In this Figure both the attacks as shown in Fig. 8 are shown but for the case when we have two separate models for each sensor. It can be seen that the attacks are isolated to the particular sensor under attack.

4.4 Reduction in False Alarm Rate via Ensemble

From the results above we have seen that the bank of models (BoM) can detect as well as isolate the attacks on the sensors. However, we thought to make use of more information by combining the BoM and Joint models termed as Ensemble model here as outlined in Algorithm 1. Last two columns in Table 2 shows the results for the Ensemble of both the models. It is seen that using the information about residual vectors from two different models and obtaining an ensemble increase the information at hand and can led in reduced false alarms. Observing column TNR-Ensemble and comparing with other TNR columns reveal that the false alarm rate has significantly reduced as compared to prior results.

5 Discussion

TPR and TNR Accuracy: The reason for low TPR and TNR in some cases is that as soon as an attack is ended, we start considering the behavior/ground truth to be a normal operation. But our detection system still raises alarms and these alarms are treated as False positives. In reality, this is the time required by the system to come back to a normal operating range. More so, since we do not record that as a rightful attack detection then it is also counted as wrongful TNR reducing the TNR. For example, as shown in Fig. 10 we can observe that as soon as an attack is removed, we observe post-attack effects which persist for some time. In this region, we assume the attack is over but due to attack effects, our detector keeps raising an alarm thus reducing the TNR value. From a defender's perspective, it might be acceptable since operators would be involved even from the first alarm raised. However, from an attacker's perspective this observation highlights, how important it is to terminate attacks in a way to reduce the number of alarms. This is in line with earlier works that have highlighted how important it is to time an attack [27], similarly, it is important to terminate attack as such to avoid abrupt changes.

Scalability: An important consideration is the practicality of the proposed technique for real-world plants. Since the proposed method does not use any extra hardware, scalability is not an issue. Previously in the literature bank of observers has been used for hundreds of sensors, similarly, the proposed idea of a bank of models can be used as it is grounded in the mathematical formulation and software. Practical demonstration in the real-world water treatment testbed also shows the applicability of the proposed technique to real systems without any overhead.

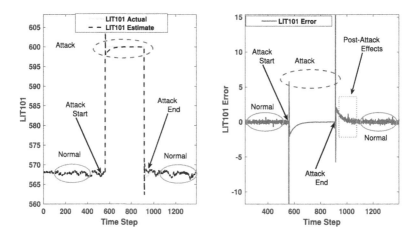

Fig. 10. Explanation for low TPR/TNR dues to post-attack effects.

6   Related Work

Machine Learning-based Approaches: There have been a lot of efforts towards attack detection in the context of ICS. Most of the works took a machine learning-based approach. Most techniques took classification approach and either used unsupervised or semi-supervised machine learning algorithms to detect attacks in an ICS [18, 19, 23, 24, 26, 40]. In particular, some of them have used data from Secure Water Treatment (SWaT) testbed [33]. The design of an anomaly detector for ICS is treated as a "one-class classification problem" and several unsupervised learning methods are effectively employed [24]. Unsupervised learning approaches construct a baseline for normal behavior through feature learning and monitor whether the current behavior is within the specified range or not. Although these techniques can detect zero-day vulnerabilities, they generate high false alarms due to the existence of several hyperparameters and the multivariate nature of ICS data. Similarly, for one class SVM, authors in [24] have fine-tuned the parameters, namely c and γ for better performance on the SWaT dataset. Although there exist several automated approaches, such as grid search, randomized search, and metaheuristic optimization techniques for fine-tuning, a significant challenge faced by these techniques is overfitting. Generally, the error rate during the validation process should be less for the trained model; a higher validation error for the model trained with a large volume of data implies that the model is over-fitted. A context-aware robust intrusion detection system is proposed by [41]. Given the amount of work done in this domain this related worklist is by no means exhaustive but tried to cover the related work tested on the SWaT testbed. These techniques do not include a feature of attack isolation that is the core of this work.

System and Process Model: There have been efforts from the system and the process model perspective. Krotofil et al. [29] detect the spoofed measurements using the correlation entropy in a cluster of related sensors. Most of the work focused on system model-based approaches, the literature volume is huge and it is not possible to cover all the studies here but a few representative [17, 32, 39]. These works capture the process dynamics in the form of system models and use the point change detection methods to detect attacks in the process data. A similar recent approach [49] does isolate the attack but only the attacks on the actuators. Sensor fusion [36] and multi observer techniques[45] are recent efforts on attack isolation problem in simulated environments. However from the results in Sect. 3.2 it is noticed that the sensor attacks could be isolated using the idea of a bank of observers but it would not detect the case when the attack is in multiple sensors at the same time, e.g., multi-point single-stage attacks in an ICS. Our work is the first effort demonstrating a bank of models on a live water treatment plant.

7   Conclusions and Future Work

The problem of attack isolation is critical in terms of system response and recovery in an event of attack detection. We demonstrated that using the bank of models (BoM) the attack isolation problem on multiple sensors at a time could be solved. This work strengthens the previous studies and provides a novel solution to the problem of determining the source of the attack in a complex industrial control system. In future, we plan to extend this work using bigger city scale process plant. Moreover, we propose to automate the process of data-based system modelling.

Acknowledgements. This research is supported by the National Research Foundation, Singapore, under its National Satellite of Excellence Programme "Design Science and Technology for Secure Critical Infrastructure" (Award Number: NSoE_DeST-SCI2019-0002). Any opinions, findings and conclusions or recommendations expressed in this material are those of the author(s) and do not reflect the views of National Research Foundation, Singapore.

References

1. Ahmed, C.M., A.Sridhar, M., A.: Limitations of state estimation based cyber attack detection schemes in industrial control systems. In: IEEE Smart City Security and Privacy Workshop, CPSWeek (2016)
2. Ahmed, C.M., Mathur, A.P.: Challenges in machine learning based approaches for real-time anomaly detection in industrial control systems. In: Proceedings of the 6th ACM on Cyber-Physical System Security Workshop. p. 23–29. CPSS '20, Association for Computing Machinery, New York, NY, USA (2020). https://doi.org/10.1145/3384941.3409588
3. Ahmed, C.M., Murguia, C., Ruths, J.: Model-based attack detection scheme for smart water distribution networks. In: Proceedings of the 2017 ACM on Asia Conference on Computer and Communications Security, pp. 101–113. ASIA CCS '17, ACM, New York, NY, USA (2017). https://doi.org/10.1145/3052973.3053011
4. Ahmed, C.M., et al.: Noiseprint: Attack detection using sensor and process noise fingerprint in cyber physical systems. In: Proceedings of the 2018 on Asia Conference on Computer and Communications Security, pp. 483–497. ASIACCS '18, ACM, New York, NY, USA (2018). https://doi.org/10.1145/3196494.3196532
5. Ahmed, C.M., Zhou, J.: Challenges and opportunities in cyberphysical systems security: a physics-based perspective. IEEE Secur. Privacy **18**(6), 14–22 (2020)
6. Aström, K.J., Wittenmark, B.: Computer-controlled Systems, 3rd edn. Prentice-Hall Inc, Upper Saddle River, NJ, USA (1997)
7. Athalye, S., Ahmed, C.M., Zhou, J.: A tale of two testbeds: a comparative study of attack detection techniques in cps. In: International Conference on Critical Information Infrastructures Security, pp. 17–30. Springer (2020). https://doi.org/10.1007/978-3-030-58295-1_2
8. Cardenas, A., Amin, S., Lin, Z., Huang, Y., Huang, C., Sastry, S.: Attacks against process control systems: Risk assessment, detection, and response. In: 6th ACM Symposium on Information, Computer and Communications Security, pp. 355–366 (2011)
9. Case, D.U.: Analysis of the cyber attack on the ukrainian power grid (2016)
10. Chang, C.C., Lin, C.J.: LIBSVM: a library for support vector machines. ACM Trans. Intell. Syst. Technol. **2**, 1–27 (2011) www.csie.ntu.edu.tw/cjlin/libsvm
11. Chen, Y., Poskitt, C.M., Sun, J.: Learning from mutants: using code mutation to learn and monitor invariants of a cyber-physical system. IEEE Security and Privacy 2018 abs/1801.00903 (2018). arxiv.org/abs/1801.00903
12. CNN: Staged cyber attack reveals vulnerability in power grid (2007). edition.cnn.com/2007/US/09/26/power.at.risk/index.html, year

13. Dan, G., Sandberg, H.: Stealth attacks and protection schemes for state estimators in power systems. In: Smart Grid Communications (SmartGridComm), 2010 First IEEE International Conference on, pp. 214–219. IEEE (2010)
14. Ding, S.X.: Model-based fault diagnosis techniques: design schemes, algorithms, and tools. Springer Sci. Business Media (2008)
15. Esfahani, P.M., Vrakopoulou, M., Andersson, G., Lygeros, J.: A tractable nonlinear fault detection and isolation technique with application to the cyber-physical security of power systems. In: Proceedings of the 51st IEEE Conference on Decision and Control, pp. 3433–3438 (2012)
16. Falliere, N., Murchu, L., Chien, E.: W32 stuxnet dossier. symantec, version 1.4 (2011). www.symantec.com/content/en/us/enterprise/media/security
17. Fawzi, H., Tabuada, P., Diggavi, S.: Secure estimation and control for cyber-physical systems under adversarial attacks. IEEE Trans. Autom. Control **59**(6), 1454–1467 (2014)
18. Filonov, P., Kitashov, F., Lavrentyev, A.: Rnn-based early cyber-attack detection for the tennessee eastman process. arXiv preprint arXiv:1709.02232 (2017)
19. Filonov, P., Lavrentyev, A., Vorontsov, A.: Multivariate industrial time series with cyber-attack simulation: fault detection using an lstm-based predictive data model. arXiv preprint arXiv:1612.06676 (2016)
20. Garcia, L., Brasser, F., Cintuglu, M.H., Sadeghi, A.R., Mohammed, O., Zonouz, S.A.: Hey, my malware knows physics! attacking plcs with physical model aware rootkit. In: 24th Annual Network and Distributed System Security Symposium (NDSS) (Feb 2017)
21. Goh, J., Adepu, S., Junejo, K.N., Mathur, A.: A dataset to support research in the design of secure water treatment systems. In: Havarneanu, G., Setola, R., Nassopoulos, H., Wolthusen, S. (eds.) Critical Information Infrastructures Security, pp. 88–99. Springer International Publishing, Cham (2017)
22. Gollmann, D., Krotofil, M.: Cyber-physical systems security, pp. 195–204. Springer, Berlin Heidelberg (2016). https://doi.org/10.1007/978-3-662-49301-4_14
23. Huda, S., Yearwood, J., Hassan, M.M., Almogren, A.: Securing the operations in scada-iot platform based industrial control system using ensemble of deep belief networks. Appl. Soft Comput. **71**, 66–77 (2018)
24. Inoue, J., Yamagata, Y., Chen, Y., Poskitt, C.M., Sun, J.: Anomaly detection for a water treatment system using unsupervised machine learning. In: 2017 IEEE International Conference on Data Mining Workshops (ICDMW), pp. 1058–1065. IEEE (2017)
25. iTrust: Sutd security showdown. itrust.sutd.edu.sg/scy-phy-systems-week/2017-2/s317-event/ year = 2017
26. Kravchik, M., Shabtai, A.: Detecting cyber attacks in industrial control systems using convolutional neural networks. In: Proceedings of the 2018 Workshop on Cyber-Physical Systems Security and Privacy, pp. 72–83. ACM (2018)
27. Krotofil, M., Cárdenas, A.A.: Is this a good time? deciding when to launch attacks on process control systems. In: Proceedings of the 3rd International Conference on High Confidence Networked Systems, p. 65–66. HiCoNS '14, Association for Computing Machinery, New York, NY, USA (2014). https://doi.org/10.1145/2566468.2576852
28. Krotofil, M., Cárdenas, A.A., Manning, B., Larsen, J.: Cps: driving cyber-physical systems to unsafe operating conditions by timing dos attacks on sensor signals. In: Proceedings of the 30th Annual Computer Security Applications Conference, p. 146–155. ACSAC '14, Association for Computing Machinery, New York, NY, USA (2014). https://doi.org/10.1145/2664243.2664290

29. Krotofil, M., Larsen, J., Gollmann, D.: The process matters: ensuring data veracity in cyber-physical systems. In: Proceedings of the 10th ACM Symposium on Information, Computer and Communications Security, pp. 133–144. ASIA CCS '15, ACM, New York, NY, USA (2015). https://doi.org/10.1145/2714576.2714599
30. Krotofil, M., Gollmann, D.: Industrial control systems security: what is happening? In: 2013 11th IEEE International Conference on Industrial Informatics (INDIN), pp. 670–675 (2013). https://doi.org/10.1109/INDIN.2013.6622964
31. Li, X., Ye, N.: Decision tree classifiers for computer intrusion detection. J. Parallel Distrib Comput Practices **4**(2), 179–190 (2001)
32. Liu, Y., Ning, P., Reiter, M.: False data injection attacks against state estimation in electric power grids. In: Proceedings of the 16th ACM Conference on Computer and Communications Security, pp. 21–32 (2009)
33. Mathur, A.P., Tippenhauer, N.O.: Swat: a water treatment testbed for research and training on ics security. In: 2016 International Workshop on Cyber-physical Systems for Smart Water Networks (CySWater), pp. 31–36 (2016). https://doi.org/10.1109/CySWater.2016.7469060
34. Mo, Y., Sinopoli, B.: Secure control against replay attacks. In: 2009 47th Annual Allerton Conference on Communication, Control, and Computing (Allerton), pp. 911–918 (2009). https://doi.org/10.1109/ALLERTON.2009.5394956
35. Mo, Y., Sinopoli, B.: Integrity attacks on cyber-physical systems. In: Proceedings of the 1st International Conference on High Confidence Networked Systems, pp. 47–54. HiCoNS '12, ACM, New York, NY, USA (2012). https://doi.org/10.1145/2185505.2185514
36. Mohammadi, A., Yang, C., Chen, Q.w.: Attack detection/isolation via a secure multisensor fusion framework for cyberphysical systems. Complexity 2018 (2018)
37. NIST: Cyber-physical systems (2014). www.nist.gov/el/cyber-physical-systems
38. Overschee, P.V., Moor, B.D.: Subspace identification for linear systems: theory, implementation, applications. Kluwer Academic Publications, Boston (1996)
39. Pasqualetti, F., Dorfler, F., Bullo, F.: Attack detection and identification in Cyber-Physical Systems, models and fundamental limitations. IEEE Transactions on Automatic Control **58**(11), 2715–2729 (2013)
40. Rubio, J.E., Alcaraz, C., Roman, R., Lopez, J.: Analysis of intrusion detection systems in industrial ecosystems. In: SECRYPT, pp. 116–128 (2017)
41. Sethi, K., Sai Rupesh, E., Kumar, R., Bera, P., Venu Madhav, Y.: A context-aware robust intrusion detection system: a reinforcement learning-based approach. Int. J. Inf. Secur. **19**(6), 657–678 (2019). https://doi.org/10.1007/s10207-019-00482-7
42. Shoukry, Y., Martin, P., Yona, Y., Diggavi, S., Srivastava, M.: Pycra: physical challenge-response authentication for active sensors under spoofing attacks. In: Proceedings of the 22Nd ACM SIGSAC Conference on Computer and Communications Security, pp. 1004–1015. CCS '15, ACM, New York, NY, USA (2015). https://doi.org/10.1145/2810103.2813679
43. Sommer, R., Paxson, V.: Outside the closed world: on using machine learning for network intrusion detection. In: 2010 IEEE Symposium on Security and Privacy, pp. 305–316. IEEE (2010)
44. Urbina, D.I., et al.: Limiting the impact of stealthy attacks on industrial control systems. In: Proceedings of the 2016 ACM SIGSAC Conference on Computer and Communications Security, pp. 1092–1105. ACM (2016)
45. Wang, X., Luo, X., Zhang, M., Jiang, Z., Guan, X.: Detection and isolation of false data injection attacks in smart grid via unknown input interval observer. IEEE Internet of Things J. **7**(4), 3214–3229 (2020). https://doi.org/10.1109/JIOT.2020.2966221

46. Wei, X., Verhaegen, M., van Engelen, T.: Sensor fault detection and isolation for wind turbines based on subspace identification and kalman filter techniques. Int. J. Adapt. Control Signal Process. **24**(8), 687–707 (2010). https://doi.org/10.1002/acs.1162

47. Welch, P.: The use of fast fourier transform for the estimation of power spectra: a method based on time averaging over short, modified periodograms. IEEE Trans. Audio Electroac. **15**(2), 70–73 (1967)

48. Wired: A cyberattack has caused confirmed physical damage for the second time ever (2015). www.wired.com/2015/01/german-steel-mill-hack-destruction/

49. Yang, T., Murguia, C., Kuijper, M., Nešić, D.: An unknown input multi-observer approach for estimation, attack isolation, and control of lti systems under actuator attacks. In: 2019 18th European Control Conference (ECC), pp. 4350–4355 (2019). https://doi.org/10.23919/ECC.2019.8796178

Super Detector: An Ensemble Approach for Anomaly Detection in Industrial Control Systems

Madhumitha Balaji[1], Siddhant Shrivastava[1(✉)], Sridhar Adepu[2], and Aditya Mathur[1]

[1] iTrust Center for Research in Cyber Security, Singapore University of Technology and Design, Singapore, Singapore
madhumitha_balaji@mymail.sutd.edu.sg,
{shrivasatava_siddhant,aditya_mathur}@sutd.edu.sg
[2] Bristol Cyber Security Group, University of Bristol, Bristol, England
sridhar.adepu@bristol.ac.uk

Abstract. Industrial Control Systems encompass supervisory systems (SCADA) and cyber-physical components (sensors/actuators), which are typically deployed in critical infrastructure to control physical processes. Their interconnectedness and controllability leaves them vulnerable to cyber-physical attacks which could have detrimental impacts on the safety, security, and service of the infrastructure. Detection and defense against these attacks is, therefore, of utmost importance. Existing detection methods often fail to detect cyber-physical attacks of certain types, or produce false alarms by design. This paper proposes a novel anomaly detection method called the Super Detector for the robust prediction of cyber-physical attacks in these complex systems by design. It fuses the inputs from the real-time operational data from the system as well as individual anomaly detectors. The methods tested for the first prototype of Super Detector entail a stacked ensemble of Random Forest, Bagging with k-Nearest Neighbors and Gaussian Naïve Bayes algorithms to classify normal and anomalous data. This results in high accuracy of detection and a lower number of false alarms. The training and validation of our method has been carried out on the SWaT dataset collected during a real live-fire international cyber exercise. The operational and attack data is obtained from a real small-scale replica of an industrial water treatment plant. We present that Super Detector achieves much higher accuracy and a lower false alarm rate as compared to individual anomaly detection approaches.

Keywords: Attack detection · Decision fusion · Industrial control systems · Critical infrastructure · Anomaly detection · Cyber-physical attacks · Cybersecurity · Water systems

1 Introduction

Industrial Control System (ICS) is the collective term for different types of control systems and associated instrumentation, which includes the devices, systems,

© Springer Nature Switzerland AG 2021
D. Percia David et al. (Eds.): CRITIS 2021, LNCS 13139, pp. 24–43, 2021.
https://doi.org/10.1007/978-3-030-93200-8_2

networks, and controls used to operate and/or automate industrial processes. These are highly interconnected cyber-physical systems (CPS) integrating computational, networking, physical, and human components. These are vital components of critical infrastructure assets such as water treatment and distribution systems, chemical plants, power generation, transmission, and distribution facilities, etc. An ICS typically consists of a subsystem called the Supervisory Control and Data Acquisition (SCADA) system. SCADA systems are typically composed of devices such as Programmable Logic Controllers (PLC) or other commercial hardware modules that are distributed in various locations to provide control at the supervisory level. These systems can acquire and transmit data and are integrated with a Human Machine Interface (HMI) that enables operators to interact with the devices. In a SCADA, a setpoint is sent to the controller that is capable of instructing actuators (such as valves, pumps, etc.) to operate in a manner such that the desired setpoint is maintained. Local operations are often controlled by field devices such as sensors and controllers (like remote telemetry units or RTUs) that receive supervisory commands from remote stations. [29]

Context of the Problem: Since many of these ICSs are networked for remote control and monitoring, they become susceptible to cyber-attacks. An attacker who breaches the network security could corrupt the operations of the system in question and lead to catastrophic outcomes. For example, the Stuxnet computer virus attack against critical infrastructure targeted PLCs and disrupted the Iranian nuclear program by damaging centrifuges used to separate nuclear material. In December 2015, hackers compromised electric grids in Ukraine using BlackEnergy malware, leading to a six-hour power outage [27]. Given these disastrous consequences, and the rising number of reported cyber-attacks in today's digital world, much research focuses on the development of anomaly detection techniques for improving the endurance of ICS to cyber-attacks and physical malfunction. Several types of ICS-specific anomaly detection methods have been developed in recent years, such as behavior-based [12], network-based [6], and process-based methods [3]. In reality, however, an ICS with multiple anomaly detectors runs into the problem of **decision fusion** - a situation where different detectors report the same event in a conflicting manner i.e., some detectors report the event as an anomaly/attack while others report it as normal. Furthermore, on one hand, some attacks remain undetected by these detectors, whereas on the other, the detectors produce false alarms, reporting an anomaly when there is none, thereby misleading system operators.

Overview of our Approach: The key idea behind our approach is the use of ensemble methods to solve the problem of decision fusion. Super Detector takes in inputs from the plant alongside inputs from existing detectors. This enables it to differentiate between false alarms and actual anomalies, providing a more reliable decision to the operator. The meaning of 'ensemble' here is two-fold. Super Detector not only combines the output from existing detectors, but also uses a stacked ensemble of Random Forest, Bagging and Gaussian Naïve Bayes classifiers at its core. Figure 1 provides an illustration of the data input to Super

Detector, showing the receipt of data from SWaT as well as three existing detectors.

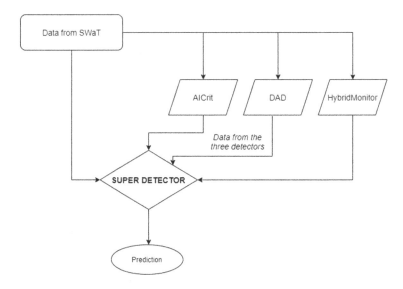

Fig. 1. Data input to Super Detector; Operational data from sensors/actuators together with data from existing anomaly detectors (DAD, AICrit, HybridMonitor).

Our Contribution: The aim of this paper is to present a novel technique for anomaly detection in an ICS. The novelty of our approach is as follows:

- Our work is in the area of water treatment as a critical infrastructure. Our prediction model is based on data obtained from the Secure Water Treatment (SWaT) testbed (located at iTrust Centre for Research in Cyber Security in the Singapore University of Technology and Design), a scaled down replica of an industrial water treatment plant, thereby resembling a real plant in terms of complexity.
- Our model not only takes input from the water treatment plant but also three other pre-existing anomaly detectors in place at iTrust, in order to provide a combined, reliable decision with a lower rate of false alarms as well as undetected attacks. Our technique has thereby been named the 'Super Detector'.
- The Super Detector approach involves the development of an ensemble machine learning model based on three individual supervised machine learning models, resulting in improved accuracy.
- The validation of the proposed method has been carried out on the SWaT dataset across two realistic cyber exercises [10,11].

By taking inputs from existing detectors, Super Detector not only seamlessly integrates into the existing infrastructure but also acts as a check on the prevailing detection techniques. Super Detector can be put to use even in an ICS that does not have detectors currently in operation. There exists a variety of safety alarms in every SCADA system that operators must check manually. In such a situation, Super Detector can analyse the existing alarms and provide a final, reliable indication to the operator. Attackers can bypass pre-configured hard-coded safety alarms with cyber attacks. Super Detector understands plant behavior and takes decision on estimated values (and not the falsified network values). The trust of the operator should be in a system that evolves over time.

Organization: The remainder of this paper is organized as follows. We discuss related works in Sect. 2. Section 3 presents the architecture of the SWaT system, the data obtained for training and testing purposes. In Sect. 4, the mathematical background of the algorithms used is explained. Section 5 describes the methodology we adopted, and Sect. 6 presents the results and their analysis. Section 7 concludes the paper.

2   Related Work

Several attack scenarios could lead to malicious process anomalies, including 1) *Bad data injection* [2]: an attacker may launch a Man-in-the-Middle (MITM) attack and send bad sensor data to one or more PLCs, which may use the deceptive data and plan anomalous command accordingly; 2) *Bad command injection* [4]: an attacker may compromise the link between the PLC and an actuator, or the PLC itself, and directly send a command to an actuator. Those commands may lead an operational plant into an unsafe state either immediately or sometime later.

Alongside conventional anomaly detection mechanisms that defend against known physical weaknesses [19], a vast majority of detection techniques adopt data-driven approaches. The development of machine learning and deep learning techniques for anomaly detection in ICSs has seen a rapid increase lately. Machine learning algorithms such as support vector machines, k-nearest neighbors and decision trees [5] provide high sensitivity to attacks with precise detection. However, due to the difficulty in obtaining labelled data for supervised methods, there has been a shift towards semi-supervised and unsupervised techniques. Semi-supervised techniques use data pertaining to one class, mostly the 'normal' system operation data for training containing no attack scenarios. MADICS: A Methodology for Anomaly Detection in Industrial Control Systems [25] is based on a semi-supervised anomaly detection paradigm and makes use of deep learning algorithms to model ICS behaviors. [28] proposes a hybrid semi-supervised method for high-dimensional data that consists of two parts: a deep autoencoder and an ensemble k-nearest neighbor graphs based anomaly detector.

Unsupervised learning methods, especially neural networks [13] are increasingly adopted due to their ability to effectively detect attacks without requiring any labelled data. Li et al., [18] proposed unsupervised multivariate anomaly detection with Generative Adversarial Networks (MAD-GAN) to capture the spatial-temporal correlations between sensors and actuators in the system.

Deep Neural Networks and Support-Vector Machines specifically adapted to time-series data [15] show high precision. One-dimensional convolutional neural networks and autoencoders coupled with Principal Component Analysis have proven to be an efficient cyber-attack detection method [16].

In [21] presents a review of deep learning-based anomaly detection (DLAD) mechanisms in CPS. The state-of-the-art ensemble DLAD presented here is the Multi-Branch Predictor Framework [33] which aggregates the predictions of two models - a statistical model named TBATS (Trigonometric Box-Cox transform, ARMA errors, Trend, and Seasonal components) and a' multi-branch deep neural network (built of encoders and LSTM cells). While this method significantly outperformed baseline methods such as Stacked LSTM and Regularized LSTM when evaluated on a SCADA water supply system, the high computational cost to an ICS is a considerable drawback. The lengthy training time is an another con of such an approach. Ensemble machine learning models, on the other hand, are quick to train [31]. For instance, Super Detector completes the entire training process in 8 min (timed using Python's *timeit* module), whereas the training time for LSTM-based neural networks typically ranges from a few hours to a few days.

Ensemble machine learning methods are gaining popularity due to their low computational complexity and high accuracy in anomaly detection. Zhiruo [32] proposed a method that uses bootstrapping and improvised Random Forest algorithm to better detect anomalies. Random Forest is shown to result in better performance than other machine learning techniques in [24]. Bagging ensembles have been used for feature selection in high-dimensional and noisy datasets in [17]. In this study, we propose a stacking ensemble of Random Forest, Bagging and Gaussian Naïve Bayes algorithms that are trained on an integrated dataset obtained from the water treatment plant and its existing anomaly detectors. To the best of our knowledge, our work is the first to adopt such an approach.

3   SWaT: The Secure Water Treatment Plant

3.1   Architecture

SWaT is a scaled-down water treatment testbed with a six-stage purification process [22]. It closely mimics modern treatment plants. It is used to investigate the response to cyber attacks and experiment with novel designs of defense mechanisms such as the ones described in [23,27].

Its architecture is depicted in Fig. 2. The entire treatment process is controlled by a set of 28 sensors and 27 actuators. The process begins by taking in raw water and storing it in a tank. In the second stage, water characteristics such as pH and reduction potential are controlled through the dosing of chemicals such as HCl, NaOCl and NaCl in a static mixer. The third stage involves the removal of impurities across fine membranes in the Ultra Filtration(UF) system. This is followed by the fourth stage, where the water is de-chlorinated using

Ultraviolet lamps. Subsequently, the water is pumped into the Reverse Osmosis (RO) system to remove smaller contaminants in the fifth stage. A backwashing process uses the water produced by RO to clean the membrane in the UF. In the last stage, the clean water from the RO system is stored and ready for distribution. The cyber portion of SWaT consists of a layered communications network, PLCs, HMIs, SCADA workstation, and a Historian.

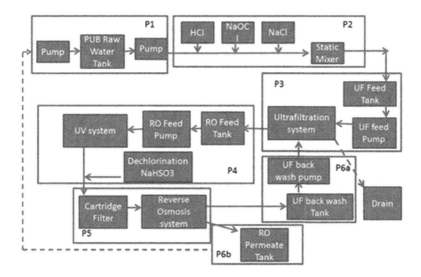

Fig. 2. Architecture of the six-stage water treatment process

3.2   Existing Anomaly Detectors

To improve our predictions, we have used the reports of three pre-existing detectors, namely DAD, AICrit and Hybrid Monitor, that are in place at iTrust.

DAD: Distributed Attack Detection (DAD) [1] is an attack detection system developed by a team of researchers in iTrust. It is a host-based intrusion detection system. DAD collects data on the various sensor measurements of processes such as water pH, water level and flow indicator of the plant for analysis and anomaly detection in processes. It can detect single-stage multi-point and multi-stage multi-point cyber-attacks in a distributed control system.

AICrit: AICrit [26] is a unified framework for real-time process monitoring to preserve the control behavior integrity of the ICS. It precisely learns the normal spatio-temporal relationship among the components through the application of unsupervised machine learning algorithms. First, it models the normal behaviour of continuous-valued state variables (sensors) through temporal dependencies. Second, it models the non-linear correlation among the discrete and continuous type state variables (cross-correlation among the sensors and actuators) during the normal plant operation. By combining these two, the functional dependencies of the sensors and actuators are monitored continuously.

Hybrid Monitor: Hybrid Monitor [9] tool is a black-box modelling approach to detect deviations from expected behavior. It relies on two different tools: HybModeller and HybMonitor. HybModeller uses data from SWaT Historian and creates a model of the normal behavior of the system. The second component (HybMonitor) uses the created models to predict 'normal' behavior of the system under test. It reads the actual state of the system, identifies the operational mode, and predicts sensor readings. HybMonitor can also predict state transitions in a controller based on prior knowledge.

3.3   Cyber Exercise

The Critical Infrastructure Security Showdown (CISS) is an annual international cyber exercise held in the years 2019 and 2020 [10,11]. Super Detector was tested on the datasets obtained from these cyber exercises. The exercise involves several red teams participating in their assigned time slots throughout the fortnight-long exercise. They attempt to attack the IT (Information Technology) and OT (Operational Technology) infrastructure of SWaT.

The attacker profiles of red teams range across nation-states, cybersecurity agencies, professional red team organizations, private operational security establishments, academic researchers, and student-led red teams. Each red team brings their unique perspective and style of cyber-physical attacks that get reflected in the datasets. The diversity of these attacks help to stress test the performance of individual detectors. Each individual detection technology has its strengths and weaknesses to different classes of attacks which are established in these datasets. Super Detector aims to fuse the strengths and minimize the weaknesses of individual detectors.

Each red team gets four hours to discover attack targets, identify vulnerabilities, establish persistence, traverse across networks to ultimately compromise the cyber-physical operation of SWaT. A judging panel coordinates with the attackers and scores them based on the following characteristics of an attack - novelty, cyber impact, physical impact, stealthiness, and success rate. The scoring system incentivizes the red teams to craft a range of attacks and minimize similar approaches. This encourages creativity and results in a vibrant dataset that is described in the next section.

All the network traffic and operational data from the historian and detectors is logged during the cyber exercise. The blue teams (or detection/defense teams) stealthily operate throughout the duration of the exercise and publish their alarm status in response to each state of SWaT.

This time-series dataset is then used for scoring the red teams and shared widely with the community to bolster cybersecurity research.

3.4   Dataset

The CISS 2019 dataset contains SWaT data under normal operation as well as under attack over the period of 4 d. On each day, the plant was run for 8 h from 0900–1300 h and 1400–1800 h. (On the last day, the plant was only run from 0900–1300 h). The CISS 2020 dataset also contains SWaT data under normal operation and under attack over the period of 9 d, with the plant running from 0900–1300 h and 1400–1830 h on each day. Each row in both the datasets contains measurements from all sensors and actuators as recorded in the SWaT Historian sampled at 1-second intervals.

Reports from the three aforementioned detectors - DAD, AICrit and Hybrid Monitor collected during the entire run of CISS 2019 and 2020 sampled at 1-second intervals over the same time period were then collated with the corresponding timestamps in the respective datasets.

With the help of Python scripts, the data was labelled based on the attack information collected during CISS 2019 and 2020 exercise for supervised learning. We added a final column to the dataset - the target column - with the label "Attack" representing the presence of an attack and the label "Normal" denoting the absence of anomalies.

For illustration, a sample of a few rows and columns of the compiled dataset are shown in Table 1. The nomenclature of the components mentioned are as follows. 'AIT' refers to the Analyzer Indication Transmitters that provide as indication of the pH, conductivity and oxidation reduction potential of raw water. 'FIT' refers to the Flow Indication Transmitters, which indicate the water flow rate to the UF tank. 'LIT', i.e., the Level Indication Transmitters indicate water level, as its name suggests. 'MV' refers to Motorised Valves and 'P' refers to Pumps. 'PIT', or Pressure Indication Transmitters, monitor the difference between inlet and outlet pressure in the tanks. 'AICrit Report', 'HybMon Report' contain the reports of the aforementioned detectors. The last column, 'Plant Status', describes whether the plant is under attack or in normal operation. This is the column that is used as the ground truth for supervised learning.

Table 1. A snippet of the dataset used for training.

Timestamp	AIT201	FIT201	LIT101	MV101	P101	PIT501	AICrit report	DAD rport	HybMon rport	Plant sate
2020–07–30 09:04:26	199.6924	0.000256	697.8355	1	1	237.8877	No alarm	No alarm	No alarm	Normal
2020–07–30 09:04:27	199.6924	0.000256	697.9141	1	1	237.8877	No alarm	Alarm	No alarm	Normal
2020–07–30 09:04:28	199.6924	0.000256	697.9141	1	1	237.6154	Alarm	No alarm	No alarm	Normal
2020–07–30 09:04:29	199.6924	0.000256	698.4636	1	1	237.4231	Alarm	No alarm	No alarm	Normal
2020–07–30 09:04:30	199.6924	0.000256	698.4636	1	1	237.4231	No alarm	No alarm	No alarm	Normal
2020–07–30 09:04:31	199.6924	0.000256	698.7776	1	1	237.2148	No alarm	No alarm	No alarm	Normal

4   Learning Algorithms Used in the Approach

This section presents the machine learning algorithms used in this work.

4.1   Random Forest

The Random Forest (RF) [14] algorithm uses decision trees as its base estimator. In machine learning terminology, decision trees are binary trees that learn how to best split the dataset into smaller and smaller subsets to predict the target value. N decision trees are built with N bootstrap samples i.e., samples randomly drawn from the original set. When splitting at each node, only a random subset of features is considered (without replacement). The split is made by choosing the best numerical or categorical feature based on an appropriate impurity criterion.

   Impurity is a measure of homogeneity of labels at a node. We calculate the Gini impurity criterion in our model. Gini impurity [20] is a measure of how often a randomly chosen element from the set would be incorrectly labelled if it were randomly labelled according to the distribution of labels in the subset.

For a set of items with J classes, suppose $i \in \{1, 2, ..., J\}$, and let p_i be the fraction of items labelled with class i in the set, the Gini impurity I_G is calculated as follows.

$$I_G = \sum_{i=1}^{J}\left(p_i \sum_{k \neq i} p_k\right) = \sum_{i=1}^{J} p_i(1 - p_i) = \sum_{i=1}^{J}(p_i - p_i^2) = \sum_{i=1}^{J} p_i - \sum_{i=1}^{J} p_i^2 = 1 - \sum_{i=1}^{J} p_i^2$$

As the splitting at each node continues, each decision tree is grown to its largest. The final prediction of the random forest is given aggregating the predictions of the N individual trees by majority voting.

4.2   Gaussian Naïve Bayes

The Naïve Bayes classifier [7] is a probabilistic classifier that is based on the Bayes' Theorem with the assumption that each feature makes an independent and an equal contribution to the outcome. Consider an input feature vector $X = (x_1, x_2, ..., x_n)$ which are iid, i.e., independent of each other and identically distributed (in other words, drawn from the same distribution), and a class variable C_k. Bayes Theorem states that:

$$P(C_k \mid X) = \frac{P(X \mid C_k)P(C_k)}{P(X)} \ for \ k = 1, 2, ..., K$$

The naïve conditional independence assumption, which assumes that input features are independent of each other, is stated as:

$$P(C_k \mid x_1, ..., x_n) = \frac{P(C_k)P(x_1 \mid C_k)P(x_2 \mid C_k)...P(x_n \mid C_k)}{P(x_1)P(x_2)...P(x_n)}$$

The posterior probability can then be written as:

$$P(C_k \mid x_1, ..., x_n) \ \alpha \ P(C_k) \prod_{i=1}^{n} P(x_i \mid C_k)$$

The Naïve Bayes classification problem can then be formulated as

$$C = \arg \max_{C_k} P(C_k) \prod_{i=1}^{n} P(x_i \mid C_k)$$

In other words, Naïve Bayes outputs the class C_k with maximum probability.

Gaussian Naïve Bayes assumes that continuous values are sampled from a Gaussian/Normal distribution. In mathematical terms, for input feature vector $X = x_i$ for i = 1,2,...,n with mean μ_i and output y with standard deviation σ_y, it assumes that

$$P(x_i \mid y) = \frac{1}{\sqrt{2\pi\sigma_y}}exp(-\frac{(x_i - \mu_i)^2}{2\sigma_y^2})$$

4.3 Bagging with k-nearest Neighbors

Bagging is an ensemble learning method [8], an acronym for Bootstrap Aggregation. In this algorithm, N bootstrap samples i.e., randomized subsets of the original data are drawn from the training set. These samples are trained on N learning models, also known as base estimators, that use the k-nearest neighbors algorithm. This algorithm is based on the assumption that similar data points occur close to each other when plotted on a graph. It predicts the output based on the Euclidean distance between the query point and its k-nearest neighbors. Some instances are sampled several times, some are not sampled at all. These samples are called out-of-bag (OOB) instances. After training on bootstrap samples, OOB instances are used to evaluate the performance of the ensemble. Predictions collected from the N individual estimators are aggregated by majority voting to produce the final output.

4.4 Stacking Classifier

The stacking algorithm [30], as illustrated in Fig. 3, is as follows.

1. Specify a list of M base models (with a specific set of model parameters) and a meta learning algorithm.
2. Train each of the M base algorithms on the training set.
3. Perform k-fold cross-validation on each of these learners and collect the cross-validated predicted values from each of the M algorithms.
4. The M cross-validated predicted values from each of the models can be combined to form a new p x M matrix, where p is the number of rows in the training set. This matrix, along with the original target vector, is called "level-one" data.
5. Train the meta learning algorithm on the level-one data to produce the final output.

The above algorithms were chosen based on the following considerations. Random Forests are a popular choice for anomaly detection due to their ability to model both linear and non-linear relationships well without being too sensitive to outliers. They implicitly perform feature selection and generate uncorrelated decision trees, making them a great choice for working with a high-dimensional dataset like the SWaT dataset. Since the model's principle is to average the results across the multiple decision trees it builds, it reduces variance. k-nearest

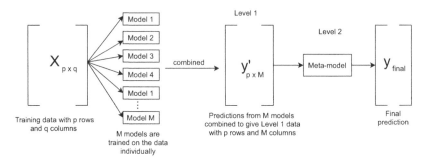

Fig. 3. The stacking classifier

neighbors is another algorithm apt for detecting anomalies. Since it uses underlying patterns in the data to make predictions, any errors in these predictions are thus telltale signs of data points which do not conform to overall trends. Bagging several k-nearest neighbor classifiers results in a stable and more robust classifier. This also lowers variance and prevents overfitting. Gaussian Naïve Bayes is selected due to its lightweight implementation that provides good results while remaining computationally efficient, making it ideal for real-time prediction. It is resilient to noise and irrelevant features. It is especially great for large datasets because it scales linearly with data. Stacking ensemble allows us to use the strength of each individual estimator and diminish their weaknesses by using their output as input to a final estimator. The default Logistic Regression algorithm is used as the meta-learner that outputs the final prediction of the Stacked Classifier because it is a simple and efficient linear model that doesn't require much engineering overhead.

5   Methodology

5.1   Data Pre-processing

It is important to note that the 2 aforementioned classes - 'Attack' and 'Normal' are severely disproportionate, with the portion of attack scenarios with respect to all the non-attack scenarios being approximately 1%. The following preprocessing steps were carried out keeping this in consideration.

First, data records with missing and/or invalid values were removed. Since the CISS datasets contained the plant status at 1-second intervals, they were rather large in size and resulted in a high training time, especially for a distance-based algorithm like k-nearest neighbors. To resolve this, the initial approach adopted was to aggregate the data over 60s to reflect the plant status at every minute. This was done by taking the average of over 60s for numerical features and taking the mode over 60s for categorical features using Excel Pivot Tables and Macros. However, this failed to represent the data and the underlying patterns in the sensor and actuator values correctly. Sudden changes in the values could not be captured.

Therefore, we sampled the data at 10-second intervals, and also included all the attacks that occured on that day so as to not reduce the already low number of attack samples. This was done for each of the 4 d of CISS 2019. For CISS 2020, however, we only included data from 5 selected days out of 9 d of CISS 2020, because the sheer volume of the dataset tremendously increased training time. The 5 d were selected such that number of attacks launched on these days were higher than the others. In the rest of this paper, it is these condensed datasets that we refer to when we mention CISS 2019 and CISS 2020 datasets.

The data cleaning process was followed by feature engineering to encode categorical features using the One-Hot Encoding technique. This was applied to the columns containing the reports of the three detectors - DAD, AICrit and Hybrid Monitor, which were categorical in nature with "Alarm" signifying the report of an anomaly, and "No alarm" signifying no detection. Furthermore, each individual feature has a different range. For example, FIT101 typically ranges from 0 to 2.6 whereas LIT101 ranges from 0–900. Hence, all the data was normalised to be on the same scale using scikit-learn's StandardScaler to prevent the domination of some features over the others.

Since the dataset was highly imbalanced, we adopted the method of SMOTE (Synthetic Minority Oversampling Technique). This is a statistical technique for increasing the number of minority cases in the dataset in a balanced way. It works by generating new instances from existing minority cases. The new instances are not just copies of existing cases, instead, the algorithm takes samples of the feature space for each target class and its nearest neighbors and generates new examples that combine features of the target case with features of its neighbors. The number of minority cases generated was set to be atleast 25% of the number of majority cases. This proportion was carefully chosen so as to provide suffi-cient samples for the model to learn from, at the same time preventing it from developing a bias towards the minority case and raising false alarms.

5.2   Training

The collated data was split into training and test sets, wherein 15% of the training data was held out for testing. Three individual models - Random Forest, Bagging ensemble with k-nearest neighbors, and Gaussian Naïve Bayes were trained on the data. Hyperparameters of each of the models were optimized by performing a Randomized Search cross validation, followed by Grid Search cross validation to select those that resulted in the highest accuracy, precision and recall score. The three optimized models were fed into a Stacking Classifier with scikit-learn's default Logistic Regressor as the meta model to produce the final prediction as shown in Fig. 4.

Figure 5 summarizes the steps taken to pre-process and train the Super Detector.

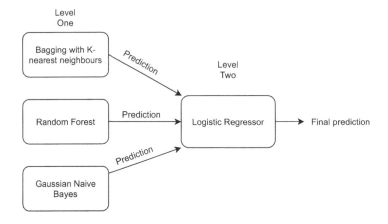

Fig. 4. An illustration of Super Detector's learning model.

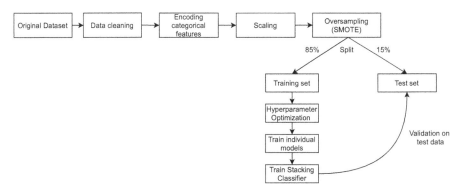

Fig. 5. The pre-processing and training process

6   Results and Analysis

We use two methods to evaluate the predictive power of the model, namely, confusion matrix and classification report. A confusion matrix is a table used to describe the performance of a classification model. For a 2-class classification, the matrix has 4 values. The top-left value indicates the number of true positives, i.e., the number of positive observations that were predicted correctly (where the positive and negative classes are defined by the user). Similarly, the bottom right value represents the number of negative observations that were predicted correctly or true negatives. The top-right value indicates the number of positive observations that were predicted to be negative by the model. Likewise, the bottom-left value is the number of negative observations that the model predicted to be positive. In a classification report, the following metrics are listed. Precision refers to the ratio of correctly predicted positive observations to the total predicted positive observations. A recall is the ratio of correctly predicted positive observations to all observations actually in the positive class. F1-score is the weighted average of precision and recall. Accuracy refers to the ratio of the number of correctly predicted observations to the total number of observations. In our work, we define the 'Attack' class as the positive class and the 'Normal' class as the negative class.

We first include the results of prediction by the individual models - Random Forest Classifier, Bagging Classifier and Gaussian Naïve Bayes, and perform a comparison with the result obtained from Super Detector on the CISS 2020 dataset. The classification performance of the individual models is summarized in Table 2.

Table 2. Prediction performance of Random Forest, Bagging ensemble and Gaussian Naïve Bayes models on the CISS 2020 dataset.

	Random forest		Bagging		Gaussian Naïve Bayes	
	Predicted 'Attack'	Predicted 'Normal'	Predicted 'Attack'	Predicted 'Normal'	Predicted 'Attack'	Predicted 'Normal'
Actual 'Attack'	468	32	471	29	496	4
Actual 'Normal'	21	1977	82	1916	1808	190

To further analyse the efficacy of each model, we compare the following metrics obtained from the respective classification reports. Figure 6 shows that Random Forest achieves the highest precision of 96% in detecting attacks. Gaussian Naïve Bayes achieves a high recall score of about 99%, rightly detecting nearly all attack cases, but also misclassifying an alarmingly high number of normal cases, as observed from the confusion matrix above. Random Forest also achieves the highest F1-score of 95%.

It is also important to analyze the performance of the individual detectors - AICrit, DAD and HybMon to realise the improvement that Super Detector achieves in terms of performance. Table 3 shows the confusion matrices produced by these detectors on the CISS 2020 dataset. AICrit achieves a precision of 2% and recall of 89%, resulting in a large false alarm rate. DAD and HybMon result in precision of 5% and 2%, and recall of 14% and 8% respectively, owing to the misclassification of majority of the attacks as normal cases. It is worth noting that the data was not oversampled before analysing detector performance because this would not be a true reflection of their performance.

Table 3. Prediction performance of AICrit, DAD and HybMon detectors on the CISS 2020 dataset.

	AICrit		DAD		HybMon	
	Predicted 'Attack'	Predicted 'Normal'	Predicted 'Attack'	Predicted 'Normal'	Predicted 'Attack'	Predicted 'Normal'
Actual 'Attack'	26	11	5	32	2	35
Actual 'Normal'	1676	788	100	2364	216	2248

The confusion matrix and classification report of Super Detector's predictions on CISS 2019 and 2020 data are summarised in Tables 4 and 5.

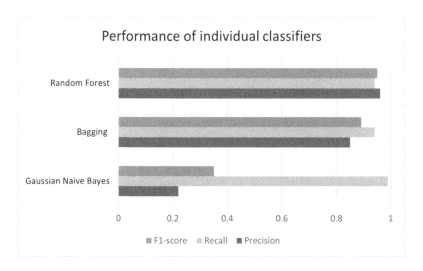

Fig. 6. A comparison of the precision, recall and F1-score achieved by Random Forest, Bagging ensemble and Gaussian Naïve Bayes on the CISS 2020 dataset.

Table 4. In the CISS 2019 dataset, Super Detector predicted 363 attacks and 340 normal cases correctly, whereas 17 attacks were predicted to be 'Normal' and 14 normal cases were predicted to be 'Attack'. In the CISS 2020 dataset 479 attacks and 1979 normal cases were predicted correctly, while 21 attacks were predicted to be 'Normal' and 19 normal cases were predicted to be 'Attack'.

	CISS2019		CISS2020	
	Predicted 'Attack'	Predicted 'Normal'	Predicted 'Attack'	Predicted 'Normal'
Actual 'Attack'	363	17	479	21
Actual 'Normal'	14	340	19	1979

Table 5. Super Detector achieved an accuracy and precision of 96% and recall of 95% on the CISS 2019 dataset and 98% accuracy and 96% precision and recall on the CISS 2020 dataset.

	CISS2019			CISS2020		
	Precision	Recall	F1-Score	Precision	Recall	F1-Score
Attack	0.96	0.95	0.95	0.96	0.96	0.96
Normal	0.98	0.99	0.98	0.99	0.99	0.99
Accuracy	0.96			0.98		
Macro average	0.97	0.96	0.97	0.98	0.97	0.97
Micro average	0.97	0.97	0.97	0.98	0.98	0.98

We describe one of the attacks from the CISS 2019 dataset. The attacker manipulated level sensor LIT101 value and set its value to 222 mm, much lower than its normal operating range of 500 mm–800 mm. This resulted in activation of raw water inlet valve MV101 (i.e., changing its status from close to open) and water pump P101 is stopped (changing its status from ON to OFF). The detectors AICrit raised an alarm, but DAD and Hybrid Monitor failed to do so. Super Detector, however, rightly identified the attack. Figure 7 shows the status of there components and detector reports. Here, the attack was launched at 10:41:00 am. In the bottom-right plot, '1' indicates the no alarm produced by the detector, and '2' indicates that an alarm was produced.

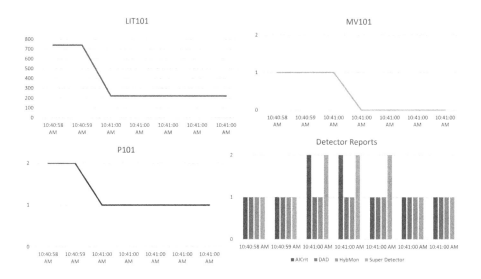

Fig. 7. An attack scenario detected by Super Detector

It is easily observable that Super Detector outperforms individual models in terms accuracy and precision, and significantly lowers the false positive rate.

6.1   Analysis

We analyse the reasons to understand why our model is able to achieve better anomaly detection performance. Firstly, the incorporation of reports from existing anomaly detectors in addition to data from the SWaT plant provides us an edge over detectors trained solely on plant data. When the same model architecture is trained without the reports of the three detectors, it achieved a lower accuracy of 92% and a recall of 91% compared to the 95% accuracy and 94% recall achieved by Super Detector. The inclusion of information from these detectors along with plant operation data proves to output a more reliable decision.

Secondly, the adoption of ensemble machine learning algorithms allowed us to improve the prediction performance of individual models. Furthermore, since our model is trained on a dataset that contains samples over a significant period of time in short intervals, it could capture many underlying patterns in sensor and actuator values, increasing its suitability for real water treatment plants. Lastly, our model is simple in nature and quick to train, which makes it easy to understand and adapt to other plants.

We notice that in some cases, our detector performed better than the existing detectors - predicting 'Normal' correctly despite the three detectors raising an alarm (Table 6) and also detecting an attack when none of the detectors raised an alarm (Table 7). The 'Super Detector' column is the label predicted by our detector. This shows that Super Detector has extracted and learnt the right patterns from plant operation data, and can detect the anomalous values even in the absence of accurate information from the pre-existing detectors. Thereby, Super Detector is able to tackle the problem of decision fusion effectively.

Super Detector's improved performance also stems from the fact that its hyperparameters were carefully tuned according to the labelled training data. When dealing with the detection of anomalies in real-world ICSs, generation of the ground truth data corresponding to all sorts of anomalies is not practically possible. In such a scenario, where training on labelled data i.e., supervised training is not an option, we suggest tapping into existing historical data of the ICS collected from its normal day-to-day operation. This will allow the detector to learn the expected behavior of the system, reporting an anomaly anytime a deviation from this behavior is observed.

Table 6. Super Detector correctly classifies the data point as 'Normal' whereas AICrit, DAD, and Hybrid Monitor have produced a false attack alarm

Timestamp	AIT201	FIT201	LIT101	MV101	AICrit report	DAD report	HybMon report	Plant state	Super Detector
2020–08–03 18:24:18	191.6496	2.291097	759.2661	1	Alarm	Alarm	Alarm	Normal	Normal
2020–08–03 18:27:30	191.3612	2.281485	670.3586	1	Alarm	Alarm	Alarm	Normal	Normal

Table 7. Super Detector successfully detects the attack whereas AICrit, DAD and Hybrid Monitor have produced a false negative of 'No alarm'

Timestamp	AIT201	FIT201	LIT101	MV101	AICrit report	DAD report	HybMon report	Plant state	Super Detector
2020–07–28 18:57:50	23.67982	0.000256	656.4239	1	No alarm	No alarm	No alarm	Attack	Attack

It's important to recognize the challenges when using such a method in its current form. As with all supervised machine learning methods, our model requires a large amount of labelled data which is often difficult to obtain in reality, especially attack data. Moreover, a balanced dataset is required to prevent the model from developing a bias towards the majority class. Despite optimization, we were unable to achieve a near-zero false positive rate. Additionally, since the data has been considered at 10-second intervals, sudden drops or spikes in values that occurred within a fraction of second could have been missed.

Machine learning approaches typically employ transfer learning to improve their learning rate. However, in the setting of an ICS, training on data previously collected data i.e., training on CISS 2019 data and testing on CISS 2020 data (or vice versa) is not advisable. This can be attributed to the *ageing effect* (wear and tear) of sensors and actuators in the treatment plant over time, causing the range of values in datasets from different years to be significantly different. Therefore, transfer learning is not a viable option.

Another major challenge we faced was the insufficiency of attack data. The tremendous volume of 'Normal' data collected in comparison to the tiny proportion of attacks made it extremely difficult to attain a good accuracy without sampling at longer intervals or using the oversampling technique. The available attack data too was difficult to interpret due to ambiguous and incomplete attack logging. Some of the attacks were not logged instantaneously due to which they may not correspond to the right timestamp. This lowered the accuracy of the labelled training data.

Future Work: Through experimentation in a live scenario, we discovered that while using supervised learning, the model tends to learn the signature of each attack case while training. This leads to the detection of only the attacks with the same signature as those in the training dataset when deployed. Attacks unseen by the model, no matter how severe, go undetected. We propose training unsupervised learning models as future work. Such an approach would involve training the model solely on the normal scenario and using it for the prediction of outliers. This way, any deviation from normalcy can be detected effectively. Furthermore, to tackle the ageing effect of the components, we have also decided to adopt a continuous learning approach wherein Super Detector will update its model on a daily basis.

We plan to test the Super Detector approach in a real-time setting in upcoming cyber exercises.

7   Conclusion

Anomaly detection and securing ICS from cyber-attacks are of high importance to many institutions and even government organizations. In this paper, we have proposed a novel approach for detecting attacks on operational technology using ensemble learning. We successfully demonstrated that our approach achieves reliable performance through testing on data from a realistic testbed. Our approach can also be extended to a wide variety of applications outside of water treatment. The principle of sensor fusion, broadly speaking, will be important as multiple detection mechanisms are installed in critical infrastructures in the future.

Another potential future prospect for our work is further tuning to reduce the false alarm rate and further training to identify the component(s) that show an anomalous value as well.

References

1. Adepu, S., Mathur, A.: Distributed detection of single-stage multipoint cyber attacks in a water treatment plant. In: Proceedings of the 11th ACM on Asia Conference on Computer and Communications Security, pp. 449–460 (2016)
2. Adepu, S., Mathur, A.: An investigation into the response of a water treatment system to cyber attacks. In: 2016 IEEE 17th International Symposium on High Assurance Systems Engineering (HASE), pp. 141–148. IEEE (2016)
3. Adepu, S., Mathur, A.: Distributed attack detection in a water treatment plant: method and case study. IEEE Trans. Dependable Secure Comput. (2018)
4. Adepu, S., Mathur, A.: Safeci: avoiding process anomalies in critical infrastructure. Int. J. Critical Infrastruct. Prot. **34**, 100435 (2021)
5. Al-Madani, B., Shawahna, A., Qureshi, M.: Anomaly detection for industrial control networks using machine learning with the help from the inter-arrival curves. arXiv preprint arXiv:1911.05692 (2019)
6. Angséus, J., Ekbom, R.: Network-based intrusion detection systems for industrial control systems. Master's Thesis (2017)
7. Bayes, F.: An essay towards solving a problem in the doctrine of chances. Biometrika **45**(3–4), 296–315 (1958)
8. Breiman, L.: Bagging predictors. Mach. Learn. **24**(2), 123–140 (1996)
9. Castellanos, J.H., Zhou, J.: A modular hybrid learning approach for black-box security testing of CPS. In: Deng, R., Gauthier-Uma, V., Ochoa, M., Yung, M. (eds.) Applied Cryptography and Network Security. ACNS 2019. LNCS, vol. 11464. Springer, Cham (2019). https://doi.org/10.1007/978-3-030-21568-2_10
10. CISS 2019: CISS. itrust.sutd.edu.sg/ciss/ciss-2019/
11. CISS 2020: CISS. itrust.sutd.edu.sg/ciss/ciss-2020-ol/
12. Das, T.K., Adepu, S., Zhou, J.: Anomaly detection in industrial control systems using logical analysis of data. Comput. Secur. **96**, 101935 (2020)
13. Goh, J., Adepu, S., Tan, M., Lee, Z.S.: Anomaly detection in cyber physical systems using recurrent neural networks. In: 2017 IEEE 18th International Symposium on High Assurance Systems Engineering (HASE), pp. 140–145. IEEE (2017)
14. Ho, T.K.: Random decision forests. In: Proceedings of 3rd International Conference on Document Analysis and Recognition, vol. 1, pp. 278–282. IEEE (1995)
15. Inoue, J., Yamagata, Y., Chen, Y., Poskitt, C.M., Sun, J.: Anomaly detection for a water treatment system using unsupervised machine learning. In: International Conference on Data Mining Workshops, pp. 1058–1065. IEEE (2017)
16. Kravchik, M., Shabtai, A.: Efficient cyber attack detection in industrial control systems using lightweight neural networks and pca. IEEE Trans. Dependable Secure Comput. (2021)
17. Lazarevic, A., Kumar, V.: Feature bagging for outlier detection. In: Proceedings of the Eleventh ACM SIGKDD International Conference on Knowledge Discovery in Data Mining, pp. 157–166 (2005)
18. Li, D., Chen, D., Jin, B., Shi, L., Goh, J., Ng, S.K.: MAD-GAN: Multivariate anomaly detection for time series data with generative adversarial networks. In: Tetko, I., Karpov, P., Theis, F. (eds.) Artificial Neural Networks and Machine Learning ICANN 2019: Text and Time Series. ICANN 2019. LNCS, vol. 11730. Springer, Cham (2019). https://doi.org/10.1007/978-3-030-30490-4_56
19. Li, T., Hankin, C.: Effective defence against zero-day exploits using bayesian networks. In: International Conference on Critical Information Infrastructures Security, pp. 123–136. Springer (2016)

20. Loh, W.Y.: Classification and regression trees. Wiley Interdiscipl. Rev. Data Mining Knowl. Discovery **1**(1), 14–23 (2011)
21. Luo, Y., Xiao, Y., Cheng, L., Peng, G., Yao, D.: Deep learning-based anomaly detection in cyber-physical systems: progress and opportunities. ACM Comput. Surv. (CSUR) **54**(5), 1–36 (2021)
22. Mathur, A.P., Tippenhauer, N.O.: Swat: a water treatment testbed for research and training on ics security. In: 2016 International Workshop Cyber Physical Systerm Smart Water Network (CySWater), pp. 31–36. IEEE (2016)
23. Maw, A., Adepu, S., Mathur, A.: Ics-blockops: blockchain for operational data security in industrial control system. Pervasive Mobile Comput. **59** (2019)
24. Mokhtari, S., Abbaspour, A., Yen, K.K., Sargolzaei, A.: A machine learning approach for anomaly detection in industrial control systems based on measurement data. Electronics **10**(4), 407 (2021)
25. Perales Gómez, Á.L., Fernández Maimó, L., Huertas Celdrán, A., García Clemente, F.J.: Madics: A methodology for anomaly detection in industrial control systems. Symmetry **12**(10), 1583 (2020)
26. Raman, M.G., Dong, W., Mathur, A.: Deep autoencoders as anomaly detectors: method and case study in a distributed water treatment plant. Comput. Secur. **99**, 102055 (2020)
27. Shrivastava, S.: Blackenergy-malware for cyber-physical attacks. Singapore **74**, 115 (2016)
28. Song, H., Jiang, Z., Men, A., Yang, B.: A hybrid semi-supervised anomaly detection model for high-dimensional data. Comput. Intell. Neurosci. (2017)
29. Stouffer, K., Falco, J.: Guide to supervisory control and data acquisition (SCADA) and industrial control systems security. National Inst. Standards Technol. (2006)
30. Wolpert, D.H.: Stacked generalization. Neural Netw. **5**(2), 241–259 (1992)
31. Xin, Y., et al.: Machine learning and deep learning methods for cybersecurity. IEEE access **6**, 35365–35381 (2018)
32. Zhao, Z.: Ensemble methods for anomaly detection, Syracuse University (2017)
33. Zohrevand, Z., Glässer, U., Tayebi, M.A., Shahir, H.Y., Shirmaleki, M., Shahir, A.Y.: Deep learning based forecasting of critical infrastructure data. In: Proceedings of the 2017 ACM on Conference on Information and Knowledge Management, pp. 1129–1138 (2017)

Optimal Man-In-The-Middle Stealth Attack

Luca Faramondi, Gabriele Oliva$^{(\boxtimes)}$ (iD), and Roberto Setola

Automatic Control Unit, Department of Engineering, Universitá Campus Bio-Medico di Roma, via Álvaro del Portillo 21, 00128 Rome, Italy
`g.oliva@unicampus.it`

Abstract. In this paper we propose an optimal Man-In-The-Middle attack strategy to maliciously manipulate information transmitted from the field to a centralized control unit. The aim of the attacker is to significantly deviate the system's behavior from its nominal trajectory and, at the same time, avoid that thew attack can be recognized. Specifically, we consider a scenario where an attacker is able to intercept and manipulate data transmitted from a remote sensor to a centralized state estimator equipped with a bad data detector. As shown in the paper, under the assumption of perfect information, the attacker, by solving a non-concave maximization problem, can cause a large discrepancy between the actual state and the estimated one without being discovered. By developing local optimality conditions for the problem at hand, we are able to design an algorithm to find an approximated solution. The paper is concluded by an example showing the best strategy for the attacker.

Keywords: Cyber attack · Cyber security · Cyber-physical systems · Critical infrastructures · Operational technologies

1 Introduction

In last decades, the pervasive adoption of network-based remote control solutions has exposed industrial systems, such as plants or infrastructures, to unprecedented cyber-security threats, able to compromise their correct functioning. Despite the adoption of countermeasures based on network traffic monitoring for intrusion detection, cyber threats still represent one of the main vulnerabilities for industrial plants and SCADA systems. In last 10 years, several malwares have been designed specifically to affect industrial control systems, the most relevant being Stuxnet (2010), Havex (2014), Black Energy (2015), Clash Override (2016), and Triton (2017) [15]. Stuxnet is a malware able to identify a specific industrial controller in order to alter the rotational speed of some motors. The malware Havex is used as a support for more complex attacks, as it is able to scan the network via legitimate functionalities in the OPC protocol, with the aim to identify the network devices and their addresses. Black Energy is able to acquire data about the industrial process; specifically, the malware monitors the Human-Machine Interface (HMI) to extract relevant information from

D. Percia David et al. (Eds.): CRITIS 2021, LNCS 13139, pp. 44–59, 2021.
https://doi.org/10.1007/978-3-030-93200-8_3

the graphical representation of the plant and about the activities performed by SCADA operators. Crash Override, like the latest version of Blackenergy, is able to introduce legitimate commands, manipulating the behavior of the electricity network with the aim to create a black-out. Finally, Triton is designed for SIS systems (Safety Instrumental System), i.e., particular industrial control systems, generally separated from the general purpose ones, that are used to prevent catastrophic events. However, the most effective attack has been those against the Colonial pipeline in may 2021 which halted the 2200 km gasoline and jet fuel pipeline for more than a week [5].

1.1 Related Works

For that which concerns attacks able to compromise measurement and actuator data by intercepting the communication channel, according to [1], one can consider two classes of attack: *block* (aimed to degrade data availability) and *deception* attacks (which aim is to compromise data integrity). The first one, generally based on DoS (Denial of Service) attacks, are able to interrupt the exchange of information among the control center and the Remote Terminal Units (RTUs) and this might induce a degradation or even a stop in the plant [4]. In [21], DoS attacks against state estimators are performed via jamming techniques, with the aim to increase the estimation error and in [9] a game-theoretic framework is provided with the aim to detect jamming attacks.

On the other side, an attack able to alter the integrity of the exchanged data has the potential to induce more dramatic consequences, being the plant driven to operate in dangerous conditions. Such attacks are relatively easy to be performed due to the lack of authentication and cryptography mechanism in several industrial protocol (e.g. Modbus). Simple attacks are based on replay attack, i.e., the attacker accesses, records, and replays the sensor data [11,12]. However, such attacks can be easily detected in the presence of a state estimator as illustrated by [22], where an extended Kalman filter is adopted to detect bias injection or replay attacks. In [18,19] the vulnerability of state estimators in power systems with respect to attacks performed against the communication infrastructure is analyzed, moreover the authors define security metrics that quantify the importance of individual substations and the cost of attacking individual measurements. In [16] bad data detection schemes are developed as a support for cyber threats identification; such schemes, based on measurement redundancy, represent a support to the state estimator with the aim to identify a set of simple cyber attacks and detect random outliers in the measurement data. In [2], cyber attacks based on measurements or actuators' signals modifications are studied; in particular, the authors characterize the maximum number of attacks that can be detected and corrected providing a necessary condition for the state reconstruction in case of multiple attacks. In [13], data injection attacks against state estimators are considered where false signals are injected in order to compromise the integrity of the Kalman filter used to perform state estimation. The work presented in [20] describes the design of an optimal input injection scheme based on switching attacks, where the adversary aims to maximize the deviation of the plant's state from nominal condition by suitable input injection and location switching. An attack strategy based on zero-dynamics and stealthy data injection attacks on control systems is discussed in [17]. Specifically, in [17] the authors characterize and analyze the stealthiness properties of attacks to linear time-invariant systems and provide detection strategies based on the modification of the structure of the system; moreover, necessary and sufficient conditions about the identification of zero-dynamics attacks are provided. In [6], the behavior of a malicious attacker aiming to compromise linear state estimators is studied. In particular, the authors of [6] consider a systems with a state estimator based on Kalman filter and a residual-based intrusion detectors. For such systems, they analyze the effects of intermittent data integrity improvements, such as the use of message authentication codes. In [8] the design of a robust state estimation scheme for continuous-time linear dynamical systems is addressed; the method correctly estimates the states under sensor attacks thanks to the sensor redundancy, and guarantees a bounded estimation error despite measurement noises and process disturbances. In [14], an attacker aims at maximize the error of a state estimator of a multi-agent system by introducing noise in a subset of the communication channels of the network.

1.2 Contribution and Paper Outline

In this paper we take the standpoint of an attacker that modifies via a Man-In-The-Middle (MITM) attack the measurements received by the SCADA system in order to cause discrepancies in the state estimation of the plant without being discovered by the Bada Data Detector (BDD) system. As a result, the SCADA user is mislead into performing wrong actions due to the fact that it is observing a fake state of the system. The outline of the paper is as follows: In Sect. 2 we describe the formulation of the proposed attack strategy. In Sect. 3 we provide a sufficient and a necessary conditions for local optimal solution for the problem into account. Results and discussions are collected in Sect. 4 with the aim to validate the proposed formulation; finally some conclusive remarks are collected in Sect. 5.

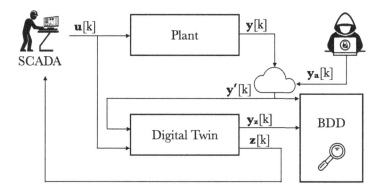

Fig. 1. State estimation under the envisaged MITM attack.

1.3 Preliminaries: Notation and Definitions

We denote vectors by boldface lowercase letters and matrices with uppercase letters. We refer to the (i,j)-th entry of a matrix A by A_{ij}. We represent by $\mathbf{0}_n$ and $\mathbf{1}_n$ vectors with n entries, all equal to zero and to one, respectively. Moreover, we denote by I_n the $n \times n$ identity matrix. The set of positive real numbers is denoted by $\mathbb{R}_{>0}$.

2 Optimization Formulation

Let us consider a plant described by the following discrete-time system where k represents the time step

$$\begin{cases} \boldsymbol{x}[k+1] &= A\boldsymbol{x}[k] + B\boldsymbol{u}[k], \\ \boldsymbol{y}[k] &= C\boldsymbol{x}[k] \end{cases}$$

with $\boldsymbol{x}[k] \in \mathbb{R}^n$, $\boldsymbol{u}[k] \in \mathbb{R}^p$, $\boldsymbol{y}[k] \in \mathbb{R}^q$, and matrices A, B, C of compatible dimensions. Let us assume that the pair (A, C) is observable (i.e., the observability matrix $O = [C^T, A^T C^T, \ldots (A^T)^{n-1} C^T]^T$ is full rank) and that, in the nominal case, the SCADA receives the output $\boldsymbol{y}[k]$ of the plant via a communication network that is used also to send the control input $\boldsymbol{u}[k]$ from the SCADA to the plant. Let us consider a scenario where the SCADA implements an Luenberger-like observer [10] to estimate the plant's state $\boldsymbol{x}[k]$ in order to perform supervisory activities, detect faults and elaborate the control input $\boldsymbol{u}[k]$. Specifically the plant's state is reconstructed via the following equation

$$\begin{cases} \boldsymbol{z}[k+1] &= A\boldsymbol{z}[k] + B\boldsymbol{u}[k] + L(\boldsymbol{y}[k] - \boldsymbol{y}_z[k]), \\ \boldsymbol{y}_z[k] &= C\boldsymbol{z}[k]. \end{cases}$$

As usual, the SCADA system implements also some BDD strategy in order to detect anomalous data. In particular, the BDD is aimed to emphasize large discrepancies between the actual and estimated outputs. To this end, let us define the *residue* $r[k]$ as

$$r[k] = y'[k] - y_z[k]; \tag{1}$$

where $y'[k]$ is the measure received from the field. The BDD triggers an alarm whenever the condition $\|r[k]\| > \theta$ is met, $\theta \in \mathbb{R}_{>0}$ being a threshold that is tailored to the particular plant.

As mentioned in the introduction, the aim of the attacker is to implement an optimal stealth attack, i.e., an attack that causes the maximum discrepancy between the real state and the one estimated by the SCADA's observer, without triggering the alarm condition. Let us now consider a scenario where an attacker performs a MITM attack altering the information transmitted by the plant towards the SCADA system as depicted in Fig. 1. Specifically, the attacker replaces the real output value $y[k]$ with a maliciously altered value

$$y'[k] = y[k] + y_a[k]$$

with the aim to significantly degradate the estimation accuracy, but avoiding being discovered by the BDD. Notice that, for the sake of simplicity, in this work we assume that the attacker is in the same communication network, hence is able to read and modify all the sensors measures. Moreover, notice that, in this scenario we do not encode the magnitude of exchanged data via physical quantity (e.g. voltage, current) and we suppose the adoption of network protocols for the transmission of sensors data. Hence, the attacker is able to compromise the measures without constraints about the magnitude. As a consequence of the attack, the dynamics of the observer used by the SCADA becomes

$$\begin{cases} z[k+1] &= Az[k] + Bu[k] + L(y'[k] - y_z[k]), \\ y_z[k] &= Cz[k]. \end{cases}$$

Let us consider the estimation error $e[k]$, defined as the discrepancy between the plant's state and the estimated one, i.e., $e[k] = x[k] - z[k]$. Under the MITM attack, the estimation error dynamics is

$$e[k+1] = x[k+1] - z[k+1] = (A - LC)e[k] - Ly_a[k]. \tag{2}$$

To this end, the attacker need to solve the following optimization problem.

Problem 1. Let $A, B, C, L, \theta, u[k], y[k], e[k]$ be given. Find $y_a^*[k] \in \mathbb{R}^q$ such that

$$y_a^*[k] = \arg\max_{y_a[k] \in \mathbb{R}^q} \frac{1}{2} \|e[k+1]\|^2, \quad \text{Subject to} \quad \|r[k+1]\| \leq \theta. \tag{3}$$

Notice that $e[k+1]$ can be expressed in terms of $e[k]$ and $y_a[k]$ via Eq. (2); similarly, by using Eq. (1) we have that

$$r[k+1] = y'[k+1] - y_z[k+1] = Ce[k] + y_a[k].$$

At this point we observe that, in typical working conditions, sufficient time has elapsed so that the transients of the SCADA's observer have vanished; in this case, the attacker may assume that $e[0] = \mathbf{0}_n$. Consequently, the attacker is able to calculate $e[k]$ as follows

$$e[k] = -\sum_{m=0}^{k-1} (A - LC)^{k-m-1} L y_a^*[m]. \tag{4}$$

From an operative point of view, in the remainder of this paper we equivalently formulate the above problem expressing $y_a^*[k]$ in terms of a new variable $w^*[k]$ and we take the square of both sides in the constraint. As discussed later, the reason for expressing $y_a^*[k]$ in terms of a new variable $w^*[k]$ is twofold: firstly, the formulation in terms of the new variable does not depend on C; moreover, the constraint is simplified in that the search space reduces to the unit ball in $\mathbb{R}^q$. In particular, as shown in the next section, since the objective function is convex, the search space reduces to the boundary of the unit ball, i.e., any local maximum $w^*[k]$ is such that the constraint $\|w^*[k]\| = 1$. The equivalent formulation is as follows.

Problem 2. Let $A, B, C, L, \theta, u[k], y[k], e[k]$ be given. Find $y_a^*[k] \in \mathbb{R}^q$ such that

$$y_a^*[k] = \theta w^*[k] - Ce[k], \tag{5}$$

where

$$w^*[k] = \arg\max_{w \in \mathbb{R}^q} \frac{1}{2} \|Ae[k] - \theta Lw\|^2 \quad \text{Subject to} \quad \|w\|^2 \le 1. \tag{6}$$

Remark 1. Notice that the Hessian matrix of the objective function of the above problem is

$$\nabla_{ww} \left(\frac{1}{2} \|Ae[k] - \theta Lw\|^2 \right) = \theta^2 L^T L,$$

which is positive semi-definite by construction. Hence, the objective function of the problem is convex and, since the problem is a maximization one, KKT conditions characterize local optimality.

Remark 2. The above problem always admits a feasible solution. In fact it can be noted that $w = \mathbf{0}_q$ trivially satisfies the constraint.

3   Local Optimality and Attack Strategy

As noted in Remark 1, the maximization problem at hand is non-concave; hence, it is quite challenging to find a global optimal solution. In this section, we first provide a necessary and a sufficient local optimality condition for the problem at hand based on the KKT first and second order conditions (see the appendix for details); then, we rely on such conditions to design an approximated algorithm to solve Problem 2.

3.1   Necessary Local Optimality Condition

Theorem 1. *A necessary condition for* $\boldsymbol{w}^*$ *to be a local maximum for Problem 2 is that*

$$\|\boldsymbol{w}^*\| = 1 \tag{7}$$

and

$$f(\boldsymbol{w}^*) = P(\boldsymbol{w}^*)\boldsymbol{w}^* - L^T A e[k] = \boldsymbol{0}_q, \tag{8}$$

where

$$P(\boldsymbol{w}) = \theta L^T L + \left(\boldsymbol{w}^T L^T A e[k] - \theta \boldsymbol{w}^T L^T L \boldsymbol{w}\right) I_q. \tag{9}$$

Proof. In order to prove the result, we claim that any local maximum $\boldsymbol{w}^*$ must satisfy Eq. (7). In view of a contradiction, let us assume that there is as local maximum $\boldsymbol{w}^*$ with $\|\boldsymbol{w}^*\| < 1$. Since the objective function is convex and $\boldsymbol{w}^*$ is a local maximum, we have that any $\boldsymbol{w}^\dagger$ in an infinitesimal neighborhood of $\boldsymbol{w}^*$ with $\|\boldsymbol{w}^\dagger\| > \|\boldsymbol{w}^*\|$ must have larger objective function than $\boldsymbol{w}^*$. At this point we observe that, for $\boldsymbol{w}^*$ to be a local maximum, any of such points $\boldsymbol{w}^\dagger$ must violate the constraint, i.e., it must hold $\|\boldsymbol{w}^\dagger\| > 1$. However, since we assumed $\|\boldsymbol{w}^*\| < 1$, we have that at least one of such points exists with $\|\boldsymbol{w}^\dagger\| \leq 1$. This is a contradiction; hence, our claim is verified. Let us now elaborate on the KKT first order necessary condition. First of all we observe that the gradient of the constraint, evaluated at a local maximum $\boldsymbol{w}^*$, is equal to $2\boldsymbol{w}^*$, which is nonzero because we established that $\|\boldsymbol{w}^*\| = 1$. Therefore, the problem satisfies the Linear Independence Constraint Qualification (LICQ) condition. Notice that the Lagrangian function for Problem 2 is

$$\mathcal{L}(\boldsymbol{w}, \lambda) = \frac{1}{2} \|A e[k] - \theta L \boldsymbol{w}\|^2 + \lambda \left(1 - \|\boldsymbol{w}\|^2\right).$$

According to KKT theory, a necessary condition for $\boldsymbol{w}^*$ to be a local maximum is that it is feasible for Problem 2 (i.e., $\|\boldsymbol{w}^*\| \leq 1$) and there is a $\lambda^* \geq 0$ such that the gradient of $\mathcal{L}(\boldsymbol{w}, \lambda)$ with respect to $\boldsymbol{w}$ (we assume the gradient is a column vector), evaluated at $\boldsymbol{w}^*, \lambda^*$, satisfies

$$\nabla_w \mathcal{L}(\boldsymbol{w}, \lambda)\Big|_{\boldsymbol{w}=\boldsymbol{w}^*, \lambda=\lambda^*} = \boldsymbol{0}_m \tag{10}$$

and it holds

$$\lambda^* \left(\|\boldsymbol{w}^*\|^2 - 1\right) = 0. \tag{11}$$

In particular, treating the gradient as a column vector and recalling that

$$\nabla_p \boldsymbol{p}^T A \boldsymbol{p} = (A + A^T)\boldsymbol{p}$$

and

$$\nabla_p \boldsymbol{p}^T \boldsymbol{q} = \boldsymbol{q},$$

Eq, (10) becomes

$$\theta^2 L^T L \boldsymbol{w}^* - \theta L^T A e[k] - 2\lambda^* \boldsymbol{w}^* = \boldsymbol{0}_q. \tag{12}$$

By Eq. (7), we have that Eq. (11) is satisfied by any $\lambda^* \geq 0$. Let us first assume that $\lambda^* > 0$. By pre-multiplying both sides of Eq. (12) by $\boldsymbol{w}^*[k]^T$, we get

$$2\lambda^* \boldsymbol{w}^*[k]^T \boldsymbol{w}^*[k] - \theta^2 \boldsymbol{w}^*[k]^T L^T L \boldsymbol{w}^*[k] + \theta \boldsymbol{w}^*[k]^T L^T A\boldsymbol{e}[k] = 0. \qquad (13)$$

By Eq. (7), we have that $\boldsymbol{w}^*[k]^T \boldsymbol{w}^*[k] = 1$ and thus we can simplify Eq. (13) as

$$\lambda^* = \frac{\theta^2}{2} \boldsymbol{w}^*[k]^T L^T L \boldsymbol{w}^*[k] - \frac{\theta}{2} \boldsymbol{w}^*[k]^T L^T A\boldsymbol{e}[k]. \qquad (14)$$

At this point we observe that, when $\lambda^* = 0$, Eq. (12) yields

$$\theta L^T L \boldsymbol{w}^*[k] = L^T A\boldsymbol{e}[k];$$

hence, we can express λ^* as in Eq. (14) also in this case. The proof is complete by plugging Eq. (14) into Eq. (12). $\qquad \square$

3.2   Sufficient Local Optimality Conditions

Let us now elaborate on the KKT second order sufficient local optimality conditions discussed in the preliminaries.

Theorem 2. *Let $\boldsymbol{w}^*[k]$ be a solution to Problem 2 that satisfies the necessary local optimality conditions from Theorem 1. If $P(\boldsymbol{w}^*[k])$ is negative semi-definite (negative definite) then $\boldsymbol{w}^*[k]$ is a local maximum (strict local maximum).*

Proof. From KKT theory, we know that a sufficient local optimality conditions for $\boldsymbol{w}^*[k]$ is that $\boldsymbol{w}^*[k]$ satisfy the first order KKT and the LICQ conditions (which correspond to those in Theorem 1) and

$$\nabla_{\boldsymbol{w}\boldsymbol{w}} \mathscr{L}(\boldsymbol{w}, \lambda)\big|_{w=\boldsymbol{w}^*[k], \lambda=\lambda^*}$$

is negative semi-definite (the local optimality is strict if the above Hessian sub-matrix is negative definite). For the problem at hand, we have that

$$\nabla_{\boldsymbol{w}\boldsymbol{w}} \mathscr{L}(\boldsymbol{w}, \lambda)\big|_{w=\boldsymbol{w}^*[k], \lambda=\lambda^*} = 2\theta P(\boldsymbol{w}^*[k]).$$

Hence a sufficient local optimality condition for $\boldsymbol{w}^*[k]$ is that $P(\boldsymbol{w}^*[k])$ is negative semi-definite, while strict local optimality is obtained if $P(\boldsymbol{w}^*[k])$ is negative definite. $\qquad \square$

Remark 3. Note that, by construction, a local maximum $\boldsymbol{w}^*[k]$ must be such that $\|\boldsymbol{w}^*[k]\| = 1$, and this implies that $\lambda^* \geq 0$. However, when $\lambda^* = 0$ we have that $P(\boldsymbol{w}^*[k]) = \theta L^T L$, i.e., $P(\boldsymbol{w}^*[k])$ is positive semi-definite. Therefore, when $\lambda^* = 0$, the second order KKT sufficient conditions are inconclusive.

3.3 Attack Strategy

Let us now discuss the procedure adopted by the attacker for finding an approx-imated solution to Problem 2. Such a procedure, based on the condition in Theorem 1, is summarized in Algorithm 1. According to the above theorem, candidate local optimal solutions to Problem 2 can be obtained by solving a set of nonlinear algebraic equations. However, finding the analytical solutions of such equations is a challenging task, thus calling for approximated approaches. Since $P(\boldsymbol{w})$ is differentiable, a possible approach is to resort to the Netwon-Raphson method (e.g., see [7]). In particular, if we choose a point $\boldsymbol{w}(0)$ sufficiently close to a root of $f(\cdot)$, then the equation

$$\boldsymbol{w}(t+1) = \boldsymbol{w}(t) - \nabla_{\boldsymbol{w}(t)}(f(\boldsymbol{w}(t)))^{-1} f(\boldsymbol{w}(t)) \tag{15}$$

converges to a root of $f(\cdot)$. Notice further that, since by Theorem 1 we know that any local maximum must lie on the boundary of the unit ball, a possible approach is to select initial points on the boundary of the unit ball, i.e., such

---

Algorithm 1. Attacker procedure

  ▷ Initialization
$\boldsymbol{w}_{\text{best}} \leftarrow \emptyset$
$\text{Obj}_{\text{best}} \leftarrow 0$
  ▷ Main Cycle
for $i = 1, \ldots, h$ **do**
    Sample $\boldsymbol{w}^{(i)}[0]$ from the unit ball in $\mathbb{R}^m$
    $t \leftarrow 1$
    exitcondition $\leftarrow$ false
    while not(exitcondition) **do**
        Compute $w^{(i)}(t), z^{(i)}(t)$ via Eq. (16)
        if $\|w^{(i)}(t) - w^{(i)}(t-1)\| < \delta$ or $t > t_{\max}$ **then**
            exitcondition $\leftarrow$ true
        else
            $t \leftarrow t + 1$
        end if
    end while
    $\overline{w}^{(i)} \leftarrow z^{(i)}(t)$
    Compute objective function Obj_i at $\overline{w}^{(i)}$
    if $\text{Obj}_i > \text{Obj}_{\text{best}}$ **then**
        $\boldsymbol{w}_{\text{best}} \leftarrow \overline{w}^{(i)}$
        $\text{Obj}_{\text{best}} \leftarrow \text{Obj}_i$
    end if
  end for
  $\boldsymbol{y}_a \leftarrow \theta \boldsymbol{w}_{\text{best}} - Ce[k]$
  return $\boldsymbol{y}_a$

---

that $\|\boldsymbol{w}(0)^{(h)}\| = 1$, and then normalize the Newton-Raphson iteration at each step; with this modification, the Newton-Raphson iteration becomes

$$\begin{cases} \boldsymbol{w}(t+1) & = \boldsymbol{z}(t) - \nabla_{\boldsymbol{w}(t)}(f(\boldsymbol{z}(t)))^{-1}f(\boldsymbol{w}(t)) \\ \boldsymbol{z}(t) & = \dfrac{\boldsymbol{w}(t)}{\|\boldsymbol{w}(t)\|}. \end{cases} \tag{16}$$

Using the above iteration, the attacker can compute $\boldsymbol{z}(t)$ until a stopping criterion is met, i.e., until $\|\boldsymbol{z}(t) - \boldsymbol{z}(t-1)\| < \delta$ or $t \geq t_{\max}$, thus obtaining an approximate solution $\overline{\boldsymbol{w}}$. Then, the attacker can approximate the solution of Problem 2 by selecting the point $\overline{\boldsymbol{w}}$ with largest corresponding objective function, and consequently identify the value $y_a[k]$ to be added to the actual measurements in order to perform the stealth attack. Note that, as discussed in Section IV.B, if $P(\overline{\boldsymbol{w}})$ is negative (semi-)definite, then the attacker can conclude that a local maximum has been found.

4   Example

In order to show the effectiveness of the MITM attack, let us consider the plant described by the discrete-time LTI system characterized by the following matrices.

$$A = \begin{bmatrix} 0.8 & 0 & 0 & 0.1 & 0.1 \\ 0 & 0.9 & 0.1 & 0 & 0 \\ 0 & 0.1 & 0.8 & 0 & 0.1 \\ 0.1 & 0 & 0 & 0.9 & 0 \\ 0.1 & 0 & 0.1 & 0 & 0.8 \end{bmatrix}, \quad B = \begin{bmatrix} 0.1 & 0 & 0 & 0 & 0 \end{bmatrix}^T, \quad C = \begin{bmatrix} 1 & 0 & 0 & 1 & 1 \\ 0 & 1 & 1 & 0 & 0 \end{bmatrix}.$$

Moreover, let us assume that $u[k] = sin(0.5k)$. Notice that the system is observable; hence the SCADA user is able to reconstruct the state via a Luenberger-type observer. In particular, the SCADA implements an observer with gain matrix L equal to

$$L = \begin{bmatrix} 101.8393 & 58.6912 \\ -177.6906 & -94.7608 \\ 78.0621 & 36.3658 \\ -300.1788 & -158.5921 \\ 298.7553 & 159.0812 \end{bmatrix}.$$

Finally, the threshold chosen by the SCADA user for the residue of the BDD is $\theta = 0.2$.

Figure 2 shows the value of the objective function of Problem 2 for $e[0] = \boldsymbol{0}_n$, i.e., $\|\theta L \boldsymbol{w}\|^2 / 2$, evaluated on the boundary of the unit circle. It can be noted that, among the points on the boundary of the unit ball, the best solutions are in the form $\boldsymbol{w}^*[0] = \pm \begin{bmatrix} 0.8831 & 0.4692 \end{bmatrix}^T$, with objective function equal to 5.83×10^3. In particular, we argue that both the above solutions are indeed global maxima for the objective function; this stems from the consideration that $\|L \boldsymbol{w}^*[0]\| = \|L\| = 5.39 \times 10^2$, i.e., the maximum of $\|L \boldsymbol{w}\|$ over all vectors of

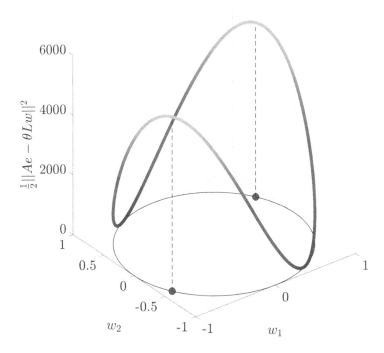

Fig. 2. Objective function of Problem 2 for the example discussed in Sect. 4 and for $k = 0$, evaluated at the boundary of the unit circle. The largest values are reported via small circles.

norm one is attained at $\boldsymbol{w}^*[0]$. Notice that it is possible to conclude that both points are local maxima (not in a strict sense), because they both satisfy the condition in Theorem 1 and, as per Theorem 2, in both cases matrix $P(\cdot)$ is negative semi-definite.

Figure 3 shows the results of the procedure summarized in Algorithm 1, considering 10 initial points uniformly spaced on unit circle (represented by asterisks). For each initial point we show by an arrow the result obtained for $\delta = 10^{-4}$ and $t_{\max} = 1000$. Notice that all solutions found are admissible and, in particular six solutions correspond to a global maximum (we show the global maxima by small circles); moreover, we observe that both global maxima are found by Algorithm 1. Therefore, the attacker is able to find one global optimal solution in an approximated way. Notably, by using the standard Newton-Raphson iteration in Algorithm 1 (i.e., Eq. (15) instead of Eq. (16)), only three initial points converge to a local maximum (only one of the two global maxima is found), and the iteration diverges for one of the initial points. The results suggest that, relying on the fact local maxima have unit norm can improve considerably the effectiveness of the Newton-Raphson approach.

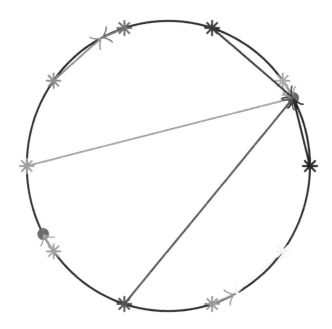

Fig. 3. Example of application of the procedure discussed in Sect. 3.3, considering the modified Newton-Raphson iteration in Eq. (16) and 10 initial points sampled uniformly on the unit circle. The initial points are shown by asterisks, while the arrow shows the result obtained for 1000 iterations of the Newton-Raphson method. The global optimal solutions $\boldsymbol{w}^*[0] = \pm[0.8831,\ 0.4692]^T$ are shown by small circles.

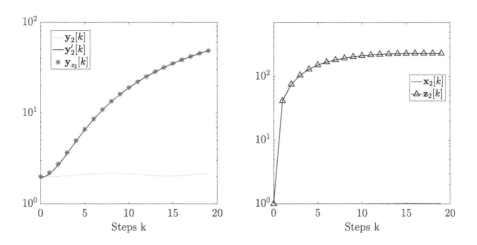

Fig. 4. Left panel: trajectories of $y_2[k]$, $y_2'[k]$ and $y_{z2}[k]$. Right panel: trajectories of $x_2[k]$ and $z_2[k]$.

Let us now show the effect of iterating the MITM attack, i.e., we consider a situation where the attacker modifies the plant's output at each time step k, computing $\boldsymbol{y}_a[k]$ via Algorithm 1. In the left panel of Fig. 4, for the sake of readability, we report just one output variable; i.e. $y_2[k]$, the measurements modified by the attacker ($y_2'[k]$) and the measurements ($y_{z2}[k]$) computed by the SCADA; similarly, in the right panel of Fig. 4 we show the evolution of one of the states $x_2[k]$ and the state $z_2[k]$ estimated by the SCADA. According to the figure, the attack causes the estimated state $\boldsymbol{z}[k]$ to differ significantly from the actual state $\boldsymbol{x}[k]$; at the same time, the attack is done by replacing the actual measurements $\boldsymbol{y}[k]$ with altered values $\boldsymbol{y}'[k]$ that are very close to the values $\boldsymbol{y}_z[k]$ computed at the BDD based on the estimated state $\boldsymbol{z}[k]$. Fig. 5 further highlights the effectiveness of the attack. Specifically, in the left panel, we report the evolution of the norm of the estimation error $\boldsymbol{e}[k]$. The plot emphasizes that the discrepancies between the plant's state $\boldsymbol{x}[k]$ and the estimated state $\boldsymbol{z}[k]$ increase considerably; however, as shown by the right panel in Fig. 5, the norm of the residue $\boldsymbol{r}[k]$ remains below, but very close to, the threshold $\theta = 0.2$, i.e., the attack is not noticed by the BDD.

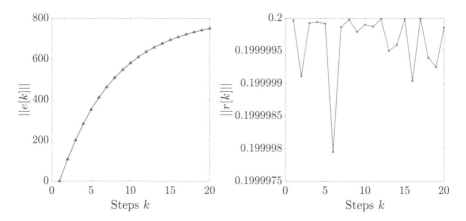

Fig. 5. Effect of the iterated MITM attack on the system considered in Sect. 4. Left panel: evolution of the norm of the estimation error. Right panel: norm of the residue.

5   Conclusions

In this paper we propose a strategy to design an optimal Man-In-The-Middle attack to a networked plant. Specifically, the attacker is able to replaces the real outputs with altered values that generate large discrepancies in the state estimated by the SCADA without being discovered by the BDD system. In particular, we formulate the attacker strategy in terms of a non-concave maximization problem for which we give local optimality conditions. Based on such conditions, we develop an algorithm to find an approximated solutions. The proposed example shows the effectiveness of the envisaged attack strategy, in that the estimated state differs considerably from the real one, but the SCADA system is not able to spot the attack. Future work will be aimed to relaxing the hypothesis of perfect information from the attacker and at considering nonlinear systems affected by noise, so as to modify the proposed formulation in order to find a global optimal solution.

Acknowledgement. This work was supported by POR FESR Lazio Region Project RESIM A0375-2020-36673 (CUP: F89J21004860008).

Appendix: KKT Local Optimality Conditions

In this appendix we review the Karush-Kuhn-Tucker (KKT) local optimality conditions for non-concave maximization problems (the reader is referred to [3] for a comprehensive overview of the topic). Specifically, we consider optimization problems in the form

$$\max_{\boldsymbol{x} \in \mathbb{R}^n} f(\boldsymbol{x}) \quad \text{Subject to} \quad g(\boldsymbol{x}) \leq 0, \tag{17}$$

where f, g are continuous, differentiable and, in general, non-concave scalar functions. Note that in order to resort to the KKT conditions, the constraints of the problem must satisfy some *constraint qualification* criteria. For simplicity, here we consider the *Linear Independence Constraint Qualification* (LICQ), i.e., the requirement that the gradients of the *active* inequality constraints (i.e., those holding as an equality), evaluated at the local maximum, must be linearly independent. Notice that, when only one constraint is present as in the case of Eq. (17), the LICQ condition is equivalent to requiring that, if the constraint is active, its gradient evaluated at the local maximum is nonzero.

Let us now review the Karush-Kuhn-Tucker (KKT) first order necessary conditions for local optimality.

Theorem 3 (KKT First Order Necessary Condition). *Consider a constrained optimization problem as in Eq. (17) and let the Lagrangian function $\mathscr{L}(\cdot)$ be defined as*

$$\mathscr{L}(\boldsymbol{x}, \lambda) = f(\boldsymbol{x}) - \lambda g(\boldsymbol{x}),$$

where $\lambda \in \mathbb{R}$ is the Lagrangian multiplier that corresponds to the constraint $g(\boldsymbol{x}) \leq 0$. Suppose the point $\boldsymbol{x}^*$ satisfies the LICQ condition. If the point $\boldsymbol{x}^* \in \mathbb{R}^d$ is a local maximum for the problem then there exist a $\lambda^* \in \mathbb{R}$ such that the following conditions hold true:

$$\nabla_{\boldsymbol{x}} \mathscr{L}(\boldsymbol{x}, \lambda)\Big|_{\boldsymbol{x}=\boldsymbol{x}^*, \lambda=\lambda^*} = 0, \tag{18}$$

$$\lambda^* g(\boldsymbol{x}^*) = 0 \tag{19}$$

$$g(\boldsymbol{x}^*) \leq 0 \tag{20}$$

$$\lambda^* \geq 0. \tag{21}$$

We now review the KKT second order sufficient conditions for local optimality.

Theorem 4 (KKT Second Order Sufficient Condition). *Consider a constrained optimization problem as in Eq. (17) and suppose that there is a point $\boldsymbol{x}^* \in \mathbb{R}^d$, together with a Lagrangian multiplier $\lambda^* \in \mathbb{R}$, satisfying the KKT first order necessary condition. Denote by $\nabla_{\boldsymbol{xx}}\mathscr{L}(\boldsymbol{x},\lambda)|_{\boldsymbol{x}=\boldsymbol{x}^*,\lambda=\lambda^*}$ the sub-matrix of the Hessian matrix of the Lagrangian function involving only partial derivatives with respect to the entries of $\boldsymbol{x}$. If the above sub-matrix is negative semi-definite (definite), then $\boldsymbol{x}^*$ is a (strict) local maximum.*

References

1. Cardenas, A., Sastry, S.: Secure control: towards survivable cyber-physical systems. In: Proceedings 28th International Conference Distributed Computing Workshops, pp. 495–500 (2008)
2. Fawzi, H., Tabuada, P., Diggavi, S.: Secure estimation and control for cyber-physical systems under adversarial attacks. IEEE Trans. Autom. Control **59**(6), 1454–1467 (2014)
3. Floudas, C.A.: Nonlinear and Mixed-Integer Optimization: Fundamentals and Applications. Oxford University Press, New York (1995)
4. Gupta, L., Basar, T.: Optimal control in the presence of an intelligent jammer with limited actions. In: 49th IEEE Conference on Decision and Control (CDC), pp. 1096–1101. IEEE (2010)
5. Hobbs, A.: The colonial pipeline hack: exposing vulnerabilities in US cybersecurity (2021)
6. Jovanov, I., Pajic, M.: Relaxing integrity requirements for attack-resilient cyber-physical systems. IEEE Trans. Autom. Control **64**(12), 4843–4858 (2019)
7. Kelley, C.T.: Iterative Methods for Linear and Nonlinear Equations, vol. 16. Siam (1995)
8. Lee, C., Shim, H., Eun, Y.: Secure and robust state estimation under sensor attacks, measurement noises, and process disturbances: observer-based combinatorial approach. In: 2015 European Control Conference (ECC), pp. 1872–1877. IEEE (2015)
9. Li, Y., Shi, L., Cheng, P., Chen, J., Quevedo, D.E.: Jamming attacks on remote state estimation in cyber-physical systems: a game-theoretic approach. IEEE Trans. Autom. Control **60**(10), 2831–2836 (2015)
10. Luenberger, D.: An introduction to observers. IEEE Trans. Autom. Control **16**(6), 596–602 (1971)
11. Miciolino, E.E., Setola, R., Bernieri, G., Panzieri, S., Pascucci, F., Polycarpou, M.M.: Fault diagnosis and network anomaly detection in water infrastructures. IEEE Des. Test **34**(4), 44–51 (2017)
12. Mo, Y., Sinopoli, B.: Integrity attacks on cyber-physical systems. In: Proceedings 1st International Conference High Confidence Networked Systems, pp. 47–54 (2012)
13. Mo, Y., Garone, E., Casavola, A., Sinopoli, B.: False data injection attacks against state estimation in wireless sensor networks. In: 49th IEEE Conference on Decision and Control (CDC), pp. 5967–5972. IEEE (2010)
14. Ren, X., Wu, J., Dey, S., Shi, L.: Attack allocation on remote state estimation in multi-systems: structural results and asymptotic solution. Automatica **87**, 184–194 (2018)

15. Setola, R., Faramondi, L., Salzano, E., Cozzani, V.: An overview of cyber attack to industrial control system. Chem. Eng. Trans. **77**, 907–912 (2019)
16. Teixeira, A., Amin, S., Sandberg, H., Johansson, K.H., Sastry, S.S.: Cyber security analysis of state estimators in electric power systems. In: 49th IEEE Conference on Decision and Control (CDC), pp. 5991–5998. IEEE (2010)
17. Teixeira, A., Shames, I., Sandberg, H., Johansson, K.H.: Revealing stealthy attacks in control systems. In: 2012 50th Annual Allerton Conference on Communication, Control, and Computing (Allerton), pp. 1806–1813. IEEE (2012)
18. Vuković, O., Sou, K.C., Dán, G., Sandberg, H.: Network-layer protection schemes against stealth attacks on state estimators in power systems. In: 2011 IEEE International Conference on Smart Grid Communications (SmartGridComm), pp. 184–189. IEEE (2011)
19. Vukovic, O., Sou, K.C., Dan, G., Sandberg, H.: Network-aware mitigation of data integrity attacks on power system state estimation. IEEE J. Sel. Areas Commun. **30**(6), 1108–1118 (2012)
20. Wu, G., Sun, J., Chen, J.: Optimal data injection attacks in cyber-physical systems. IEEE Trans. Cybern. **48**(12), 3302–3312 (2018)
21. Zhang, H., Cheng, P., Shi, L., Chen, J.: Optimal denial-of-service attack scheduling with energy constraint. IEEE Trans. Autom. Control **60**(11), 3023–3028 (2015)
22. Zhao, J., Mili, L., Abdelhadi, A.: Robust dynamic state estimator to outliers and cyber attacks. In: 2017 IEEE Power & Energy Society General Meeting, pp. 1–5. IEEE (2017)

GNSS Positioning Security: Automatic Anomaly Detection on Reference Stations

Stéphanie Lebrun[1,2] , Stéphane Kaloustian[1(✉)] , Raphaël Rollier[1] ,
and Colin Barschel[2]

[1] Swisstopo, 3084 Wabern, Switzerland
{stephane.kaloustian,raphael.rollier}@swisstopo.ch
[2] Cyber Defence Campus - Armasuisse, 3602 Thun, Switzerland
colin.barschel@armasuisse.ch

Abstract. The dependency of critical infrastructures on Global Navigation Satellite Systems (GNSS) keeps increasing over the years. This over-reliance brings concerns as those systems are vulnerable and consequently prone to human-made perturbations, such as jamming and spoofing attacks. Solutions for detecting such disturbances are therefore crucially needed to raise GNSS users' awareness and protection. This paper suggests an approach for detecting anomalous events (i.e., potentially an attack attempt) based on measurements recorded by Continuously Operating GNSS Reference Stations (CORS). Precisely, the anomaly detection process first consists in modeling the normal behavior of a given signal thanks to a predictive model which combines the *Seasonal and Trend decomposition using LOESS* and *ARIMA* algorithms. This model can then be used to predict the upcoming measurement values. Finally, we compare the predictions to the actual observations with a statistical rule and assess if those are normal or anomalous. While our anomaly detection approach is intended for real-time use, we assess its effectiveness on historical data. For simplicity and independence, we also focus on the *Carrier-to-Noise Ratio* only, though similar methods could apply to other observables. Our results prove the sensitivity of the proposed detection on a reported case of unintentional disturbance. Other anomalies in the historical data are also uncovered using that methodology and presented in this paper.

Keywords: GNSS · CORS · RINEX · Jamming · Spoofing · Anomaly detection · Carrier-to-Noise Ratio · Critical infrastructure protection

1 Introduction

The Global Navigation Satellite Systems (GNSS) refer to groups of artificial satellites enabling a user to determine its position and time, anywhere and anytime on Earth. Today, almost every mode of transportation relies on GNSS, including aviation, maritime, and railway sectors [1]. Moreover, navigation satellites carry on board atomic clocks, all synchronized to a master clock. This

ⓒ The Author(s) 2021
D. Percia David et al. (Eds.): CRITIS 2021, LNCS 13139, pp. 60–76, 2021.
https://doi.org/10.1007/978-3-030-93200-8_4

precise source of timing provides a reference for a range of processes in telecommunication networks, electrical power grids, and financial transactions [2,3]. It is also a critical component in rescue operations, for instance, to locate the source of an incident [4]. Due to their global availability, performance, ease of use, and low cost, GNSS are the preferred - and often unique - source of navigation and timing information in many critical applications.

Nevertheless, GNSS are increasingly targeted by cyber-attacks (e.g., [6,7]). The ability to automatically detect and report such events is vital to ensure a continuity of navigation service and identify the sources of disruption.

Since the growth in popularity of satellite navigation, many countries have established a network of Continuously Operating Reference Stations (CORS) to enhance GNSS activities. AGNES[1] is one such CORS network comprising 31 GNSS static stations distributed across Switzerland. The purpose of this paper is to investigate whether the data that these stations continuously collect could contribute to the automatic real-time detection of potentially malicious events.

It is noteworthy that this research does *not* intend to provide the one solution to all GNSS security issues, nor to cover a specific scenario of attack. It rather aims at contributing to the general security enhancement of GNSS users by monitoring signal parameters and providing information on detected anomalies.

The anomaly detection scheme we propose works as follows. Each station continuously tracks GNSS satellites from multiple constellations and transmits signal measurements. Since the stations are static, some of the measurements, e.g., the *Carrier-to-Noise Ratio*, have a predictable behavior at a given station. Therefore, a signal measurement patterns can be learned by fitting a predictive model on past data. Hence, the model can predict future values accurately. Next, the actual values of the given measurement are compared to the predicted ones. Using a statistical rule based on how well the model usually predicts, we can assess whether the observed values are normal or anomalous. An anomaly may indicate the occurrence of an attack around the station or some other kind of malfunction possibly impacting GNSS users.

To study the feasibility of such a scheme, in this research, we work on the historical data of the *Carrier-to-Noise Ratio* parameter recorded in so-called RINEX files for two constellations (GPS and GLONASS) by different stations. One reported case of disturbance allows confirming the anomaly detection is effective. Then, we discover other anomalous events.

In comparison to related work, our approach presents two significant benefits. Its simplicity first, as our only assumption is that the stations are static. Second, we leverage high-level information available on every GNSS receiver. Therefore, the same methodology applies to any other static GNSS receiver without the need for new hardware.

The remainder of this paper consists of six sections. Section 2 reviews the basic principles behind GNSS technology and its vulnerabilities. Related work is then discussed in Sect. 3. Next, the methodology proposed to detect anomalies in an automated way is outlined in detail in Sect. 4. The results are presented

---

[1] Automated GNSS NEtwork for Switzerland.

in Sect. 5. Limitations and future work are discussed in Sect. 6. The final section summarizes the paper and draws its conclusions.

2   Background Theory on GNSS

In this section, we briefly present the basics of GNSS technology and its principal vulnerabilities.

2.1   Technology Basics

GNSS are groups of satellites (*constellations*) continuously sending signals to the Earth, allowing positioning and timing services over a wide geographical area. Today, four systems provide global coverage: the American GPS, the Russian GLONASS, the European Galileo, and the Chinese BeiDou. The principle of operation remains the same across all systems and is illustrated in Fig. 1. Each transmitted signal encodes a Navigation Message from which the satellite's position at a given time can be determined (quantity (a) in Fig. 1). Then, other signal characteristics, e.g., propagation time, allow computing the distance between the satellite and the receiver (quantity (b)). Given that information for at least four satellites, the receiver can derive its position (quantity (c)) and adjust its clock.

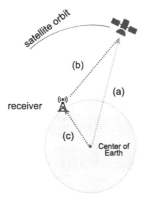

Fig. 1. Satellite-based positioning principle. Adapted from [8].

For each constellation, multiple parts of the L-band (which ranges from 1 GHz to 2 GHz) are allocated for the satellites to transmit their signals at different frequencies.

Upon the reception of a signal, the receiver measures and records the *Carrier-to-Noise Ratio* (C/N_0). It consists of the ratio of the received desired satellite signal power to the noise power per unit bandwidth. It is often used to measure signal quality and the noise environment of GNSS observations [9].

The C/N_0 and other signal measurements are commonly stored at a receiver in files written under the standard human-readable format named Receiver Independent Exchange Format (RINEX).

2.2   Vulnerabilities

GNSS signals may experience perturbations that are *naturally* or *intentionally* entailed [10]. Regarding the latter, two well-known malicious actions can harm a GNSS user, namely *jamming* and *spoofing*. Jamming refers to the intentional emission of interference to prevent the processing of legitimate signals and deny the availability of GNSS service [11]. Due to the long distance they travel, signals reach the ground receivers with a low power level and can be easily overshadowed. On the other hand, a spoofing attack can occur because *civilian* GNSS signals (in contrast to signals in military use) are neither encrypted nor authenticated, and the signal's specifications are publicly available [12]. It is then possible for an attacker to impersonate a satellite and transmit counterfeit signals, misleading a receiver to compute a wrong position or time [13]. One way to achieve a spoofing attack in spite of encryption is to acquire an authentic signal and to replay it with some delay or from another location [14]. This type of spoofing is referred to as *meaconing*.

It should be noted that GNSS service providers are currently developing solutions against spoofing that rely on cryptographic mechanisms (e.g., Galileo OS-NMA, PRS, GPS CHIMERA) [15,16]. For example, the cryptographic authentication of GNSS signals would ensure a user that they were generated by a satellite [15]. While this is an important step towards greater security for GNSS users, this approach may not protect against meaconing since authentic signals are re-broadcasted [17]. Moreover, such systems are not fully operational yet. In any case, we believe that there is no silver-bullet solution to the threats against GNSS. Therefore, any means of detection may contribute to increase the protection by rising the awareness level in case of disturbance.

2.3   Attacks Incentives

From fraud to terrorism, the motivations for initiating an attack against GNSS are numerous. Both theory and practice demonstrated the feasibility of the attacks described in the previous section.

For example, in 2011, Iranian forces captured a flying US drone by spoofing it to spy on the drone's technology [18]. For terrorist purposes, an attacker could also consider steering off the course of a larger vehicle, such as a ship. The workability of such a scenario was demonstrated by [19], and several reported real-world events are suspected of being the result of this kind of attack, e.g., in June 2017, GPS receivers of several ships navigating in the Black Sea all derived the same incorrect position [7]. Besides, a jamming attack around an airport could prevent a plane and air traffic controllers from knowing its position and making take-off and landing operations difficult and unsafe. Several disruptions of this kind were reported in the past (e.g., [6,20]).

3   Related Work

Both academia and industry have developed several systems for automatically detecting attacks on GNSS. In the signal processing domain, some of the proposed algorithms include the monitoring of the receiver power spectrum (e.g., [21]), the Automatic Gain Control level (e.g., [22]), or the signal correlation peak (e.g., [23]). These solutions all imply access and modification of the receiver firmware [24] and thus increase the complexity of the detection method. The present work involves monitoring parameters easily accessible in RINEX files and therefore does not require any receiver update.

Many of the proposed systems also require the deployment of sensors (e.g., [21,25]). Our research leverages the data from a network of stations already operating and can handily work on top of any existing station.

Moreover, to our knowledge, previous work focuses either on the jamming or the spoofing issue. In this study, we do not restrict the detection to a specific kind of attack but rather attempt to pinpoint any anomalous deviation from what is expected in terms of GNSS parameters.

The closest work to the present one is a recently published article [26], where anomalies in the C/N_0 measurements extracted from RINEX files are automatically detected to identify (unintentional) interferences. They do not target the discovery of intended disruptions. Their detection algorithm uses 15-minutes duration files and uncovers interference events lasting a few seconds. In this paper, we build an expectation of future observations based on days of history. This lets us believe that their system and ours would be complementary since we could detect longer events, e.g., a spoofing attack that slowly settles. Finally, their work addresses the C/N_0 parameter only, whereas we emphasize that our approach applies to other parameters.

Regardless of the differences between our work and the literature, it is worth mentioning that this research was *not* initiated by the wish of filling a gap in research with novel technology. Instead, it was motivated by the existence of an infrastructure (the AGNES network), available, delivering real-time and historical data in quantity, and the well-recognized need to improve the resilience of GNSS-dependent services. Robustness of defense calls for a diversity of protection mechanisms [27]. Our work demonstrates the value of GNSS reference stations as possible contributors to the set of solutions.

4   Data and Methodology

This section presents the available data and the methodology developed to process them and uncover anomalies within them. The complete procedure is summarized in Fig. 2.

4.1   Data

We study the data from AGNES, a network of static reference stations continuously tracking GNSS satellites, receiving signals, and storing measurements in RINEX files. For each station, those files are processed using the `G-nut/Anubis` software.[2] This tool, free and open-source for most of its functionalities, is

---

[2] https://www.pecny.cz/gop/index.php/gnss/sw/anubis.

designed to allow a quality check of GNSS observations. For each constellation and frequency tracked by a station, it provides a number of indicators (e.g., the C/N_0 per satellite, the mean C/N_0 over all satellites, a position solution) at the requested sampling rate (e.g., a data point per minute) and for the duration of the files given in input. These time series can then be analyzed with the system we developed to detect potential anomalies.

In this research, we focus on the data recorded during 2017, which include the signals received from GPS and GLONASS constellations, respectively on two different frequencies. This leads to the analysis of four different signals: GPS L1, GPS L2, GLONASS L1, and GLONASS L2. For each of them, we have at hand one time series per GNSS parameter, made of one data point per minute.

It is important to stress that in a CORS network, the stations' site locations are selected where the environment is favorable, i.e., there are as few topographic obstructions and reflective bodies as possible [28]. This means that the data collected have the benefit of being naturally relatively clean.

4.2 Indicator Selection

For the sake of simplicity, we decided to narrow down the research to a single indicator to handle univariate time series (i.e., the temporal sequence of a single variable). Our choice fell on the C/N_0 indicator (more precisely, the mean C/N_0 over all visible satellites' signals for each constellation and frequency). The procedure to detect anomalies outlined below can, however, be applied to other GNSS data parameter. A focus on the C/N_0 parameter is relevant for mainly two reasons. Firstly, this parameter would necessarily be affected in case of intentional interference (by definition) and potentially in a spoofing attack too. To succeed, a spoofer must indeed force its target to follow its forged signals. To that end, s/he might send signals with a stronger power. Therefore, a sudden increase in the recorded C/N_0 may indicate a spoofing attempt [29]. However, this technique would turn out ineffective if the attacker can increase the receiver noise power level simultaneously [30]. Secondly, when considering static stations, the C/N_0 patterns do not depend on other external quantities, as opposed to other measurements that would require incorporating additional data, e.g., ephemerides or weather data. This makes it a more straightforward parameter to study.

As a result of this choice, for a given station, the work essentially amounts to an anomaly detection performed on the mean C/N_0, per minute over a year (i.e., 525 600 data points) for each of the four signals.

4.3 Anomaly Detection Scheme

There are generally two main ways to identify abnormalities in a system [31]. First, if some anomalies were already encountered in the past, their signatures can be captured. On that basis, one can verify if such patterns re-appear. The second method consists in learning the "profile of a normal behavior" in the data [32]. Anything that deviates too much from this normality can be considered an anomaly. In the present research context, we do not have any signature of attack having targeted the network stations studied. We have the historical data of each station at our disposal but no knowledge on whether they were affected or not at some point. Besides, the outdoor simulation of attacks to generate signatures is complex, and such an experiment requires a license due to GNSS spectrum regulations. As a result, the second technique is preferred.

The challenge of this approach lies in the definition and modeling of this normal behavior. The decided strategy to this effect in our research is to build and validate a predictive model on historical data. It is the most common approach in univariate time series anomaly detection, according to [33].

The anomaly detection process we suggest thus takes place in three stages, as explained in Fig. 2. First, for a given data indicator such as the C/N_0, a forecast model relying on the Seasonal and Trend decomposition using LOESS (STL) is trained to make accurate predictions. Second, future values for that indicator are predicted using that model. Finally, actual observations are compared to the predictions, and we decide whether they look normal or anomalous using a statistical rule based on the InterQuartile Range. We provide more details about the C/N_0 forecasting and statistical rule in the following sections.

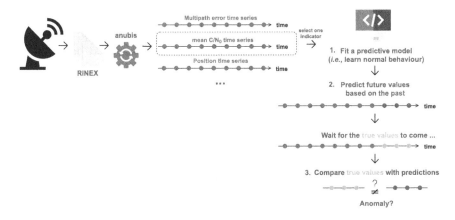

Fig. 2. Proposed anomaly detection scheme on GNSS data for a given station. The time history of different parameters recorded by each station is easily accessible through RINEX files. A prediction-based anomaly detection can then be applied on a specific parameter's time series.

Carrier-to-Noise Ratio Forecasting

Model Selection. Since the GNSS satellites' trajectories repeat over time, the relative position between a static station and the satellites is periodically the same (every sidereal day for GPS, every eight sidereal days for GLONASS [8]). Consequently, a given signal's mean C/N_0 time series presents a seasonality, i.e., a pattern that repeats at regular intervals. It should be emphasized that this would not necessarily be the case for a mobile GNSS receiver. The methodology we propose is intended for static receivers only.

The Seasonal and Trend decomposition using LOESS (STL) forecast model is selected for its ability to handle seasonal time series. Other more traditional methods, such as the SARIMA model, were considered. However, they appeared inappropriate for implementation reasons due to the high sampling rate of our dataset (a data point per minute) and the seasonal period value.

Introduced in [34], the STL algorithm uses a locally weighted regression (LOESS) to decompose a time series into three components: the trend, seasonal and residual components. Figure 3 presents an example of such decomposition applied on GPS L2 signal's mean C/N_0 time series over 15 days.

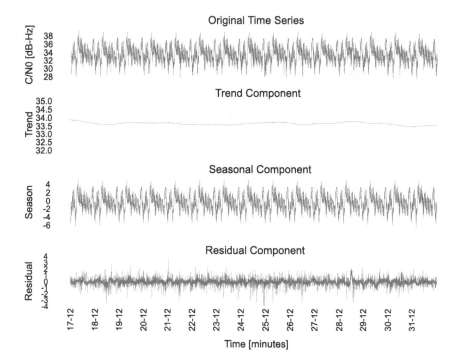

Fig. 3. STL decomposition applied on GPS L2 signal's mean C/N_0 time series on a duration of 15 days (2017 data). The upper graph shows the original signal. The three others respectively indicate the trend, the seasonal and residual components.

To obtain a forecast, the seasonal component is first estimated with STL and removed from the original time series. Predictions for the resulting *seasonally adjusted time series* are then made using an ARIMA model. Lastly, the seasonal component is added back to get final predictions [35].

The method involves a set of parameters that were optimized using a grid search. It should be noted that for simplicity, this optimization has solely been conducted on the data gathered by a specific station. The mean absolute deviation (MAD) metric is used to quantify the prediction error.

Prediction Implementation Choices. Several decisions regarding which past data to use for the prediction tasks, how much, and the length of the period to predict (the *forecast horizon*) are presented and discussed in this section. The final setting is illustrated in Fig. 4.

Some models age well over time and do not need to be retrained (*static* models), while others require a continuous revision, i.e., they are *dynamic* [36]. In the case of GNSS data, a dynamic model is preferred. The solar activity is, for instance, a parameter that can influence the signals and that fluctuates over the years [37]. It would probably be inaccurate to make predictions for a given day using a model fitted on data from previous years. Therefore, a *rolling forecast approach* is adopted, where the model is updated for each new prediction.

Moreover, the amount of GNSS historical data for training the model should be large enough to capture the patterns. For the same reasons as just outlined, all history is certainly not relevant to predict the C/N_0 at a given minute. Two different sizes for the training set are experimented and compared, namely the past 7 and 31 days for GPS data, past 16 and 24 days for GLONASS (the difference between the constellations is due to the longer ground track repeatability of GLONASS satellites). Table 1 provided in the Appendix shows that in any case, the resulting error is almost equivalent. As the use of fewer past data is faster and allows to test the anomaly detection scheme on more data, the past 7 and 16 days are used for each prediction.

Finally, for a real-time anomaly detection system (which is the long-term goal of this research), predicting the next minute or next ten minutes would be appropriate. Nevertheless, to visually inspect the STL model performance, the forecast horizon is set to one day.

Fig. 4. Forecast implementation choices: illustration of the rolling forecast approach.

Hence, for a given signal, the previous 7 days (GPS) or 16 days (GLONASS) of mean C/N_0 provided per minute are used to predict values of the next day. The process takes around 1 min for a GPS signal and 8 min for GLONASS, so it could be performed in almost real-time as new data come. An example of prediction results for a randomly selected day on two signals is provided in Fig. 5. Predictions for each signal induce a MAD of 0.4201 dB-Hz regarding GPS L2 signal and a MAD of 0.4096 dB-Hz for GLONASS L1 signal. Given that the mean C/N_0 of GPS L2 and GLONASS L1 signals over 2017 is on average 33.6203 dB-Hz and 46.1642 dB-Hz, the above MAD values should be considered as a good forecasting performance. For additional verification, predictions of other fifteen randomly selected days in 2017 with the same setting were made. The average prediction error for each signal is provided in Table 1, given in the Appendix. The results confirm the model's accuracy.

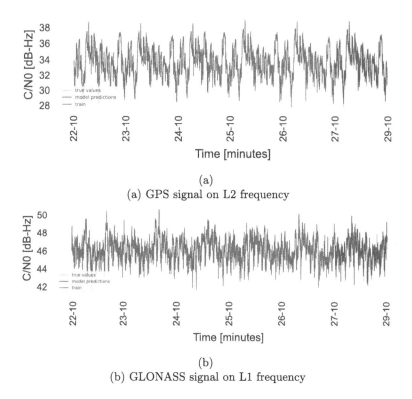

(a)

(a) GPS signal on L2 frequency

(b)

(b) GLONASS signal on L1 frequency

Fig. 5. Mean C/N_0 predictions per minute during one day for two types of signals, for a given station. The end of past data used for training the model appear in dark blue, predictions are highlighted in brown, true values are given in light blue. (Color figure online)

Statistical Rule. An anomaly should be declared when observations deviate significantly from the expectations provided by the predictive model. This implies the definition of a threshold above which the distance between an actual value and the estimated one (the prediction error) is not tolerable. For that purpose, the InterQuartile Range (IQR), defined as

$$IQR = Q3 - Q1, \tag{1}$$

is computed over the distances of the previous N predictions. The first quartile $Q1$ and the third quartile $Q3$ correspond respectively to the value under which

25% and 75% of the data lie. Anomalies are defined as observations whose distance to expectation falls below $Q1 - 1.5 \cdot IQR$ or above $Q3 + 1.5 \cdot IQR$. This is a commonly used rule in statistical-based anomaly detection, developed by [38]. Finally, we decide to inspect if collections of anomalies appear (as opposed to isolated anomalies). After flagging each prediction error as normal or anomalous, the density of anomalies is computed over a rolling window W. If more than k anomalies occur within W, the window is declared an *anomalous period*. Practically speaking, the predictions over the previous $N = 15$ days are used to compute the IQR. Thus, for any new station/receiver, only a few days would be necessary before the real-time detection process could start on incoming data.

5   Results

In this section, we first show the effectiveness of the procedure outlined above on a GPS signal using an event of reported accidental interference. Then, we present other anomalies successfully unveiled in the stations' data.

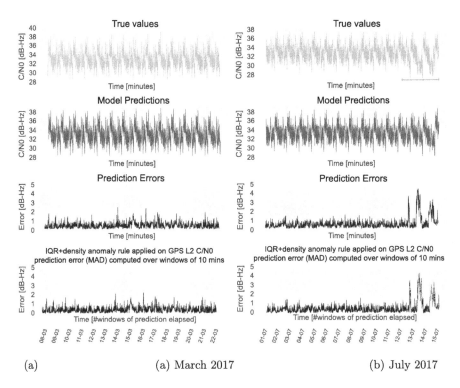

Fig. 6. True values of mean C/N_0 for GPS L2 signal (top figures), predictions of mean C/N_0 (second), MAD prediction error (third) and detected anomalous periods on the prediction error, highlighted in orange (lower figures). Each column of figures refers to one specific month. (Color figure online)

5.1 Proof of Effectiveness

The upper graph in Fig. 6 (a) shows the evolution of the mean C/N_0 per minute of GPS signals received on L2 frequency by a given station during March 2017. The C/N_0 observations seem regular. Predictions using the STL model are given in the second graph. Since the observations and predictions for these days are close, the corresponding prediction error represented in the third graph is low and stable. No anomaly is detected (lower graph).

On the other hand, in July 2017, unintentional interference in the GNSS frequency bands affected two stations of the AGNES network. In the upper graph of Fig. 6 (b), it can be observed that the mean C/N_0 parameter is indeed disturbed compared to the other days (perturbations are indicated with an orange brace). What is observed deviates from what was expected (provided in the second graph). The prediction error (third graph) consequently increases at the time of the interference. Those data points are identified as anomalous and are highlighted in the lower graph.

It should be noted that the occurrence of anomalies will bias the following predictions. Such behavior stems from selecting a rolling forecast approach and can already be seen in the presented case. The anomalous data should therefore be filtered before forecasting the following days.

This example confirms that we can effectively learn from a GNSS reference station's historical data to detect potential anomalous events. The monitoring of the distance between observed and expected values obtained through a predictive model indeed successfully reveals anomalies.

5.2 Detected Anomalies

The same procedure applied to the data collected by multiple AGNES network stations allowed discovering several anomalies in the mean C/N_0 behavior. Figure 7 shows four of them. At some point in time and during several hours, the mean C/N_0 experiences an unusual decrease compared to other days. The anomalies presented in (a) and (b) graphs affect the two GPS signals but only the GLONASS L1 signal. The ones in (c) and (d) affect all types of signals.

Interestingly, the disturbance in April 2017 was felt on stations 2 and 3, which are neighboring stations. Other cases of perturbations affecting two stations at a time were encountered.

Investigations with the CORS network operators revealed that those disturbances were caused by a snow accumulation on the stations' antenna. The reason why the GLONASS L2 signal was not affected by the anomaly exposed in Fig. 7 (a) and (b) still needs to be clarified. Although not being cases of intentional disturbances, those examples still highlight the detector's sensitivity to unusual events.

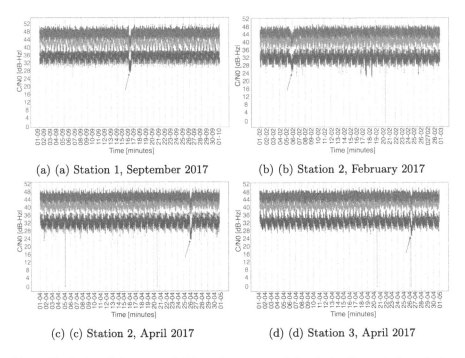

(a) (a) Station 1, September 2017

(b) (b) Station 2, February 2017

(c) (c) Station 2, April 2017

(d) (d) Station 3, April 2017

Fig. 7. Evolution of the mean C/N_0 on four types of signals for three stations during different periods of the year. The blue and orange curves correspond to signals from GLONASS constellation respectively on L1 and L2 frequencies. The green and red curves correspond to signals received from GPS satellites respectively on L1 and L2 frequencies. Anomalies were detected in these data and are indicated with an arrow. (Color figure online)

6 Limitations and Perspectives

The present research is subject to some limitations. To begin with, the STL prediction model appeared to be suitable, but other more recent and advanced forecasting methods could be considered instead, for instance, an autoencoder-based solution. It should be noted that the primary goal of this research was *not* to test every possible predictive model and find the perfect one for our data. Then, regarding the anomaly detection itself, the statistical rule to assess the observations' regularity should be refined. The addition of an "anomaly filter" step also constitutes a necessary enhancement. The detected anomalies should indeed not be taken into account for the following predictions.

Further research in automatic anomaly detection systems on GNSS data might consider investigating the following aspects. First, the same process could be repeated on other signals' parameters than the C/N_0. It is very likely that monitoring multiple indicators simultaneously would improve the detection accuracy. The signals' Doppler shift, the satellites' orbital trajectories, and detected cycle slips in the signals' phase measurements are examples of such parameters. Besides, since several anomalies were found to affect two stations at a time, we believe that monitoring at the network level rather than station level by cross-referencing the stations' data could be another interesting area of study. The spatial relationships between the stations in the network have indeed not been exploited in the present work. Moreover, the anomaly detection scheme should be further applied to more recent data and data coming from the two other global constellations, i.e., Galileo and BeiDou. Finally, future work could be devoted to the simulation of attacks to evaluate the detection process in adversarial conditions.

7   Conclusions

Today, the dependency of critical infrastructures on GNSS is greater than ever. However, it is by design a fundamentally insecure technology that may be threatened in different ways, e.g., jamming or spoofing attacks. Therefore, it is imperative to monitor any anomaly that may the sign of an attack attempt.

This paper presented how GNSS reference stations' data could be leveraged to that end. Specifically, training a predictive model on the past data for a given GNSS parameter allows encapsulating its normality profile and predicting what we expect to observe next. When the actual observations significantly deviate from those predictions, which is quantified by the prediction error, it indicates that the underlying data might be abnormal.

Besides its simplicity, this methodology offers the benefit of operating with high-level information from RINEX files and can therefore be easily applied to any static station's data easily without requiring hardware or firmware modification. Practically, only a few days of data are required in order to start the anomaly detection process. Moreover, it does not reduce to the detection of one specific human-made manipulation but rather aims to uncover any kind of irregular activity.

The effectiveness of such a detection scheme was demonstrated on the mean C/N_0 parameter using a reported case of unintentional interference. Finally, it allowed pinpointing other anomalies.

Acknowledgment. We would like to express our gratitude to PNAC and swipos teams from swisstopo, as well as SAPOS Baden-Würtenberg and SAPOS Bayern for their valuable technical and logistic support during this research.

Appendix

Table 1. Average MAD error (expressed in dB-Hz) resulting from C/N_0 predictions over fifteen randomly selected days on GPS and GLONASS signals, using the STL forecast method. Comparison between the use of two sizes for the training set.

	GPS L1	GPS L2		GLONASS L1	GLONASS L2
7 days	0.4221	0.5266	16 days	0.6664	0.6930
31 days	0.4263	0.5316	24 days	0.69598	0.7527

References

1. United Nations Office for Outer Space Affairs page on Global Navigation Satellite Systems. https://www.unoosa.org/oosa/en/ourwork/psa/gnss/gnss.html. Accessed 11 May 2021
2. European Space Agency page on Precise Time Reference. https://gssc.esa.int/navipedia/index.php/Precise_Time_Reference. Accessed 11 May 2021
3. Analytica, O.: Global reliance on GPS creates new risks. Expert Briefings (2019). https://doi.org/10.1108/OXAN-DB241765
4. Homeland Security presentation: GPS Use in U.S. Critical Infrastructure and Emergency Communications. United States Technical Training Institute (USTTI). https://www.gps.gov/multimedia/presentations/2012/10/USTTI/graham.pdf. Accessed 10 May 2021
5. Cybersecurity and Infrastructure Security Agency, National Risk Management page on PNT. https://www.cisa.gov/pnt. Accessed 6 May 2021
6. New Jersey Star-Ledge: N.J. man fined $ 32K for illegal GPS device that disrupted Newark airport system. https://www.nj.com/news/2013/08/man_fined_32000_for_blocking_newark_airport_tracking_system.html. Accessed 13 May 2021
7. Galileo GNSS: Mass GPS Spoofing Attack in Black Sea? https://galileognss.eu/mass-gps-spoofing-attack-in-black-sea/. Accessed 11 May 2021
8. Hofmann-Wellenhof, B., Lichtenegger, H., Wasle, E.: GNSS - Global Navigation Satellite Systems, 1st edn. Springer, Wien (2008). https://doi.org/10.1007/978-3-211-73017-1
9. Jin, S., Qian, X., Wu, X.: Sea level change from BeiDou navigation satellite system-reflectometry (BDS-R): first results and evaluation. Global Planet. Change **149**, 20–25 (2017)
10. European GNSS Global Navigation Satellite Systems Agency (GSA): GNSS User Technology Report, Issue 1 (2016)
11. Jones, M.: The civilian battlefield, protecting GNSS receivers from interference and jamming. Inside GNSS **6**, 40–99 (2011)
12. Petovello, M.: What is navigation message authentication? Inside GNSS (2018)
13. Jafarnia-Jahromia, A., Broumandan, A., Nielsen, J., Lachapelle, G.: GPS vulnerability to spoofing threats and a review of Antispoofing techniques. Int. J. Navig. Obs. (2012)
14. Ranganathan, A., Ólafsdóttir, H., Capkun, S.: SPREE, a spoofing resistant GPS receiver. In: MobiCom 2016: Proceedings of the 22nd Annual International Conference on Mobile Computing and Networking, pp. 348–360, New York City (2016)

15. Neish, A., Walter, T.: Securing GNSS - a trip down cryptography lane. Inside GNSS (2020)
16. AZO - Space of Innovation story page: GNSS Jamming and Spoofing: Hazard or Hype? https://space-of-innovation.com/gnss-jamming-and-spoofing-hazard-or-hype/. Accessed 24 Aug 2021
17. Spirent white paper: GNSS Signal Spoofing: How to evaluate the risks to safety-critical and liability-critical systems (2020). https://www.spirent.com/assets/white-paper-gnss-signal-spoofing. Accessed 24 Aug 2021
18. Jansen, K., Schäfer, M., Moser, M., Lenders, V., Pöpper, C., Schmitt, J.: Crowd-GPS-Sec: leveraging crowdsourcing to detect and localize GPS spoofing attacks. In: 2018 IEEE Symposium on Security and Privacy, pp. 1018–103 (2018). https://doi.org/10.1109/SP.2018.00012
19. Bhatti, J., Humphreys, T.: Hostile control of ships via false GPS signals: demonstration and detection. J. Inst. Navig. **64**(1), 51–66 (2017)
20. Staff, T.: Disruption of GPS systems at Ben Gurion Airport resolved after 2 months. The Times of Israel (2019). https://www.timesofisrael.com/disruption-of-gps-systems-at-ben-gurion-airport-resolved-after-2-months/
21. Wende, J., Kurzhals, C., Houdek, M., Samson, J.: An interference monitoring system for GNSS reference stations. In: 15th International Symposium on Antenna Technology and Applied Electromagnetics (ANTEM), pp. 1–5. IEEE, Toulouse (2012)
22. Akos, D.M.: Who's afraid of the Spoofer? GPS/GNSS spoofing detection via automatic gain control (AGC). J. Inst. Navig. **59**, 281–290 (2012)
23. Troglia Gamba, M., Truong, M.D., Motella, B., Falletti, E., Ta, T.H.: Hypothesis testing methods to detect spoofing attacks: a test against the TEXBAT datasets. GPS Solutions **21**, 577–589 (2017)
24. Schmidt, D., Radke, K., Camtepe, S., Foo, E., Ren, M.: A survey and analysis of the GNSS spoofing threat and countermeasures. ACM Comput. Surv. **48**(4), 1–31 (2016)
25. Proctor, A.G., Curry, C.W.T., Tong, J., Watson, R., Greaves, M., Cruddace, P.: Protecting the UK infrastructure: a system to detect GNSS jamming and interference. Inside GNSS Civilian Battelfield, 49–57 (2011)
26. Stader, J., Gunawardena, S.: Leveraging worldwide, publicly-available data to create an automated satnav interference detection system. In: Proceedings of the 2021 International Technical Meeting of The Institute of Navigation, pp. 69–83 (2021)
27. U.S. Department of Homeland Security (DHS) Science and Technology: Resilient Positioning, Navigation, and Timing (PNT) Conformance Framework (2020). https://www.dhs.gov/sites/default/files/publications/2020_12_resilient_pnt_conformance_framework.pdf
28. Intergovernmental Committee on Survey and Mapping: Guideline for Continuously Operating Reference Stations. Special Publication 1 (2014). https://icsm.gov.au/sites/default/files/2018-02/Guideline-for-Continuously-Operating-Reference-Stations_v2.1.pdf
29. Jafarnia-Jahromi, A., Daneshmand, S., Lachapelle, G.: Spoofing countermeasure for GNSS receivers, a review of current and future research trends. In: 4th International Colloquium on Scientific and Fundamental Aspects of the Galileo Programme, European Space Agency, Prague (2013)
30. Jafarnia-Jahromi, A., Broumandan, A., Nielsen, J., Lachapelle, G.: GPS spoofer countermeasure effectiveness based on signal strength, noise power and C/N0 observables. Int. J. Satell. Commun. Network. **30**(4), 181–191 (2012)

31. N-able blog page on Intrusion Detection System (IDS): Signature vs. Anomaly-Based. https://www.n-able.com/blog/intrusion-detection-system. Accessed 6 May 2021
32. Paulheim, H.: Lecture on anomaly detection. (2019) https://www.uni-mannheim.de/media/Einrichtungen/dws/Files_Teaching/Data_Mining_II/FSS2019/slides/DM03-AnomalyDetection-V1.pdf. Accessed 10 May 2021
33. Blásquez-Garcìa, A., Conde, A., Mori, U., Lozano, J.: A review on outlier/anomaly detection in time series data. ACM Comput. Surv. **54**(3) (2021)
34. Cleveland, R.B., Cleveland, W.S., McRae, J.E., Terpenning, I.J.: STL: a seasonal-trend decomposition procedure based on Loess. J. Official Stat. **6**(1), 3–33 (1990). http://bit.ly/stl1990
35. Hyndman, R.J., Athanasopoulosm, G.: Forecasting: Principles and Practice, 3rd edn. Monash University, OTexts (2021)
36. Ebermann, T.: Time series prediction - a short introduction for pragmatists. https://www.liip.ch/en/blog/time-series-prediction-a-short-comparison-of-best-practices. Accessed 7 May 2021
37. Danson, E.: Managing Solar Effects in GNSS Operations. C&C Technologies (2011)
38. Tukey, J.W.: Exploratory Data Analysis. 1st edn. Addison-Wesley Pub. Co., Reading (1977)

C(I)IP Organisation, (Strategic) Management and Legal Aspects

Model-Based Risk Analysis Approach for Network Vulnerability and Security of the Critical Railway Infrastructure

Himanshu Neema[1]([⊠]) [iD], Leqiang Wang[1], Xenofon Koutsoukos[1],
CheeYee Tang[2], and Keith Stouffer[2]

[1] Vanderbilt University, Nashville, TN 37212, USA
himanshu.neema@vanderbilt.edu
[2] National Institute of Standards and Technology, Gaithersburg, MD 20899, USA
cheeyee.tang@nist.gov

Abstract. This study focuses on threat modeling, vulnerability analysis, and risk management within the critical railway transportation infrastructure. The Railway Transportation System is a highly complex, national critical infrastructure and its cybersecurity evaluation is crucial, but is still an extremely hard problem. In this paper, a novel threat modeling and risk management approach using a domain-specific modeling environment is presented. Two risk analysis techniques based on attack trees are developed to systematically model the potential risks in a cyber-physical system and provide quantitative analysis of the vulnerabilities. The automated risk assessment tool can prioritize component level vulnerabilities for potential mitigation actions. A scenario language and associated tools in the framework allow modeling and evaluation of cyber-games using a library of system exploits and mitigation actions. Cyber-games enable assessment of system-level risks and development of comprehensive risk management plans. Another key capability is the handling of dynamic network connections with variable vulnerability propagation in railway communication networks where locomotives and its devices are mobile. These capabilities are demonstrated with a case study in the railway transportation domain.

Keywords: Risk analysis · Threat modeling · Metamodeling · Vulnerability analysis · Cyber-gaming · Security · Cyber-physical system

1 Introduction

Designing and maintaining safety-critical infrastructures is a challenging task that requires minimizing risks of cyber-attacks and building resilience into their design to keep them operational despite cyber-attacks. For a reliable critical infrastructure, its security assessment and the configurations and arrangement of components must be carefully considered. As security mechanisms do impact

© Springer Nature Switzerland AG 2021
D. Percia David et al. (Eds.): CRITIS 2021, LNCS 13139, pp. 79–98, 2021.
https://doi.org/10.1007/978-3-030-93200-8_5

the system's performance [1], we must evaluate if these mechanisms are necessary and sufficient for the system's cybersecurity [2].

Vulnerability assessment and risk management of critical infrastructure is crucial in the modern world. Ongoing increases in network connectivity, distributed computing and control, and variability of network topology has dramatically increased the attack surface and made vulnerability evaluation a highly complex task, Traditional security analysis by domain experts is largely manual and relies on the judgment of professionals to qualitatively assess system vulnerability. There are several drawbacks of this approach. First, the manual assessment and reliance on personal experience, makes risk models subjective and often inconsistent among organizations. Since an attacker only needs one opportunity to succeed, this inconsistency could lead to a significant problem. Secondly, the manual approach is not scalable as the system grows larger. Considering a system as a graph, with components as its vertices and network interactions among components as its edges, the worst-case complexity of the number of edges is equal to the square of the number of vertices. For risk analysis of a system, both the relations between components and properties of individual components must be analyzed. Manually addressing this complexity is highly challenging, time-consuming, and error-prone.

In this paper, we apply Model-Integrated Computing (MIC) techniques [3] with software tools for quantitative risk analysis of Railway Transportation Systems (RTSs). Traditional Cyber-Physical Systems (CPS) are systems that involve tightly-coupled control, computation, and communication components where the CPS' functionality emerges from the interaction of components. Digital connectivity among CPS' components and their interactions makes their vulnerability assessment difficult. This is even harder in RTSs as these are geographically distributed with continuously changing network topology due to the movement of locomotives and their on-board sensors and devices. We describe our work on designing a web-based Risk Analysis Framework (RAF) for this purpose. RAF is developed using WebGME [4] – a web-based platform that allows not only metamodeling, but also developing custom visualizers and plugins. The framework develops two core components: the RAF metamodel and the risk assessment and visualization tools. The RAF metamodel allows modeling the system architecture with different system components and their network topology, network interconnections among components, the risks and vulnerabilities of CPS components, and cyber-games for dynamic risk management. The RAF analysis plugins read and calculate vulnerability scores and save the internal property data in the system model itself. The RAF visualization tools (called *visualizers*) generate and display (using a novel layout algorithm) risk propagation trees and risk values in WebGME. Both the analysis plugins and visualizers are developed in WebGME and implemented in JavaScript.

The organization of this paper is as follows. Section 2 surveys the related work in the area of cyber-physical system and threat modeling and risk analysis. Section 3 presents the system architecture with a detailed description of key technical issues in the implementation. An example from the railway domain is presented in Sect. 4. Finally, Sect. 5 concludes the paper and provides directions for future research.

2 Related Work

Threat modeling and vulnerability analysis is an established field with many works. A real-world quantitative vulnerability assessment of critical infrastructures in Norway appeared in [5]. It uses real-world tools for scanning internet connected systems and assesses their vulnerabilities. Our work is focused on *model-based risk analysis* for effective evaluation of *risk management plans*.

Standards and background knowledge for threat modeling in the railway system domain can be found in [6]. It introduces a state-of-art railway framework based on European Railway Traffic Management System (ERTMS) and elaborates the general logic when designing railway threat modeling systems including the modeling of components and processes. The basic concepts of attack trees and risk propagation techniques could be found in [7].

A metamodeling approach [8] for risk analysis in a railway temperature monitoring system model by modeling the railway system and corresponding properties aligns well with our work. This work only covers modeling the *system architecture*, while our work includes the *risk analysis algorithms* as well as *risk management planning*.

A method was presented in [9] for quantifying system-level cybersecurity risk by analyzing the risks at individual system components as well as the information and control flows among them. In our approach, we consider realistic network simulation and network topology that enables a fine-grained evaluation. In addition, our ongoing work (see Sect. 5) is on interfacing model-based risk evaluation with integrated simulation based impact assessments, which requires simulating the network and cyber-attacks.

A consideration of both cyber and physical attack paths appeared in [10]. Even though the use-cases we modeled involved only cyber-attacks, our framework can be directly applied to model physical-attacks.

The idea of chaining vulnerabilities to evaluate impact of exploitation of multiple vulnerabilities in attack paths and prioritizing attach paths was discussed in [11]. However, our approach for dynamic risk management to evaluate multiple attack paths along with mitigation actions is much broader and powerful.

An approach to model attack paths using a weighted colored petri net and modeling threat propagation using incomplete information Bayesian games appeared in [12]. In contrast, our approach uses models to intuitively specify the system architecture and network topology that mirrors what is found in real-world applications, and provides automation tools for vulnerability propagation as well as risk management using attacker-defender games.

The basic concepts of modeling threats using the attack-centric, asset-centric, and software-centric approaches were introduced in [13], and later used for designing a risk analysis method in [14].

Our paper combines theoretical problem modeling with a *real-world scenario* in the railway traffic domain and highlights the core technical issues and presents our solutions for designing a *realistic risk analysis framework*. Importantly, none of the works cited above are able to deal with *dynamic connections* that arise due to changing network topology of systems.

3   System Architecture

3.1   Modeling Approach

A *metamodel* is a model of the model, i.e., a simplified model of an actual model of a circuit, system, or software like entity [3,15]. A metamodel can be a mathematical relation or algorithm representing input and output relations. A model is an abstraction of a phenomenon in the real world; a metamodel is yet another abstraction, highlighting properties of the model itself. A model conforms to its metamodel in the way that a computer program conforms to the grammar of the programming language in which it is written. Various types of metamodels include polynomial equations, neural network, and Kriging. *Metamodeling* is the construction of a collection of *concepts* (things, terms, etc.) within a certain domain and describing how these concepts are related. Metamodeling typically involves studying the output and input relationships, the organization and association of different concepts in the domain, and then designing the right metamodel tools that capture their run-time behavior.

3.2   Modeling Environment

The RAF's metamodel is developed using WebGME [4], which is a web-based, collaborative meta-modeling environment with a centralized version-controlled model storage. WebGME is a client-server based application, where both the client (browser) and server-side (NodeJS) use JavaScript. The clients carry a significant amount of the workload and the role of the server is mainly to store and retrieve the raw model data and propagate events between collaborating clients. A simplified and partial view of RAF's metamodel is shown in Fig. 1.

3.3   Modeling Railway Infrastructure and Communications

Device Components. Devices are basic elements in a system model. A device can contain other children devices, which represents hierarchical decomposition of the system. In metamodel perspective, a device can be either high-level device or base-level device. The base-level devices are basic hardware components contained in the upper-level abstract device component. The design of device components metamodel not only consists of the metamodels for all devices (e.g., sensors and repeaters), but also includes the connections between those components, which are typically network connections (e.g., wired or wireless) only between base devices. Due to the communication property and nature of WebGME's connection type component, the connections are directional from one component to

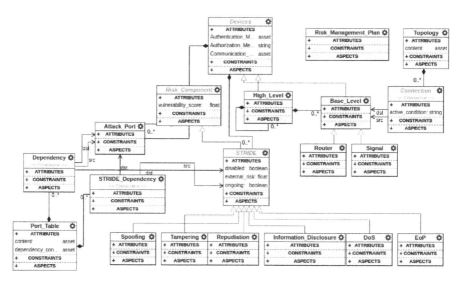

Fig. 1. RAF metamodel (simplified and partial view)

the other; even when these connections in reality are mostly bidirectional. The topology component in RAF allows connecting base-level devices.

For the devices, there is an abstract model called *Device* with a set of inherited nodes representing specific devices. For the railway networks, the device models currently include *Railway Signal, Sensor, Router, Repeater, Central Station*, and *Gateway*, and the specific network connections modeled are *WIFI, wireless*, and *IP Network*. Three properties of the *Device* meta node are inherited by all devices, viz. *authentication method, authorization mechanism*, and *communication protocol*. Authentication method and authorization mechanism both affect the risk propagated from other devices through their connections and the risk spawned within the device itself. Communication protocol is one of the key factors affecting how risks propagate among devices.

Risk Components. The risk components are abstract elements representing a risk that can occur or some intermediate event, or vulnerable points that can be exploited by malicious actors. The external risk analysis is formally modeled using a system attack graph (SAG). We provide risk dependencies and attack ports for it. Risk dependency connects different device components under the crosscut of a graph table. Crosscuts in WebGME allow viewing and connecting metamodel elements spread across containment hierarchy and different modeling pages. The *STRIDE_Dependency* is a connection component type modeled as a child of the first-class object (FCO) in WebGME and is contained in the graph table. *STRIDE_Dependency* has *STRIDE risk* [16] and *attack port* as its source and destination respectively. To model risk to risk dependencies in the dependency graph, we use a separate type of connection called *Dependency* for

STRIDE risk to attack port dependency, and this has both attack port and STRIDE risk as destination nodes, but only attack port as source nodes.

As described before, attack port is an abstraction of some potentially risky behavior that can indirectly cause risk. It can be considered as a specific potential attack surface. Attack port meta node is a direct child of the abstract type risk component, which shares the common property called *vulnerability score*. The attack ports are contained in a device component like the other risk components.

Several other meta nodes are modeled for Component Attack Trees (CAT). The *STRIDE* meta (not shown for brevity) demonstrates how meta nodes relate to risks, specifically how the internal risks, which are analyzed via CATs, are organized. In CATs, the children's risk can be combined using *AND* and *OR* relations. With AND relation, all the children risks must happen together in order to trigger the parent event.

A significant difference in a CAT from a SAG is how vulnerability scores are related. In a SAG node, if one of its children nodes' risk event occurs, its risk event is also considered to have occurred. In other words, all children's risk values are combined with an OR relationship. However, it can also be a combination of AND/OR relations which can be formalized by a logical expression. In an AND/OR logical expression, the AND operator has higher priority than the OR operator. The expression is computed using a tree logic, with AND and OR operands such that each AND operation is treated as an operation inside a bracket, which sits deeper in the computation process in the tree. The flat layer of the computation tree is always an expression combined with OR relations unless there is only one expression. Therefore, we treat a single intermediate node as a special case of the OR expression, and, by default, all children under a node are combined with OR. If there is an AND expression embedded in the whole expression, we model this by putting an *All_Combo* node on top of them, and putting those nodes under it by combining them using AND relations.

Graph Data Component. In order to facilitate easier risk analysis by users, we needed to build automation tools for both the user interaction and data processing. The risk analysis is based on CAT and SAG, both of which use tree-based data structures and their processing time grows exponentially with the system size. Visualizer should be light-weight components with low computational overhead. Therefore, we used a temporary, read-only data structure (called *Graph Data*) to store the system information, and restricted visualizer to read data lazily only before rendering the results. All devices must contain one and only one graph data component. However, as WebGME does not generate contained components while creating a parent component, we must subsequently create the graph data component if it is absent after running the plugin (described later).

The *content* property of graph data component is of *asset* type. This property type in WebGME supports values having complex data structures such as a file or a self-defined data in JavaScript. We use it to store a JavaScript dictionary with six STRIDE risks as keys and value to each key also a dictionary with key named *CAT* or *SAG*. The RAF plugin goes through the system and generates these graphs and saves them to the graph data components in devices in a structured format. When the user switches to CAT or SAG visualizer, the visualizer reads the graph data component and renders the trees in WebGME.

3.4 Component Attack Tree

A Component Attack Tree (CAT) represents how vulnerabilities propagate inside a component. The *root* node of a CAT is one of the risks in the STRIDE category (Spoofing, Tampering, Repudiation, Information Disclosure, Denial of Service, Elevation of Privilege) [16]. The *leaf* nodes are the source causes of the risk at the root node. For example, the cause *memory access* implies that if the memory for running task of a component is accessible and modifiable externally, there can be some unusual behavior caused by unexpected memory access. Between the root node and leaf nodes are *intermediate* nodes, which represent internal behavior or phenomenon caused by other leaf nodes or intermediate nodes.

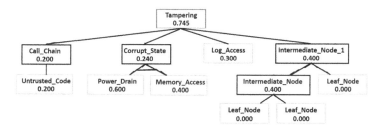

Fig. 2. Component attack tree for *Tampering* risk of a sensor

Each node contains a *vulnerability_score* property which represents the probability of exploitation and is given by domain experts that access known vulnerabilities and likelihood of those getting exploited. The vulnerability scores are propagated from bottom to top. The event of each node can occur for any combination of the occurrence of the events of its children nodes. By default, the children nodes are in an OR relationship with each other, which means if one of the children event occurs, the parent event will also occur.

Leaf nodes can contain, in addition to a vulnerability score, a mitigation score that represents a security mechanism that users put in place in order to mitigate the risk to a certain degree. For example, *Log_access* is a potential source of risk which can be a leaf node of a CAT. We can use some access control techniques, such as authentication or a privileges system, to prevent the malicious *log_access* behavior. The *mitigation_score* indicates how much these security mechanisms can prevent the vulnerability from propagating. Thus, the final vulnerability propagated to the component due to *log_access* behavior is given by: *vulnerability_score * (1 - mitigation_score)*.

Figure 2 shows an example of a CAT for Tampering risk of a sensor in the case study system described in Sect. 4. The red block on the top is the objective of this tree which is the risk itself. The children of the root node in black are intermediate nodes representing intermediate cause in one of the risk propagation paths. The leaf nodes in yellow represent the root causes of the risk.

We briefly described earlier how vulnerability scores are propagated. The *AND* logical relation among *Corrupt_State* and its children is shown by horizontal line. It implies that *Corrupt_State* can occur if and only if both *Power_Drain* and *Memory_Access* issues occur.

3.5 System Attack Graph

Similar to the CAT modeling process, the System Attack Graph (SAG) encompasses a root node, intermediary nodes, and leaf nodes. The root node corresponds to a target component STRIDE threat category, which also represents that component's CAT root node. An intermediary node represents a component *attack port*, which is used for propagating risk between components. As mentioned earlier, these attack ports are dependent on respective CAT root node risk levels, leading to the STRIDE threat categories represented by the CAT root nodes to be assigned as children leaf nodes of the attack ports. One difference in SAG from CAT is that the connections between nodes represent a path to reach a target instead of a hierarchical relationship.

When developing the SAG, the scoring assignment methodology is similar to the CAT. For the leaf nodes in the SAG, which are CAT root nodes, the score achieved from the CAT risk propagation process is used. Therefore, the score of the SAG leaf node should be the same as the CAT root node for the respective component STRIDE threat category.

Since the component attack ports do not have assigned risk scores, the intermediary nodes start as unassigned. Further, the root node also begins as unassigned. From this point, the risk from the SAG is propagated to the intermediary nodes until the root node has an assigned risk score. Next, the threat modeler can compare the SAG score for the root node to the relating CAT root node score to analyze whether the highest component threat is internal or via system-level propagation, and choose mitigation measures accordingly.

3.6 Algorithms for Vulnerability Propagation

The *EvaluateSystemLevelRisks* plugin is executed by clicking the play button in the top-left corner in WebGME and it affects the model only when executed under a Folder, Device, or a STRIDE risk component. In this section, we provide the key techniques in the plugin implementation (written in JavaScript). When this plugin is executed, WebGME creates an instance of this module and calls its *main* function. WebGME's *Core API* [4] is the major developer interface used for developing this plugin. The Core API provides the developer an interface for reading and modifying data in WebGME projects. The goal of the plugin execution is generating graph data for the visualizer. As described below, the code is organized into three parts: layered execution, reading and validation of the graph table, and generation of graphs.

Layered Execution. The *EvaluateSystemLevelRisks* plugin can be executed only inside a system folder, a device component, or a STRIDE risk within a device. Those three types have a containment relationship from top to bottom. A system folder contains devices, which contain STRIDE risks (given by domain experts based on known vulnerabilities). The execution also proceeds in a layered manner. When executed under a device, the plugin updates all the STRIDE risks under it. When executed under a system folder, the plugin collects all devices, recursively updates the devices, which in-turn updates all the STRIDE risks. We avoid repeated loading of graph data during accessing system components by putting the graph data component and its data in the function call so that the data is acquired only when it is undefined. The impact of exploitation is assessed through calculating system level risks (Sect. 3.8) and the system's safety is assessed through cyber gaming of exploitations and mitigations (Sect. 3.9).

Reading and Validating Graph Table. The graph table component under the system folder is the key for generating SAGs. When the plugin is executed, the graph table information is processed for graph generation. The plugin proceeds only when it finds no rule violations in the graph. If it finds violations, it warns the user showing the part of the graph containing errors.

The extracted data from the graph table is organized in a JavaScript dictionary. The graph table contains a directed graph of risk dependency. The keys in the dictionary are *Component ID* of the nodes under the graph table's crosscut, and the values are a list of component IDs that represent the out-degree nodes of the key's node. Since the dependency connections are a contained element of the graph table, the code iterates through all of the graph table's children, which are dependency connection components, and modifies the graph data dictionary.

Errors are collected in a list throughout the graph building process. At each dependency, the source and destination nodes are validated. Although even with a single error the SAG is not generated, the plugin still continues going through the whole dependency graph to detect and present all the errors in the model to the user for tracking the error sources. After iterating through the dependency connections and generating the graph's out-degree dictionary, the algorithm checks for any cycles in the graph.

Graphs Generation. The result of plugin execution is the CAT and SAG data. For each node in the graph, its children property lists the children trees. Both CATs and SAGs are stored in a JavaScript dictionary in the following form:

{ *"name"*: <*string*>, *"risk"*:<*string*>, *children*: [<*graph dict*>]}

Both CAT and SAG are generated recursively. For CAT, the plugin first generates the CAT for all children, then calculates the risk value based on its children's risk values, puts children in the list, and then returns the tree dictionary of current node. The RAF metamodel has specific types for *intermediate* node and *leaf* node. The leaf of the CAT tree must be of type leaf node, which represents the source cause of internal risks. If a non-leaf node does result from any leaf node cause, in the recursion it will return a NULL. During recursion, if a non-leaf node does not have children, or all children result in a NULL, the current return value will be a NULL and recursion will exit.

For SAG, the plugin generates a result dictionary from the graph table data. Dictionary data extracted from the graph table provides directed edge information. Starting from the root node, the SAG generation function recursively accesses out-degree node from the current node in the dependency graph. Similar to CAT, SAG only allows STRIDE risk as the leaf nodes of its tree structure and when recursion function is on an attack port, and if it does not have any child or all its children result in a NULL after recursion, the current return value will be NULL. The branch with attack port as leaf node will be cut off.

The CAT and SAG generated by the plugin are both tree-based structures with the same risk value propagation mechanism. In the tree, each node has a real numbered value ranging from 0 to 1 representing the probability of the risk occurrence. In both CAT and SAG, the root node is the final target for the whole tree, which is one of the STRIDE risks and is the ultimate goal of the vulnerability propagation.

3.7   Tree Visualization and Algorithms

RAF has separate visualizers for CATs and SAGs. These two visualizers differ slightly. In the sections below, we describe two major implementation issues with visualizers. The first is about handling events because the project information comes as asynchronous events and the code should handle them properly before rendering the graph. Secondly, the layout for the visualized graph must be correctly setup for efficiently and accurately rendering the graph's visual elements.

Event Handling. When switching to a visualizer, a *reload* event occurs in the browser. Upon switching the visualizer context, the client sends a request to the server for background data while refreshing the page. The requested data includes the current WebGME node and its children nodes. Loading the page content consists of several parts, each of which is processed in an asynchronous manner, and a callback is called when it is finished. Rendering cannot start as soon as the visualizer code is executed from the entry function because the key data may not be loaded by then. However, due to the asynchronicity of the loading event, we cannot determine which node is loaded last so that we can render the graph after that. Therefore, we designed a graph data component to store all the visualization information such that the visualizer only needs to load the graph data before rendering. The visualizer initializes the graph data variable as NULL. When a node is loaded, the code will render the graph only if the variable is assigned with node content. To avoid duplicated rendering, we use a flag indicating whether the graph is already rendered at current context.

Layout Method. The rendering objective is drawing a tree on a HyperText Markup Language (HTML) web page. HTML elements can be configured with width, height, and position. The key problem with the layout algorithm is how to set up the position and size information of each node's elements. We truncate the scores as they are floating-point numbers and limit string names to three units in size. The exact position of a node is determined by not only its topological position in the tree, but also the position and size of other nodes. In the visualizer, we used a recursive function to generate another tree dictionary that records layout information for all nodes.

3.8   Risk Profile

To assess the system-level risk, the *EvaluateSystemLevelRisks* plugin updates the value of a risk profile component inside a system folder. This value represents the overall risk of the whole system and six STRIDE risk values along with their corresponding weights that contribute to the overall risk assessment score.

Each STRIDE risk values in the risk profile is calculated from all the corresponding risks of top-level devices as well as lower-level devices if they are under risk and there is a path by which the risk can be propagated to the logical upper-level system. The weight represents how each kind of risk contributes to the system-level risk and it can be customized by users. The risk weights are normalized during the computation. The overall risk value is calculated by combining all normalized risk values with OR logic.

In addition, we developed a tool that computes system-level risks when one of the device's risks is being exploited. When a device risk is ongoing, its risk value is temporarily changed to 1.0 and its sibling risks are turned to 0.0. The risks in other devices remain the same. Such change can have the effect on other risks through risk propagation and result in different system-level risk values, which show how vulnerable the system is when a device risk is actually being exploited. This can help to find the weakest points in the system. The tool rank orders the system vulnerabilities by sorting the corresponding system-level risk values in descending order. These risk analysis results can be downloaded after this tool is executed. RAF generates a hyperlink in the output to directly open the associated risk components that are listed in the above priority order.

3.9   Cyber Gaming for Risk Management

We also have a metamodel (not shown for brevity) for risk management plan modeling. An example risk management plan model is shown in Fig. 3. We can further connect our risk analysis model with attack behavior models to facilitate users evaluating the effectiveness of counterattack strategies. The ultimate goal of doing risk analysis is to make the system more secure. By implementing the risk profile features, we can spot the specific points that trigger the risk easily. But the actions available for us to mitigate vulnerabilities are limited. In addition, different mitigation actions (e.g., firewall, encryption, etc.) take time to implement and also incur a cost on performance of the system. Therefore, we must consider which mitigation actions could be applied and under what circumstances. In addition, certain mitigation actions may be kept secret from potential attackers and used only when absolutely needed. Attackers usually do not just exploit one weakness in a device. Instead, a series of exploitations that interact with counterattack mitigations is used. Thus, it is important to model the attack and counterattack behaviors and analyze the risks step by step.

We developed the metamodel for risk management plans as a separate subgroup. The risk management plan allows us to model cyber gaming scenarios that allow combining and evaluating vulnerability exploitation against mitigation actions. The attack and counter-attacks can be modeled up to any depth.

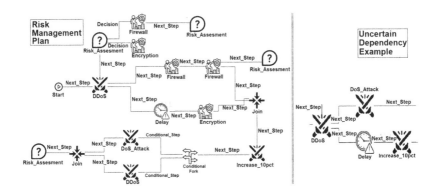

Fig. 3. Sample risk management plan with an example of uncertain dependency

The model represents a timed execution flow in which each process unit can take a certain amount of model time before its successors start running. There are two major types of processing units, exploitation and mitigation. They both associate with a risk component in the system architecture model via set relationship called *Risk_match*. An exploitation activates a certain risk by setting the vulnerability score to 1.0 and disabling the sibling risks under same device by setting their vulnerability score to 0. A mitigation reduces the chance of a device being exploited with a certain risk. Mitigation nodes have an attribute *mitigation_rate* that ranges from 0.0 to 1.0 and determines what percent of risk can the mitigation reduce. After a mitigation is processed, the vulnerability of the risk associated with the mitigation node will be reduced by the mitigation rate. In addition, RAF has a delay component that only delays the model time in the amount of specified time units. Since exploitation and mitigation are the simulation of an actual behavior, their processing time should have some associated variance. The *duration* attribute can be used to specify the time delay and *delay_variance* attribute can be used to specify the variance of the randomized processing times according to a Gaussian distribution.

Exploitation and mitigation components have a dependency limitation of what device they can be associated with. A device can be exploited with one of the risks only if any of its children is exploited. The device architecture is in a hierarchical structure – the nodes at the bottom are base devices and the others are high-level devices. At the beginning, only base devices are available for exploitation. After a risk of a device is exploited, the device's parent device is available for further exploitation. The plugin will check for a possible dependency problem that one exploitation might be associated with an unavailable device at the time of execution. Because of the parallelism in the execution and uncertainty of the process time, we cannot determine whether an exploitation is associated with an available device at the time of execution. But we can determine whether an exploitation is guaranteed to be associated with an available device. On the right side of Fig. 3, the *DoS attack* (in the upper branch) exploits a risk in base device A, and an *Increase_10_percent attack* (in the lower branch) exploits device B (which is a parent of device A). Here, if none of the exploitations on B's children were finished, B's availability will be indeterminable when *Increase_10pct attack* starts. If *DoS attack* finishes before the *Increase_10_pct attack*, then B will become unavailable for *Increase_10pct attack*. However, if *DDoS attack* (predecessor of both *DoS attack* and *Increase_10_pct attack*), exploits one of the B's children C, but is not finished, then B will still be available for *Increase_10_pct attack*. The plugin checks for device availability before executing exploitations.

As the example shows, modeling of cyber-games allows parallel branches. From one process node, the model allows multiple next steps from it. Each parallel branch represents a time independent execution flow. A *join* node serves as a synchronizing point of parallel branches. Join nodes allow multiple input flows but there is only one output flow. Each input flow will suspend on the join point until all other input flows are finished. A *conditional fork* allows *random* selection of outgoing branches based on probabilities specified on them. When the sum of probabilities on all conditional branches does not equal to 1.0, the plugin normalizes all of the probabilities.

Risk assessment node calculates the overall risk at the time point it is assigned. The risk calculation is the same as the static calculation, but it also includes dynamic connections – a key feature of RAF that existing works mentioned in Sect. 2 do not support. In each physical (network) connection, there is an *active_condition* attribute that specifies when the connection is established in model time. The *active_condition* attribute is of string type and its value is an expression using the variable t such that it must evaluate to true or false. By default, the value for this attribute is *true*, which means the connection is always active. If the attribute is $t > 3$, for example, it means the connection is active when the model time is greater than 3. The expression can also incorporate periodic patterns such as *(t%5 >1) & (t%5 <2)*, which means there is an active period with length of 1 in every 5 model time units. The overall risk value is calculated by propagating the risk through the dependency table. Each dependency is a directed connection between risks and attack ports that either relies on hierarchical relation or physical connection between the risks and ports. For those dependencies between two base devices that are connected with a physical connection, the status of this dependency depends on the active condition of the connection.

The *decision* branch after a risk assessment node uses a true/false expression to determine whether to continue with any following nodes (e.g., a mitigation).

The expression is written using the value of *variable name* attribute of previous risk assessment (which will represents the corresponding risk value). For example, if we set variable name as r, the expression on decision branches after the risk assessment can be *r >0.1, 1/r <3*, etc. When expressions on multiple decision branches are true, the nodes following them are executed in parallel.

4   Case Study from a Railway Cyber Network

4.1   Railway System Model

There are two default visualizers at the top level folder of the example project, viz. *meta* and *composition*. *Meta* is a built-in visualizer that always shows the global metamodel design at any component folder of the system and is the default one when opening the project. The *composition* visualizer next to the *meta* visualizer shows the model components, as shown in Fig. 4.

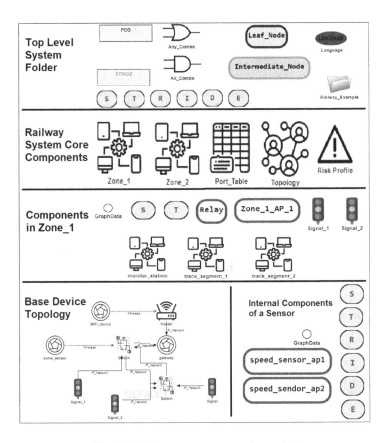

Fig. 4. Railway system example model

In the top folder of the main project, the component with a blue folder icon (named *Railway_Example*) is an example Railway Transportation System built using the metamodel described earlier. This a very simple model of a railway control system with a few sensors placed on the railway track to collect real-time signal data, a repeater for receiving, filtering, and transmitting the raw data, a gateway and a router as parts of the network, and a central station that receives all data globally and sends out control commands. The directed lines with arrows between devices show the connection from one device to another, with type names along with the line. In the example system, all connections are bidirectional, so there are always arrows at the end of lines between devices in its composition. There is also a graph table which is unique to the system and used to specify the risk propagation dependencies between attack ports and STRIDE risk components. Each type of component is assigned with an SVG icon to its metamodel. Figure 4 shows the composition of the example system, the constituents inside *Zone_1* device of the top folder, and the topology of base devices under the crosscut panel of Topology component in the system.

When double-clicking on a device component (e.g., speed_sensor) for example, the composition will show the internal component of this device, as shown in Fig. 4. The blue boxes with letters on them are STRIDE risk components, which contain a CAT organized with the folder hierarchy which will be further discussed below. The white components with red borders are attack ports. Attack ports represent certain attack behavior that can interact with an external device. For example, sending malicious packets can be an attack port of the central station because the central stations are able to send packets that may possibly cause unexpected behavior and can cause risk to the system if the packets are somehow sent with a malicious intention. If malicious packets are sent, that may further cause integrity problems in a repeater, or disrupted communication of a router or gateway, and finally result in one of the STRIDE risks in one of the devices. Such risk propagation is modeled and captured by SAG, that is described below. There is also a small circle component called *Graph Data*. This is used to store the results of computations performed by the plugin and read by visualizers to show the risk analysis graphs. It is not intended to be used by users directly.

When the user enters into one of the STRIDE risk components in a device, there may be a few children components that are in the CAT under the root node. The visualizers work for STRIDE components here and enable the *ComponentAttackTree* and *SystemAttackGraph* panels inside the STRIDE component. If the user switches to one of these visualizers, the visualized tree structure for the corresponding structure will be displayed. Figure 2 shows the CAT of *Tampering* risk of a sensor and Fig. 5 shows its SAG.

Another component is the *Graph Table*, with table like SVG icon. On selecting it, the composition view (empty) is shown, by default. However, if the user switches to the visualizer *crosscut*, a graph is shown with blue *STRIDE* components and red *attack port* components and have a directional edge between the nodes (see Fig. 5). This graph is defined by the user and it summarizes the paths of how external risks can propagate from one component to the other. The nodes of a crosscut are not contained in the graph table component but they are simply references to devices in the system folder. The connection components are included by the parent component but they are not shown in the composition due to inherited containment relationship to the Graph Table model.

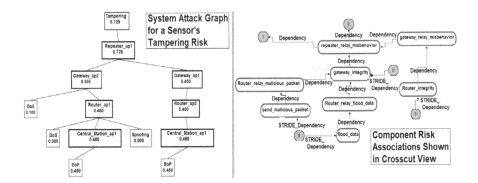

Fig. 5. SAT and risk associations

4.2 Modeling the System

To create our own model based on the project, we need to first create a Project Folder component at the top-level hierarchy of the main project. The name of a component is the metamodel's name, so it is important to rename the system folder component with a proper name for the system after creating it.

In the system folder, we can build the system topology with device components and connections. On the left there is an area with all available components in the current context are shown. Dragging an icon from the left panel to the white space can create the corresponding component. Dragging lines between device components can create connections between them. There is a prompt choice for the type of connection after drawing a line from one device to another.

Inside a STRIDE risk component, we can put intermediate nodes or leaf nodes. Those nodes are constituents of the CAT of the parent STRIDE risk device. The risk nodes inside a STRIDE risk component are organized in a tree structure based on their hierarchical relations. For each node, its children nodes are the direct causes of it. The leaf nodes require the user to input the risk values based on their domain knowledge and optionally fill the property of mitigation information.

The *EvaluateSystemLevelRiskss* plugin can be executed under three types of components: project folder, device, and STRIDE risk component. These three types of components have hierarchical relations. A project folder contains devices and a device contains STRIDE risks. When the plugin is executed under the project folder, all devices and the risks under them will be updated. If the plugin runs under a device, only the risks under the current device will be updated. If the current running environment is just one of the STRIDE risks, only the information related to this risk will be renewed. Updating globally can take a while if the system is large. If we need the result for only part of the system or if we modify only a part of the system before the update, local updates (device, risk level) can be used.

4.3   Risk Dependencies

A graph table uses the *crosscut* visualizer instead of the *composition* visualizer to model dependency relations between STRIDE risks and attack ports of various devices. In *composition*, all elements shown in the white space are direct children of the current element being inspected, and connections are created by dragging from one component to another and permissible only between nodes with a common parent. In RAF, crosscuts are used for modeling risk propagation dependencies across component hierarchies by creating connections between references of existing nodes.

The direct graph under the crosscut of a graph table must be checked for validity, so the RAF's plugin first checks that. There are three rules for the graph validity. First, there should not a cycle. The graph is built for summarizing risk dependencies and the directed edges are a representation of the potential path for risk propagation. A cycle would be logically incorrect because a risk should have its ultimate source and destination in the graph. Even if there are cycles due to the device property, the user assigning the dependency should resolve it using domain knowledge. The dependency can be from an attack port to another attack port, an attack port to a STRIDE risk, and a STRIDE risk to an attack port. For the attack port to attack port dependency, the attack ports must be from different components. For the dependency from STRIDE risk to an attack port, they cannot be within the same device. For the dependency from attack port to a STRIDE risk, they must be within the same device. This is because the graph and dependency relations are used for external risk analysis. Risk occurrence in each device is triggered by factors in other devices when the attack port is either triggered by another attack port, or internally by a risk within the device. Any errors in graph model are reported with locations.

4.4   Risk Management Plan

Figure 3 shows a full example of the risk management model. Similar to modeling the system architecture and risk node, the components are simply added from the left panel and connected by drawing from one point to the other.

From the start node, the first node is a DDoS attack and it will result in spoofing risk of one of the traffic lights. Figure 6 shows the topology associated to this example risk management plan. The device that first DDoS attacks is *Signal_1* marked by a red circle and it has an IP network connection with a switch. The active condition attribute for the marked connection from *Signal_1* to the switch is $t > 1$ & $t < 2$ which means the connection is only active during the time interval $(1, 2)$. Figure 6 shows a part of the port table associated with the risk management plan. The spoofing risk marked with a red circle is the exploited spoofing risk of *Signal_1*. The first relay is the relay inside *Signal_1* and the second relay after it is in the switch. *Signal_1* and the switch are both base devices, so the dependency between two relays is built upon this conditional connection. Such dependency inherits the condition of the connection and the dependency is also *active* when the connection is active. In this example, the tampering and spoofing risks only propagate to the top during the time interval (1, 2).

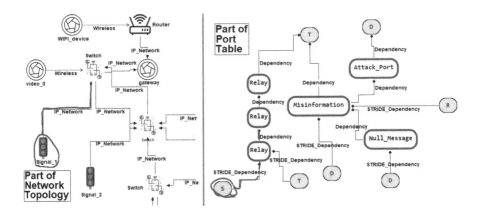

Fig. 6. Part of the network topology and port table

The risk assessment followed by next steps of mitigation nodes shows an example of the conditional action based on risk assessment result. The variable name specified in the risk assessment is *risk_var*. The first branch has the expression *risk_var >0.5 & risk_var <0.6* and second branch has *(risk_var ** 2) >0.3*. Those branches will proceed if the expression is true. In this case, the execution path is not determined before each run because there is uncertainty of the risk assessment value. The connection between *Signal_1* and the switch is only active during time interval (1,2) and whether it is active or not has impact on the overall risk value since there is a risk propagation dependency that is established upon the connection. On the other side, the actual running of first DDoS is uncertain because the actual time the exploitation takes is randomly assigned based on a normal distribution with given mean and variation. If we let the expected execution time of the DDoS exploitation be 1, the actual finish time could be somewhere around 1.0 (e.g., 0.99 or 1.01). If the risk assessment takes place at 0.99, the important dependency that propagates that risk is inactive at this time point and the exploitation will have no effect on the overall risk. Conversely, if the risk assessment runs the risk propagation at the time point at 1.01, the exploited spoofing will be propagated to the top and increase the risk value. Therefore, the action of the next step will also be random due to the randomness of risk assessment result.

After parallel branches merges at the join point, there is a conditional fork node after it. The connections that follow the conditional fork are of type *conditional step* and have a probability attribute. The sum of probabilities from the fork point should be 1.0. However, when the user enters probabilities that do not add up to 1.0, the plugin will normalize the values. Only one branch is selected during the execution, and the selection is a weighted random based on probabilities of active branches.

5   Conclusion and Future Work

In this paper, we demonstrated the use of the *model-integrated computing (MIC)* technique to build a metamodel for risk analysis and demonstrated it using a railway transportation system case study. Our web-based Risk Analysis Framework (RAF) provides a set of risk analysis and visualization tools that aim to provide a user-friendly platform for risk analysis and risk management planning.

After modeling the system architecture and network topology, risk analysis tools are used for automatically propagating the risk values, and visualization tools are used to visually inspect the component attack trees of specific component risks and system attack graphs that also consider how risks can propagate across components via their network interconnections. In addition, our automated risk assessment tool can analyze all the modeled system vulnerabilities, evaluate them for their impact on overall system-level risk, and rank order them for targeting mitigation actions against most damaging vulnerabilities. We also provided a novel approach to handle dynamic network connections for analyzing risks amidst changing network topology of infrastructure components, such as mobile locomotives and its on-board devices in the railway transportation systems. The quantitative approach to risk analysis and model-based design and automated analysis tools provides a highly powerful framework for analyzing risks of critical infrastructures, such as a railway transportation system.

It is important to note that the algorithms and approaches developed in this work are equally applicable to other types of critical infrastructures. We are currently working on applying it to energy, water distribution, and healthcare domains. Also, we are working on integrating the risk analysis framework with the networked co-simulations of dynamical systems (e.g., Cyber-Physical Systems Wind Tunnel (CPSWT) [17,18]) for validating and improving risk scores as well as for conducting informed, simulation-based cybersecurity evaluations.

Acknowledgement. This work is supported by the US National Security Agency (NSA) (award #H98230-18-D-0010) and the US National Institute of Standards and Technology (NIST) (award #70NANB20H020). No approval or endorsement of any commercial product by NSA or NIST is intended or implied. Certain commercial equipment, instruments, or materials are identified in this paper in order to specify the experimental procedure adequately. Such identification is not intended to imply recommendation or endorsement by NSA or NIST, nor is it intended to imply that the materials or equipment identified are necessarily the best available for the purpose. This publication was co-authored by United States Government employees as part of their official duties and is, therefore, a work of the U.S. Government and not subject to copyright. Any opinions, findings, and conclusions or recommendations expressed in this material are those of the author(s) and do not necessarily reflect the views of NSA or NIST.

References

1. Koutsoukos, X., et al.: Performance evaluation of secure industrial control system design: a railway control system case study. In: Resilience Week, pp. 101–108 (2016)
2. Myagmar, S., Lee, A.J., Yurcik, W.: Threat modeling as a basis for security requirements. In: Symposium on Requirements Engineering for Information Security (SREIS), vol. 2005, pp. 1–8 (2005)
3. Sztipanovits, J., Karsai, G.: Model-integrated computing. Computer **30**(4), 110–111 (1997)
4. Kecskes, T., Zhang, Q., Sztipanovits, J.: Bridging engineering and formal modeling: WebGME and formula integration. Technical report in Department of EECS, Vanderbilt University, Nashville, TN (2017)
5. Liao, Y.-C.: Quantitative information security vulnerability assessment for norwegian critical infrastructure. In: Rashid, A., Popov, P. (eds.) CRITIS 2020. LNCS, vol. 12332, pp. 31–43. Springer, Cham (2020). https://doi.org/10.1007/978-3-030-58295-1_3
6. Schmittner, C., et al.: Threat modeling in the railway domain. In: Collart-Dutilleul, S., Lecomte, T., Romanovsky, A. (eds.) RSSRail 2019. LNCS, vol. 11495, pp. 261–271. Springer, Cham (2019). https://doi.org/10.1007/978-3-030-18744-6_17
7. Saini, V., Duan, Q., Paruchuri, V.: Threat modeling using attack trees. J. Comput. Sci. Coll. **23**(4), 124–131 (2008)
8. Martins, G., Bhatia, S., Koutsoukos, X., Stouffer, K., Tang, C., Candell, R.: Towards a systematic threat modeling approach for cyber-physical systems. In: Resilience Week (RWS 2015), pp. 1–6. IEEE (2015)
9. Kavallieratos, G., Spathoulas, G., Katsikas, S.: Cyber risk propagation and optimal selection of cybersecurity controls for complex cyber-physical systems. Sensors **21**(5), 1691 (2021)
10. Stellios, I., Kotzanikolaou, P., Grigoriadis, C.: Assessing IoT enabled cyber-physical attack paths against critical systems. Comput. Secur. **107**, 102316 (2021)
11. Garg, U., Sikka, G., Awasthi, L.K.: Empirical analysis of attack graphs for mitigating critical paths and vulnerabilities. Comput. Secur. **77**, 349–359 (2018)
12. Liu, X., Zhang, J., Zhu, P., Tan, Q., Yin, W.: Quantitative cyber-physical security analysis methodology for industrial control systems based on incomplete information Bayesian game. Comput. Secur. **102**, 102138 (2021)
13. Shostack, A.: Threat Modeling: Designing for Security. Wiley, Hoboken (2014)
14. Potteiger, B., Martins, G., Koutsoukos, X.: Software and attack centric integrated threat modeling for quantitative risk assessment. In: Proceedings of the Symposium and Bootcamp on the Science of Security, pp. 99–108 (2016)
15. Garitselov, O., Mohanty, S.P., Kougianos, E.: A comparative study of metamodels for fast and accurate simulation of nano-CMOS circuits. IEEE Trans. Semicond. Manuf. **25**(1), 26–36 (2011)
16. Microsoft Security Development Lifecycle (SDL) Threat Modeling Tool. https://docs.microsoft.com/en-us/azure/security/develop/threat-modeling-tool. Accessed 27 Aug 2021
17. Neema, H., Sztipanovits, J., Steinbrink, C., Raub, T., Cornelsen, B., Lehnhoff, S.: Simulation integration platforms for cyber-physical systems. In: Proceedings of the Workshop on Design Automation for CPS and IoT, pp. 10–19 (2019)
18. Neema, H.: Large-scale integration of heterogeneous simulations. Ph.D. dissertation Research. Vanderbilt University (2018)

A Survey on Applications of Formal Methods in Analysis of SCADA Systems

Mihael Marović[(✉)] , Ante Derek , and Stjepan Groš

Faculty of Electrical Engineering and Computing, Laboratory for Information Security and Privacy, University of Zagreb, Unska 3, 10000 Zagreb, Croatia
{mihael.marovic,ante.derek,stjepan.gros}@fer.hr

Abstract. The goal of this survey is to establish how have the formal methods been applied to Supervisory Control and Data Acquisition (SCADA) systems in order to verify critical properties relevant to SCADA to a high degree of assurance. We analyze and dissect published research that attempts to formally specify and verify SCADA communication protocol or other components relevant and specific to SCADA systems. We identify areas that would benefit most from analysis by formal methods.

Keywords: SCADA · Formal methods · Verification · Protocols

1 Introduction

Supervisory Control and Data Acquisition (SCADA) systems control and monitor critical distributed infrastructure such as power generation and distribution systems, oil and gas fields, water pipelines, manufacturing plants, etc. Such systems are often distributed over a large geographic area, but allow operators at a central location fine-grained control over individual devices such as valves, switches, and pumps. Moreover, SCADA systems collect, aggregate, visualize and analyze data from individual devices and sensors.

Originally, SCADA systems were isolated from the outside world and usually used legacy protocols for communication between system components and devices. However, in recent decades, SCADA systems have transformed into heterogeneous systems where devices communicate over various wired and wireless networks using standardized protocols. Common deployment recommendations (e.g., [28]) include warnings not to connect the system or devices to the Internet, but experience shows that such air gaps are not realistic in practice [3], and examples such as Stuxnet [25] show that even air gaps cannot contain persistent threats.

This work has been supported by the European Union from the European Regional Development Fund via Operational Programme Competitiveness and Cohesion 2014–2020 for Croatia through the project Center of competencies for cyber-security of control systems (CEKOM SUS, grant KK.01.2.2.03.0019).

© Springer Nature Switzerland AG 2021
D. Percia David et al. (Eds.): CRITIS 2021, LNCS 13139, pp. 99–115, 2021.
https://doi.org/10.1007/978-3-030-93200-8_6

Due to the critical nature of the infrastructure, it is of utmost importance that the SCADA systems function as expected, i.e. that the commands sent to the devices are executed in a timely and reliable manner and that the status messages received from the devices reflect the actual condition. Moreover, these characteristics should hold even *in the face of a malicious and persistent adversary*. This makes the SCADA system and its building blocks an excellent target for analysis using formal methods.

Formal methods are used for mathematical modelling of hardware and software systems with the aim of specifying and verifying their properties. The high degree of mathematical rigour used in formal methods leads to a high degree of confidence in the verified properties, but makes the modelling and analysis of complex systems difficult and tedious. Sometimes formal methods are equipped with tools ranging from model checkers that can find counterexamples and verify properties by searching a finite state space, to full-fledged theorem provers that can provide machine-verifiable proofs of desirable properties.

The aim of this paper is to give a comprehensive and critical evaluation of research results in the area of applying formal methods to the specification and verification of critical properties of SCADA systems. Part of that process is the evaluation of research results which analyze *security* or *functional* requirements of SCADA systems. We also aim to find critical areas in SCADA systems that have not received attention from the research community and where the formal methods approach could have the most immediate and significant impact. This paper makes the following contributions to these goals:

- We conduct a comprehensive review of published research in which SCADA systems or their components have been analyzed using formal methods.
- We identify which parts of SCADA systems have had their critical properties verified in a formal way and what flaws and attacks were discovered during the analysis.
- We identify challenges in formal verification and also critical components that were not formally analyzed or if there are formal models but no attempts to verify their critical security properties.

The remainder of this paper is organized as follows. First, we give the necessary technical background on SCADA systems and formal methods in Sect. 2. We define our methodology and the scope of the survey in Sect. 3. Section 4 contains the main results of the survey. In Sect. 5 we give a further discussion on SCADA and formal methods. We address related work in Sect. 6 and conclude in Sect. 7.

2   Background

2.1   SCADA Systems

First, we give an overview of the architecture of SCADA systems (shown in Fig. 1) and list the main components of such systems. At the lowest level, we

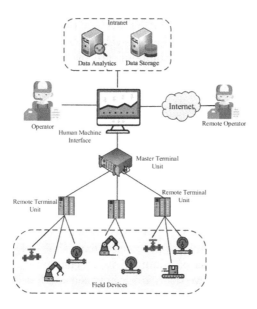

Fig. 1. A simple SCADA system layout (taken from [21])

find *field devices* that either collect data (e.g., temperature sensors), directly manage the physical elements (e.g., control valves), or both. Field devices are controlled via a digital or analog interface by *programmable logic controllers* (PLCs) or *remote terminal units* (RTUs). Both PLCs and RTUs serve as intermediaries between the central controller and the field devices and can control a large number of individual devices. In the context of SCADA systems, the roles of PLCs and RTUs overlap. However, RTUs typically provide a richer set of functions, while PLCs are simpler devices that can nevertheless individually perform complex industrial tasks.

At the level above, we find the *master terminal unit* (MTU), connected to a *human-machine interface* (HMI). The HMI is linked to the SCADA supervisory computer. System operators in a central location use the HMI to monitor and control the behavior of the overall system, including configuring and overriding the normal operation of RTUs, PLCs, and even individual field devices. In addition to communicating with the MTU, PLCs and RTUs can communicate with other PLCs/RTUs in a peer-to-peer fashion. In general, system components can be connected in different topologies, e.g. series, series-star, point-to-point, and multi-drop.

Note that in the larger context of operational technology (OT) and industrial control systems (ICS), there are other system configurations such as *distributed control systems* (DCS) that aim to control infrastructure in a smaller geographic area (e.g., a single facility) and where, among other differences, data gathering is de-emphasised when compared to SCADA. Also, in comparison to IT systems,

SCADA is specific because it is an OT system (meaning it controls physical processes). This survey is targeted exclusively on SCADA systems.

SCADA system components communicate over various types of networks using different protocols. Protocol analysis has been a fruitful application area of formal methods for many decades and therefore it is not surprising that our research shows that the protocols used in SCADA systems are the components that have been the target of most attempts of formal verification. Communication protocols can be categorized by low-level network infrastructure into *fieldbus-based protocols*, *Ethernet-based protocols*, and *serial protocols* [21]. Fieldbus is a network system used to connect field devices (sensors, actuators, etc.) to associated controllers. Common fieldbus protocols are BITBUS, PROFIBUS, and WorldFIP. Popular Ethernet based network protocols used in SCADA are Distributed Network Protocol 3 (DNP3), International Electrotechnical Commission (IEC) 61850, PROFINET, and EtherCAT. Serial protocols are protocols based on serial communication, which means that only one bit of data is sent sequentially over a bus or communication channel. A popular industrial serial protocol is Modbus (we distinguish between Modbus Serial and Modbus TCP/IP). Of the serial-based protocols, we also mention IEC 60870. Finally, it is important to know about the Open Platform Communication Unified Architecture (OPC-UA) protocol - an industrial protocol that is newer than Modbus and provides unified semantics at all levels: field, controller, and cloud. We refer the reader to the survey by Pliatsios et al. [21] for comprehensive and detailed descriptions of the protocols used in SCADA systems.

2.2 Formal Methods

Formal methods are mathematically rigorous techniques for modeling hardware and software systems, specifying and verifying their properties. Formal approaches include model checking, theorem proving, equivalence checking, assertion based verification, etc. The mathematical model of a system can be based on logic, multiset rewriting, computational or symbolic model of cryptography, process algebra, etc. The result of the formal analysis can be a counterexample showing that the properties do not hold, or formal proof. In the case of communication protocols, properties that we can describe and verify using formal methods are: secrecy, authenticity, delivery, confidentiality, integrity, availability, authorization, and others.

While formal analysis can be done in an pen-and-paper setting, it is most practical and beneficial when it is supported to some extent with automated tools. Tools that have been used for analysis of SCADA systems or components include: The Tamarin Prover (used in [5,6]), PVS Specification and Verification System (used in [7]), Symbolic Analysis Laboratory (SAL) toolkit (used in [7]), SPIN - Promela (used in [19]), AVISPA (used in [8]), ProVerif (used in [4,23]), CPN state space analysis (used in [1,2]), CPN Tools (used in [27]), UPPAAL (used in [15,18]), Prolog programming language (used in [4]), VEDA (used in [22]), Observer-Based Prover (OBP) Explorer (used in [9]) and Z3 (used in [24]).

3   Methodology

The papers included in the survey work were found using the Scopus database and the Google Scholar search engine. We started the papers that contain the keywords "SCADA" and either "formal methods", "formal analysis", "formal verification" in the title or somewhere in the text of the paper. Additionally, we used the same sources and searched for the same keywords with the name of a concrete communication protocol used in SCADA system, including all fieldbus-based protocols, Ethernet-based protocols, and serial protocols from the survey by Pliatsios et al. [21]. Starting from that initial group of papers we performed both forward and backward snowballing procedures. More precisely, we select a paper P from the initial set, we looked at all its citations and references, and manually selected the relevant papers. We repeated this procedure until no new papers were discovered.

We have to note that formal methods are used for modeling and verification of PLC hardware and software [29], but we decided not to include that area in this survey. That is because PLCs can be viewed as separate generic components and they are a research area for themselves. Similarly, there are other generic components commonly used in SCADA (for example the Transport Layer Security (TLS) protocol), but we do not include the formal analysis of such components in our survey.

For each included paper our goal was to answer the following questions: What is the target of the formal modelling or analysis? What is the mathematical foundation of the formal model? What, if any, problems or attacks were discovered or fixed by the formal analysis? What, if any, properties were formally verified by the analysis?

4   Applying Formal Methods to SCADA

In this section, we identify and describe all research efforts that apply formal reasoning to analyze SCADA systems and SCADA system components.

We find out that only few papers that we considered have entire formal model public (whether it be described in the paper or somewhere on the Internet). This includes input to the tool and output of the tool, if the tool is used. Those papers are [13,18]. There are few papers that have almost the whole model described in paper like [5] (missing the required updates for asymmetric lemmas), [9,24]. The rest of papers have formal model described in more or less detail, but we could not find the entire formal model and, hence, these results may not be easily reproducible.

Table 1 gives the summary of formal methods usage with respect to SCADA system and the results of the survey. We categorize the analysis targets into three main groups: SCADA protocols, attack detection, and SCADA architecture. In this section we address the central questions of the survey for each paper (those questions have been indicated at the end of the Sect. 3).

Table 1. This table shows the differentiation of how formal methods are used with respect to SCADA system and obtained results

Paper	Analysis target	Mathematical formalism	Attacks/problems discovered	Verified/analyzed properties	Tool(s) used	New discovery regarding analyzed properties
[6]	Modbus and OPC-UA protocols variants	Multiset rewriting rules	MITM	Authentication, delivery	The Tamarin prover	Yes
[7]	Modbus protocol	High-order logic	-	-	PVS Specification and Verification System, Symbolic Analysis Laboratory (SAL) toolkit	No
[19]	Modbus protocol	Dynamic State Machine (DSTM), computation tree logic (CTL)	MITM	-	SPIN - Promela	No
[8]	Modbus TCP and Serial	Temporal logic of actions (TLA)	MITM	Confidentiality, integrity	AVISPA	No
[27]	Modbus/TCP	Colored Petri nets (CPNs)	MITM, DoS	Integrity, authenticity	CPN Tools	No
[23]	OPC-UA protocol	a-π calculus	MITM	Authentication, secrecy	ProVerif	Yes
[2]	DNP3 protocol	Colored Petri nets (CPNs)	DoS	Availability, integrity	CPN state space analysis tool	Yes
[1]	DNP3 protocol	Colored Petri nets (CPNs), computation tree logic (CTL)	MITM	Integrity	CPN state space analysis tool	Yes
[5]	DNP3 protocol	Multiset rewrite rules	Spoofing, replay, eavesdropping	Authentication, confidentiality of keys	The Tamarin prover	Yes
[26]	DNP3 protocol	Standard XACML (eXtensible Access Control Markup Language), logic	-	Authorization	-	No
[15]	IEC 61850 protocol	Timed computation tree logic (TCTL)	-	-	UPPAAL	No
[13]	PROFINET protocol	Timing a-π calculus	-	-	-	No
[4]	Fieldubs protocols and SCADA architecture	a-π calculus	DoS	Injective agreement, non-injective agreement	ProVerif, Prolog programming language	Yes
[17]	WorldFIP protocol	Process algebra, abstract data types (ADTs)	-	-	-	No
[22]	PROFIBUS protocol	Extended finite state machine (EFSM)	-	-	VEDA	No
[16]	PROFIBUS protocol	Process algebra, extended finite state machines (EFSMs)	-	-	-	No
[18]	Attack detection	Timed temporal logic (TCTL)	Underflow or overflow attack	Underflow or overflow property	UPPAAL	Yes
[9]	SCADA architecture	Security patterns expressed in logic	-	Safety, authenticity, availability, integrity	Observer-Based Prover (OBP) Explorer	Yes
[24]	SCADA architecture	Satisfiability modulo theories (SMT)	Attacks on observability	k-Resilient observability, k-Resilient Secured observability	Z3	Yes

4.1 Formal Analysis of Protocols Used in SCADA Systems

Most of the papers we discovered are aimed to analyzing some aspect of a protocol used in SCADA systems [1,4–8,15–17,19,22,23,26,27]. As mentioned before, this is not surprising since protocol analysis has been an active area of application of formal methods for several decades. The protocol can be used for communication between SCADA components (e.g., between the MTU and the RTUs, between RTUs and field devices). Protocols that were analyzed by papers discussed in this section are: Modbus [6–8,19,27], OPC-UA [6,23], DNP3 [1,2,5,26], IEC 61850 [15], fieldbus protocols [4], WorldFIP [17] and PROFIBUS [16,22]. The common feature about Modbus, OPC-UA and DNP3 is that although they are different protocols, they all involve communication between client (master) and server (outstation).

Most papers attempt to verify the security properties of protocol (for example: secrecy, integrity, authentication). If paper uses an attacker model that model is always some variant of the so called *Dolev-Yao* attacker where the cryptography is assumed perfect and the attacker has complete control over the network. Hence, no published research attempts to verify the properties of SCADA systems in more complex models (e.g. the computational attacker model in cryptography).

4.2 The Modbus Protocol

Dreier et al. [6] analyzed two notable industrial protocols: Modbus and OPC-UA. The formal model they used is based on the multiset rewriting rules and the attacker model is the Dolev-Yao attacker model. They defined and verified security properties for different versions of the same protocol. These security properties are: non-injective message authenticity, non-injective message delivery, injective message authenticity, injective message delivery, flow authenticity, flow delivery. They obtained results regarding the security of protocols: Modbus, Modbus *Sign*, Modbus *MAC*, OPC-UA *None*, OPC-UA *Sign*, OPC-UA *SignAndEncrypt*. They also consider scenarios when the protocols are used over an insecure network and over resilient communication channels. The analysis was performed in an automated fashion by The Tamarin Prover tool and it revealed that some security properties do not hold in for some protocol variants. Specifically, they demonstrate that man in the middle (MITM) attacks such as message reordering and replay attacks are possible depending on the variant of the protocol and the assumptions on the underlying communication channels. A new discovery in this paper is that - if we assume a resilient channel (messages are always delivered) then we can guarantee formally that some properties are valid for a protocol, and those same properties are not valid if a resilient channel is not assumed. For example, for Modbus *MAC* variant flow delivery property is satisfied if a resilient channel is assumed and otherwise that property is not satisfied.

Dutertre [7] develops two formal models of the Modbus protocol. They use the PVS Specification and Verification System to build an *executable* model of the Modbus protocol as specified by the Modbus standard. The executable model can now be used as a reference when testing a specific implementation of the protocol. Their second model is based on the Symbolic Analysis Laboratory (SAL) toolkit. The authors use SAL to build a state machine model of requirements for the purpose of automated test case generation. Hence, this analysis is aimed towards verifying *functional* rather than security requirements of the Modbus protocol. Consequently, there is no attacker model and no properties of the protocol are verified.

Nardone et al. [19] use model checking techniques to generate counterexamples with respect to the security property being checked. Again, the protocol analyzed in this work is the Modbus protocol. The formal model of the protocol is based on Dynamic State Machines (DSTM). A model checker (SPIN) is used which can analyze the Promela notation, which means that the formal analysis is automated. The analysis formally demonstrates the existence of the MITM attack on the protocol—a known weakness of Modbus given the lack of security mechanisms.

Edmonds et al. [8] use formal methodology for modelling of multilayer SCADA protocols. They aim to capture subtle interactions between higher layer protocols such as Modbus and the lower layer protocols such as TCP/IP or the serial transport. The formal model is based on the use of High Level Protocol Specification Language (HLPSL)—a language that is used to describe security properties. HLPSL is based on the temporal logic of actions (TLA). This is a logic which is used for specifying and reasoning about concurrent systems. The AVISPA tool uses the HLPSL language. In summary, the security goals they have in mind for SCADA are translated into HLPSL, which can later be used by the AVISPA tool. The MITM attack is analyzed for Modbus Serial and the Modbus TCP protocol. The goal of the analysis was to find attacks and see how we can mitigate them. The authors demonstrate that MITM attacks can be mitigated with asymmetric encryption. The encryption ensures the confidentiality of the message, but for integrity we need to use (for example) a hash function.

Siddavatam et al. [27] explore testing and validation of Modbus/TCP protocol for secure SCADA communication and they use formal methods for that purpose. The formal model they used is based on colored Petri nets (CPNs) and tool used is CPN Tools. The attacker is modeled as a MITM attacker. Specifically, they analyzed and modeled formally deception attack which is a combination of MITM and Denial of Service (DoS) attack and they did that using the tool CPN Tools. Security properties are not analyzed as such, but it is concluded that since deception attack on Modbus/TCP is possible that integrity (of the data) can be compromised. Also, Modbus/TCP server does not authenticate client, so we can conclude authentication can be compromised.

4.3   The OPC-UA Protocol

Puys et al. [23] give a detailed analysis of OPC-UA. Specifically, they analyze the *OpenSecureChannel* and *CreateSession* sub-protocols. For both sub-protocols, they consider several variants depending on the cryptographic primitives used. These variants (or *security modes*) are *None, Sign, SignEnc.* In *None* mode, no encryption is used. In *Sign* mode, messages are only signed, but not encrypted. In *SignEnc* mode messages are both signed and encrypted. Additionally, they propose a new signing mechanism for the *OpenSecureChannel* sub-protocol that provides additional security guarantees. The formal method is based on using applied π-calculus. The formal analysis is automated and the authors use the ProVerif tool that can verify security properties of a protocol such as secrecy and authentication. Again, the attacker model is the Dolev-Yao model. The analysis uncovers new attacks on secrecy and authentication for both relevant modes: *Sign* and *SignEnc* (mode *None* trivially doesn't provide either secrecy or authentication). The authors also propose mitigations for discovered attacks—authentication is fixed by explicitly adding the server's public key to the messages. The problem with authentication was that identity of the server was not mentioned in the message itself, so an intruder could perform a MITM attack where it acts as the server from the client's point of view and like the client from the server's point of view. With the proposed modifications, the attacks are shown to be impossible. The secrecy problem is addressed by using the key wrapping mechanism. The proposed change is that the servers nonce is encrypt using the server's private key, and that the client nonce is encrypted analogously. For the *CreateSession* sub-protocol, the authors show by automated analysis that the use of the key wrapping mechanism in the security mode *Sign* is crucial—attacks are possible otherwise.

In Sect. 4.2 we already discussed paper by **Dreier et al.** [6] in which authors analyze Modbus and OPC-UA protocol.

4.4 The DNP3 Protocol

Amoah et al. [2] perform a formal analysis of the DNP3 protocol. DNP3 is a protocol used for communication between master stations and outstations in power grids. They distinguish between aggressive challenge response and non-aggressive challenge response (NACR) as modes of DNP3 protocol. The mathematical basis for the analysis is a formal modelling methodology called coloured Petri nets (CPNs). The formal analysis is automated using the CPN state space analysis tool. Using CPNs, they were able to translate the high-level description of DNP3-NACR into a formal model. They identified a DoS attack on the DNP3 protocol. The existence of this attack was demonstrated through a formal analysis with a CPN model and it was found that the model contains unsafe states that an attacker can exploit. It has been demonstrated that the security properties - integrity and availability can be compromised in the DNP3-NACR mode of the DNP3 protocol.

Amoah et al. [1] also perform a security analysis of the DNP3 protocol. The protocol has a security mechanism called *Secure Authentication*, which we refer to as DNP3-SA. The authors create a formal model of DNP3-SA using colored Petri nets (CPNs). The formal analysis is automated by using the CPN state space analysis tool. They were able to formally define the authentication property using computation tree logic (CTL) which is supported by the CPN tool. The attacker is modeled as a MITM attacker. The authors use the CPN based model to uncover a successful attack on DNP3-SA protocol, and propose hash-based message authentication code (HMAC) improvements to the protocol to prevent this type of attack. The attack is based on the fact that the attacker can convert a valid HMAC tag (from an old message) from one mode of operation to another, which allows him to execute commands on the outstation in the power grid. Two solutions are proposed to prevent such an attack: one is to use HMAC for challenge data in the protocol, and the other involves removing randomization in requests in the protocol.

Cremers et al. [5] have DNP3 protocol as analysis target. The formal model is based on using multiset rewriting rules. The attacker model is Dolev-Yao attacker. Analyzed properties are properties that authors named AUTH1, AUTH2, CONF. AUTH1 and AUTH2 are different authentication properties. If AUTH1 property is satisfied spoofing attack is prevented, and if AUTH2 property is satisfied replay attack is prevented. CONF is the confidentiality of keys property which means all the relevant keys (used in protocol DNP3) are confidential with respect to eavesdroppers. Their analysis in The Tamarin prover has formally verified all three of these properties. This means that they showed that attack which was claimed in paper [1] is not possible in standard as defined. Hence, Cremers et al. [5] demonstrate that the attack described in Amoah et al. [1] is due to the lack of details in the formal model is not possible in implementations of the standard.

Rysavy et al. [26] analyze the DNP3 protocol. They use the industry standard XACML (eXtensible Access Control Markup Language)—a declarative language for access control policies that can be used for an authorization framework. Thus, the goal of this paper is to improve authorization (specifically for DNP3) using role-based access control (RBAC) and it also uses formal methods as a help to achieve that goal. RBAC is an access control mechanism that is policy neutral and defined around roles and privileges. In the authorization framework proposed in this paper, each critical command is surrounded with security assertions before the command is sent to the outstation node (from the master node). Examples of such assertions exist in the SecPAL language. The SecPAL language is a logic-based declarative language for security policies. Therefore, formal analysis is automated because the SecPAL language is used for assertions.

4.5   The IEC 61850 Protocol

Kunz et al. [15] created a formal methodology to model the requirements of IEC 61850 real-time communication standard. The formal model is based on logic—they use timed computation tree logic (TCTL) and the UPPAAL model checker tool. Hence, the formal analysis is automated. The aim of the work is not to analyze the attacks on the IEC 61850 protocol, but to present a systematic and formal methodology that can help us to correctly implement the communication requirements of the protocols. Therefore, the focus is the functional rather than the security requirements of the standard. The Generic Object Oriented Substation Event (GOOSE) mappings are part of the IEC 61850 protocol. The

authors demonstrate that timed automata models can be used to model protocol components by creating a timed automata model for GOOSE Publisher and
GOOSE Subscriber.

4.6   The PROFINET Protocol

Jin et al. [13] modeled PROFINET actions formally. They did this using the
timing π-calculus, a variant of the π-calculus presented in the paper. The claimed
benefit of the timing π-calculus is that it can deal with time elapsing and
timer events. This paper does not attempt to verify the security properties of
PROFINET. Instead, the authors hope that the formal framework established in
the paper can facilitate the reliability and consistency analysis of PROFINET.
The properties of actions are also not analyzed (this is considered to be a future
task).

4.7   Fieldbus Protocols

Cheminod et al. [4] perform an analysis of networked fieldbus systems, considering both: low-level communication protocols and architecture of the system.
In the target protocols secrecy, authentication, and integrity properties protection are achieved by symmetric key cryptography and the key system they use
is hierarchical. When it comes to protocol analysis, formal models of protocol
agents are specified in this paper using the mathematical formalism of applied
π-calculus. The models are, then, analyzed in an automated fashion using the
ProVerif tool. With ProVerif they prove that (in this protocol model): injective
agreement is not true, non-injective agreement is true, and that some specifically
defined properties ("the response must be considered valid only if it is a response
to the original request" and non-injective version of that property) are not true.
The attacker model is the (standard) Dolev-Yao. With manual reasoning, the
authors discover DoS attacks on the protocol. In the rest of the paper, Prolog is
used to model the entire system infrastructure, and the focus in this part is to
analyze the vulnerabilities of a particular network configuration. They created a
model of the system, a model of the user security protocol, a case study of a small
scenario that included one user and three elements in the field network. Also,
they created an analysis of the property violations of the previously mentioned
system, and a consideration of the scalability of the analysis. Importantly for
this paper, it deals with formal verification of both: protocols and architecture.

Mariño et al. [17] analyze the WorldFIP protocol. The formal model is
based on the use of abstract data types (ADTs) and the Language Of Temporary Ordering Specification (LOTOS). LOTOS is a formal specification language
based on process algebra. Again, the focus of the work is the analysis of functional properties rather than security properties. The authors do not verify any
protocol properties in this paper, but rather consider the model to be a foundation for future work.

Poschmann et al. [22], build a formal model of the PROFIBUS protocol.
The formal model is based on the use of Estelle—a formal description technique

based on the extended finite state machine (EFSM) model. The validation of the model is done using the tool VEDA, which supports only a subset of Estelle (which is taken into account when they created the model in Estelle). The goal of the analysis is to show how formal methods can improve the protocol development cycle.

Mariño et al. [16] formally specify the PROFIBUS protocol. They build two models based on the use of LOTOS and the Specification Description Language (SDL), respectively. LOTOS is based on process algebra and SDL is based on the use of Extended Finite State Machines (EFSMs). The goal of the analysis is not verification of protocol properties, but a comparison of models in two different formalisms—the authors discuss the advantages and drawbacks of both approaches.

4.8   Formal Methods in Attack Detection

Mercaldo et al. [18] use formal methods to analyze SCADA logs for traces of undesirable events and conditions. The goal of the paper is to find attacks, not to prove the correctness of the system. The idea of the paper is to take SCADA system logs, do a discretization of the data and build a formal model (for that day). Then, for each day and each corresponding formal model, they check whether the relevant formula describing the attack is satisfied. To put it more clearly, the attacker model is a formula that checks whether an overflow or underflow attack is in progress. These attacks refer to the water level in relevant tanks in the water distribution system. For model checking, they used UPPAAL and created relevant formulas with timed temporal logic (TCTL) - they extended computation tree logic (CTL)/branching time logic with time constraints on modalities.

4.9   Formal Methods Applied on SCADA Architecture

Fadi and Dhaussy [9] build a secure architecture for a SCADA system based on an insecure architecture and they do that by using formal tools and combining *security patterns*. The formal model is based on having security patterns expressed in logic. There are 3 main elements for formal verification of security pattern composition and 3 corresponding tools: 1. Language to model the SCADA system - Format for the Embedded Distributed Component Architectures (FIACRE), 2. Formal representation of properties that would ensure the fulfillment of system requirements - Context Description Language (CDL), 3. Model explorer to explore the model and verify the properties - for this purpose Observer-Based Prover (OBP) explorer is used. Possible attacks on SCADA are mentioned in the paper, but the attacker model does not exist. However, the paper deals with verification of properties (safety, authenticity, availability, integrity) and we find out for which component certain property holds.

Rahman et al. [24] use formal methods to analyze SCADA topology models. The assumption is that IEDs or RTUs can fail due to cyber attacks, and we wish to analyze what happens to the overall system behavior in those circumstances.

Specifically, the paper introduces *k-Resilient Observability*—observability even when k field devices are not available. A related property is *k-Resilient Secured Observability*—assured observability is guaranteed even when k field devices are unavailable due to technical failures or cyber-attacks. The authors use satisfiability modulo theory (SMT) formulas to describe these properties and the Z3 SMT solver to verify them. The goal of the SMT solver is to find satisfactory associations of variable values with standard constraints. Using the approach the authors can find scenarios such as "If RTU12 fails, there is no way to observe the system".

5   Discussion

Here we summarize the findings regarding the application of formal methods in modeling and analysis of protocols used in SCADA systems.

There is a solid body of research dedicated to security analysis and the application of formal methods to the Modbus protocol (it has been studied in papers: [6–8,19,27]). The papers, in general, use a model which is based on the Dolev-Yao model and demonstrate similar attacks on the Modbus protocol. None of the results are surprising since Modbus does not come with any security mechanisms or guarantees by default.

The OPC-UA protocol has received some attention in [6,23] and has been analyzed with sufficient depth in these papers (especially in the context of Dolev-Yao attackers). However, since OPC-UA is a complex protocol (its specification has over 1000 pages and is still updated), and there should still be more room for analyzing it with formal methods.

Popular Ethernet-based protocols include DNP3, IEC 61850, PROFINET, and EtherCAT. We find that there are works that combine formal methods and DNP3 (through the papers [1,2,5] and [26]), which implies that formal methods are quite sufficiently used for this purpose. Amoah et al. [2] prove that it is possible to make DoS attack on the NACR mode of a DNP3 protocol. Amoah et al. [1] deal with secure authentication and MITM attackers. Cremers et al. [5] comes to conclusion that attack claimed by Amoah et al. [1] is not possible. Rysavy et al. [26] deal with the authorization framework and do not analyze attacks on DNP3. There is some work that connects IEC 61850 and formal methods, like [15], but it does not analyze attacks on IEC 61850, so for protocol IEC 61850 we can say that formal methods are underused. PROFINET was analyzed in Jin et al. [13], but only actions were modeled. PROFINET was not analyzed in the security context and, hence, this is one of the critical components that could benefit from security analysis by formal methods. We did not find any relevant work connecting the protocol EtherCAT and formal methods.

There are some other SCADA (fieldbus) protocols (which we mentioned in Sect. 1) such as BITBUS, PROFIBUS, WorldFIP. We have not found any papers that attempt to apply formal methods to BITBUS. For PROFIBUS there are papers [22] and [16], which are good examples of the use of formal methods, but do not analyze attacks on PROFIBUS. WorldFIP (in the sense of formal methods) is (only) analyzed in [17] and attacks on WorldFIP were not analyzed there, which means that there is an opportunity for further formal analysis of WorldFIP. The paper [4] gives a direction on how formal methods can be applied to fieldbus systems, and it seems that it just opens a whole new area of research. Note that the papers analyzing PROFIBUS [16,22] and WorldFIP [17] are not so recent, which means that research in this area is not so active anymore.

We distinguish between SCADA legacy protocols and newer standard protocols. Examples of legacy SCADA protocols are: Modbus RTU, PROFIBUS, RP-570, and Conitel. All of these protocols (except Modbus) are SCADA vendor specific, but are widely adopted and used. Modbus has been sufficiently analyzed using formal methods. PROFIBUS was analyzed, but not as extensively as Modbus, and these analyzes did not examine possible attacks on protocol communications. RP-570 and Conitel were not analyzed using formal methods. Examples of standard SCADA protocols are: IEC 60870, PROFINET, IEC 61850, and DNP3. The IEC 60870 protocol was not analyzed with formal methods. PROFINET protocol was analyzed only in paper [13] written by Jin et al., so there exists an opportunity to explore in more depth with formal methods. The IEC 61850 protocol was analyzed with formal methods, but not sufficiently. Note that there is a technical specification IEC 62351 [12] which deals with IEC 61850 protocol security, but we found no research efforts that try to formally verify proposals of that specification. The protocol DNP3 was analyzed with formal methods and the formal methods were used in above average amount (in comparison to other protocols from this paper) for this purpose.

There is no published research that addresses the verification of the properties of some SCADA protocols, and some SCADA protocols are not sufficiently analyzed with formal methods. We see the use of formal methods to analyze such protocols (including legacy protocols and newer standard protocols) as a promising area of research. That work could also be challenging since some of those protocols are not so easy to model formally (because they are complex or composed of multiple subprotocols). Also, one could argue that it could be challenging to formally analyze some protocol for the first time, since there is no reference work, and it could be hard to gather initial resources for such a purpose. This is the case for the protocols: RP-570, Conitel, IEC 60870, and EtherCAT. Also, it could be hard to analyze formally protocols: PROFINET, WorldFIP, PROFIBUS, and IEC 61850 in the context of their security for the first time (they were analyzed formally, but not in the context of security properties).

Outside of protocol analysis, specifically, SCADA systems and their components have only been analyzed using formal methods in three published papers dealing with attack detection or system architecture analysis at a higher level of abstraction. Besides these three examples, no research papers attempt to formally verify properties of a large *system* comprised of many different components—they all focus on the properties of specific components. It is well known that security properties do not compose by default and, hence, the system can have critical flaws even if all individual components are correct. We feel that this could be a great opportunity for the application of formal methods.

6   Related Work

To the best of our knowledge, this is the first survey work that deals with the use of formal methods in SCADA systems. In [11], Gnesi and Margaria give examples of usage of formal methods in the more general area of industrial critical systems. The examples are in a number of critical industrial examples such as avionics, aerospace, and railway signaling. It deals with all aspects of formal methods—specification, implementation and verification, but there is a clear emphasis on model checking. Our survey is narrower in scope compared to that work and most of the papers we discussed are not included in the mentioned survey.

We must note that formal methods are extensively used for modeling and verification of PLC hardware and software, but, as mentioned earlier, we have chosen not to include this area of research in this survey. See [29] for a review dealing with the use of formal methods in the context of PLC code, more specifically it deals with attacks on industrial control logic and defenses based on formal verification.

There are several surveys related to the general area of securing SCADA systems. Ghosh and Sampalli [10] provide a classification of possible attacks on SCADA based on network protocol layers and security requirements. Attacks can be categorized as: attacks on hardware, attacks on software, and attack on a network connection. Nazir et al. [20] provide an overview of tools and techniques that we need to discover SCADA system vulnerabilities. These tools and techniques include: scanning tools, penetration testing, machine learning, network intrusion detection systems, intrusion prevention systems, honey pots, security information and event management, ethical or white hat hacking, forensic science. Johnson [14] gives survey of SCADA security challenges and potential attack vectors. He explores SCADA system security weaknesses and current security techniques. He also proposes new tools and methods to address SCADA system security. Pliatsios et al. [21] provides an overview of the general SCADA architecture. It also gives us a description of SCADA communication protocols. They present a large number of SCADA communication protocols and arrive at the classification of SCADA protocols that we also use in this review. They also address the known security properties and issues in these protocols.

7   Conclusion

The aim of this paper is to give an overview of the application of formal methods in relation to SCADA systems. We conduct an extensive literature search and classify discovered research results in three categories—protocol analysis, attack detection, and architecture analysis. We find that the area of protocol analysis is most fruitful. However, there are both legacy protocols and new standards that have received none or very little attention from the research community. There are very few research results outside protocol analysis. We identify only three examples that deal with attempting to detect attacks and analyzing a SCADA system architecture or topology at a higher level of abstraction.

References

1. Amoah, R., Camtepe, S., Foo, E.: Formal modelling and analysis of DNP3 secure authentication. J. Netw. Comput. Appl. **59**, 345–360 (2016). https://www.sciencedirect.com/science/article/pii/S1084804515001228

2. Amoah, R., Suriadi, S., Camtepe, S., Foo, E.: Security analysis of the non-aggressive challenge response of the DNP3 protocol using a CPN model. In: 2014 IEEE International Conference on Communications (ICC), pp. 827–833 (2014)

3. Byres, E.: The air gap: Scada's enduring security myth. Commun. ACM **56**(8), 29–31 (2013). https://doi.org/10.1145/2492007.2492018

4. Cheminod, M., Pironti, A., Sisto, R.: Formal vulnerability analysis of a security system for remote fieldbus access. IEEE Trans. Industr. Inf. **7**(1), 30–40 (2011)

5. Cremers, C., Dehnel-Wild, M., Milner, K.: Secure authentication in the grid: a formal analysis of DNP3: SAv5. In: Foley, S.N., Gollmann, D., Snekkenes, E. (eds.) ESORICS 2017. LNCS, vol. 10492, pp. 389–407. Springer, Cham (2017). https://doi.org/10.1007/978-3-319-66402-6_23

6. Dreier, J., Puys, M., Potet, M.L., Lafourcade, P., Roch, J.L.: Formally and practically verifying flow integrity properties in industrial systems. Comput. Secur. **86**, 453–470 (2018). https://hal.archives-ouvertes.fr/hal-01959766

7. Dutertre, B.: Formal modeling and analysis of the modbus protocol. In: Goetz, E., Shenoi, S. (eds.) ICCIP 2007. IIFIP, vol. 253, pp. 189–204. Springer, Boston, MA (2008). https://doi.org/10.1007/978-0-387-75462-8_14

8. Edmonds, J., Papa, M., Shenoi, S.: Security analysis of multilayer SCADA protocols. In: Goetz, E., Shenoi, S. (eds.) ICCIP 2007. IIFIP, vol. 253, pp. 205–221. Springer, Boston, MA (2008). https://doi.org/10.1007/978-0-387-75462-8_15

9. Fadi, O., Dhaussy, P.: Formal verification of security pattern composition: application to SCADA. Comput. Inform. **38**(5), 1149–1180 (2019). https://hal.archives-ouvertes.fr/hal-02514951

10. Ghosh, S., Sampalli, S.: A survey of security in scada networks: current issues and future challenges. IEEE Access **7**, 135812–135831 (2019)

11. Gnesi, S., Margaria, T.: Formal Methods for Industrial Critical Systems: A Survey of Applications. IEEE, USA (2013)

12. Power Systems Management and Associated Information Exchange-Data and Communications Security Part 1: Communication Network and System Security-Introduction to Security Issues, Standard, International Electrotechnical Commission, Geneva, Switzerland (2007)

13. Jin, W., Gao, X., Li, J.: Modeling profinet actions with timing pi-calculus. In: Proceedings of the First International Conference on Information Sciences, Machinery, Materials and Energy, pp. 397–402. Atlantis Press (2015). https://doi.org/10.2991/icismme-15.2015.79

14. Johnson, R.E.: Survey of scada security challenges and potential attack vectors. In: 2010 International Conference for Internet Technology and Secured Transactions, pp. 1–5 (2010)

15. Kunz, G., Machado, J., Perondi, E., Vyatkin, V.: A formal methodology for accomplishing IEC 61850 real-time communication requirements. IEEE Trans. Industr. Electron. **64**(8), 6582–6590 (2017)

16. Mariño, P., Nogueira, J., Sigüenza, C., Poza, F., Domiünguez, M.: The profibus formal specification: a comparison between two FDTS. Comput. Netw. **37**(3), 345–362 (2001). https://www.sciencedirect.com/science/article/pii/S1389128601002079

17. Mariño, P., Poza, F., Dominguez, M., Nogueira, J.: Design of worldfip's industrial communication systems based on formal methods. In: ISIE 1999. Proceedings of the IEEE International Symposium on Industrial Electronics (Cat. No. 99TH8465), vol. 3, pp. 1427–1432 (1999)
18. Mercaldo, F., Martinelli, F., Santone, A.: Real-time scada attack detection by means of formal methods. In: 2019 IEEE 28th International Conference on Enabling Technologies: Infrastructure for Collaborative Enterprises (WETICE), pp. 231–236 (2019)
19. Nardone, R., Rodríguez, R.J., Marrone, S.: Formal security assessment of modbus protocol. In: 2016 11th International Conference for Internet Technology and Secured Transactions (ICITST), pp. 142–147 (2016)
20. Nazir, S., Patel, S., Patel, D.: Assessing and augmenting scada cyber security: a survey of techniques. Comput. Secur. **70**, 436–454 (2017). https://www.sciencedirect.com/science/article/pii/S0167404817301293
21. Pliatsios, D., Sarigiannidis, P., Lagkas, T., Sarigiannidis, A.G.: A survey on scada systems: secure protocols, incidents, threats and tactics. IEEE Commun. Surv. Tutor. **22**(3), 1942–1976 (2020)
22. Poschmann, A., Hahniche, J., Deicke, P., Neumann, P.: Experience with formal methods implementing the PROFIBUS FMS and DP protocol for industrial applications. In: Proceedings 1997 IEEE International Workshop on Factory Communication Systems, WFCS 1997, pp. 277–286 (1997)
23. Puys, M., Potet, M.-L., Lafourcade, P.: Formal analysis of security properties on the OPC-UA SCADA protocol. In: Skavhaug, A., Guiochet, J., Bitsch, F. (eds.) SAFECOMP 2016. LNCS, vol. 9922, pp. 67–75. Springer, Cham (2016). https://doi.org/10.1007/978-3-319-45477-1_6
24. Rahman, M.A., Jakaria, A.H.M., Al-Shaer, E.: Formal analysis for dependable supervisory control and data acquisition in smart grids. In: 2016 46th Annual IEEE/IFIP International Conference on Dependable Systems and Networks (DSN), pp. 263–274 (2016)
25. Rebane, J.C.: The Stuxnet Computer Worm and Industrial Control System Security. Nova Science Publishers Inc., USA (2011)
26. Rysavy, O., Rab, J., Halfar, P., Sveda, M.: A formal authorization framework for networked scada systems. In: 2012 IEEE 19th International Conference and Workshops on Engineering of Computer-Based Systems, pp. 298–302 (2012)
27. Siddavatam, I., Parekh, S., Shah, T., Kazi, F.: Testing and validation of modbus/TCP protocol for secure SCADA communication in CPS using formal methods. Scalable Comput. Pract. Exp. **18**, 313–330 (2017)
28. Stouffer, K.A., Falco, J.A., Scarfone, K.A.: SP 800-82. Guide to industrial control systems (ICS) security: supervisory control and data acquisition (SCADA) systems, distributed control systems (DCS), and other control system configurations such as programmable logic controllers (PLC). Technical report, National Institute of Standards and Technology, Gaithersburg, MD, USA (2011)
29. Sun, R., Mera, A., Lu, L., Choffnes, D.: SoK: attacks on industrial control logic and formal verification-based defenses. In: 2021 IEEE European Symposium on Security and Privacy (EuroS&P). IEEE Computer Society (2021)

The Cost of Incidents in Essential Services—Data from Swedish NIS Reporting

Ulrik Franke[1,2]([envelope]) [ORCID], Johan Turell[3], and Ivar Johansson[3]

[1] RISE Research Institutes of Sweden, SE-164 29 Kista, Sweden
`ulrik.franke@ri.se`
[2] KTH Royal Institute of Technology, SE-100 44 Stockholm, Sweden
[3] MSB Swedish Civil Contingencies Agency, SE-651 81 Karlstad, Sweden
`{johan.turell,ivar.johansson}@msb.se`

Abstract. The NIS Directive aims to increase the overall level of cyber security in the EU and establishes a mandatory reporting regime for operators of essential services and digital service providers. While this reporting has attracted much attention, both in society at large and in the scientific community, the non-public nature of reports has led to a lack of empirically based research. This paper uses the unique set of all the mandatory NIS reports in Sweden in 2020 to shed light on incident costs. The costs reported exhibit large variability and skewed distributions, where a single or a few higher values push the average upwards. Numerical values are in the range of tens to hundreds of kSEK per incident. The most common incident causes are malfunctions and mistakes, whereas attacks are rare. No operators funded their incident costs using loans or insurance. Even though the reporting is mandated by law, operator cost estimates are incomplete and sometimes difficult to interpret, calling for additional assistance and training of operators to make the data more useful.

Keywords: NIS Directive · Reporting · Incident cost · Cyber security economics · Cyber insurance

1 Introduction

Modern society depends on essential digital services for a wide range of activities. Whether we buy goods and services using payment systems, commute to work, need healthcare, or just want to relax with a glass of drinking water in the light of a lamp, these activities require dependable networks and information systems. With poor cyber security, society is vulnerable, both to accidents and to attacks.

The NIS Directive is a piece of EU-wide legislation aiming to increase the overall level of cyber security in the union [23]. More precisely, the directive focuses on disruptions (most often, but not exclusively, loss of service) at operators of essential services and digital service providers. Under the directive, all

This research was funded by the Swedish Civil Contingencies Agency (MSB).

D. Percia David et al. (Eds.): CRITIS 2021, LNCS 13139, pp. 116–129, 2021.
https://doi.org/10.1007/978-3-030-93200-8_7

member states had to establish national CSIRT units, cooperating with each other, to whom operators of essential services [23, Art. 14] and digital service providers [23, Art. 16] must report any incidents. Failure to file reports will result in penalties. As opposed to the GDPR, which is a single regulation applying equally throughout the union, the NIS Directive is a directive, which is implemented differently in each country.

The mandatory reporting scheme of the NIS Directive has attracted much attention, both in society at large and in the scientific community. An important reason for this is that although it is generally agreed that the (prospective) costs of the kind of service interruptions covered by the NIS Directive are considerable (see e.g. [20]), there is also a lack of reliable and credible statistics on such incident costs (see [1,9] for discussions of some of the methodological challenges).

This lack of data is unfortunate, because *asymmetric information* has been identified as an important explanation for cyber security failures in the literature on the economics of cyber security [2, p. 612]. In the absence of data about incidents and their costs it is difficult to make decisions improving security, such as switching from less secure to more secure vendors in procurement, investing in the best security measures, removing single points of failure, or passing effective laws.

It is against this background that this paper uses previously non-public data from Swedish NIS reporting to shed light on incident costs, thus making a unique and timely contribution. More precisely, the following research questions are investigated:

RQ1: How much do incidents in Swedish essential services, as defined in the NIS Directive, cost?

RQ2: How do the operators of Swedish essential services, as defined in the NIS Directive, fund their incident costs?

RQ3: What are the causes behind incidents in Swedish essential services, as defined in the NIS Directive?

RQ4: How can reporting be improved to raise quality?

The remainder of this paper is structured as follows: The next section describes some related work on the NIS Directive. Section 3 explains the method used before Sect. 4 describes the results. The costs found and other observations made are discussed in Sect. 5, before Sect. 6 concludes the paper.

2 Related Work

The NIS Directive is attracting scholarly attention. The literature includes both overarching considerations on cyber security regulation and governance [5,22,26] and country-specific case studies (e.g., on the NIS implementation in Greece [21] and the UK [27], the interplay between the NIS Directive and the Danish national strategy for cyber and information security [18], and the impact of the NIS Directive on cyber insurance in Norway [3]). However, to the best of our knowledge, there are no published empirical studies based on incident reporting.

This is not surprising, given the fact that the incident reports are, typically, not available for research.

As for disruption and outage incident costs more generally, a recent systematization of knowledge on quantification of cyber risk finds surprisingly few studies on outage costs [28]. One source of cost data is operational risk databases in banking (e.g. [4,15,16,25]), but these databases include incidents caused by many kinds of operational risks besides outages. One study dedicated to costs of service outages reports data from the transportation, food, and government sectors in Sweden [13], but these are a non-random sample of case-studies.

To conclude, it is evident that the NIS Directive is interesting to study, but that the relatively short time-span since its implementation and the non-public nature of the mandatory reporting has led to a lack of empirically based research. Thus, the present paper makes a unique contribution to the literature.

3   Method

In general, NIS reports are not publicly available, neither to researchers nor to the public at large. Even though Sweden has a long tradition of government transparency[1] including the world's oldest freedom of information law [19], this is the case in Sweden as well: access to NIS reports is restricted to prevent crime.

However, the fact that the NIS reports, *in full*, are classified as secret does not mean that *parts* of them, or *aggregated information* from them, cannot be made publicly available. This constitutes the basis for the method used to investigate the research questions listed in Sect. 1.

The second and third authors, employed at the Swedish Civil Contingencies Agency (MSB), have access to the NIS incident reports in their professional capacities. The aggregated data used in this paper was produced in a three-step process: (i) The second and third authors compiled data from NIS reports. (ii) The second and third authors assessed whether the resulting aggregate (descriptive statistics as shown in Sect. 4) could be released or had to remain secret. (iii) The aggregate data thus vetted was made available to the first author as well. (It should be noted, however, that under the Swedish freedom of information law, *anyone* could ask for the data, have it vetted, and released to the extent possible.)

The data set thus released and analyzed consists of all the Swedish NIS reports from 2020 (the first full year with available reports); a total of 88 mandatory reports, following incidents at service providers covered by the NIS Directive.

Out of the 88 reports, 34 contained cost information pertaining to (i) the cost of the incident, (ii) the cost of the resulting disruption, or (iii) the cost of preventive actions taken. The vast majority of these 34 reports emanate either

---

[1] Public access to official documents is enshrined in the Freedom of the Press Act: "To encourage the free exchange of opinion and availability of comprehensive information, every Swedish citizen shall be entitled to have free access to official documents." (Chapter 2, Article 1).

from (i) health and medical services, or from (ii) drinking water supply services. (This is also the case for the full set of 88 reports; the cost subset is representative in this respect.) This also means that most respondents are from the public sector, which manages much of health and medical services and almost all drinking water plants in Sweden.

Three additional caveats concerning the method should be mentioned: First, even though the reports all come from mandatory reporting, this does not mean that all reports are complete in the sense that every piece of information asked for has been provided. The 34 reports considered all include *at least one* cost estimate, but many of them exhibit considerable 'holes' in the data supplied, as will be evident in the next section. The most common cost estimate supplied was the *lowest possible cost* of incident, disruption, and preventive actions taken, respectively.

Second, incidents under the NIS Directive are first and foremost *availability* incidents (i.e. disruptions of one sort or another), not confidentiality or integrity incidents. In practice, the reported incidents have integrity consequences every now and then, whereas confidentiality aspects are almost completely absent.

Third, the confidential nature of the data and the division of labor between the authors means that even though the results reported in Sect. 4 are intended to be self-contained and interesting in their own right, part of the discussion in Sect. 5 is also informed by additional trends or details from the reports that cannot be disclosed.

4   Results

As part of the mandatory reporting, operators were asked to give a number of cost estimates. These results are reported in the following.

Giving estimates, operators could mark their numbers as being certain or not certain. In the following diagrams, visualizations that are based only on numbers that are *certain* are circumscribed with a solid line (□), visualizations that are based only on numbers that are *not certain* are not circumscribed (▨), and visualizations that are based *both* on numbers that are certain and on numbers that are not certain are circumscribed with a dotted line (▨). Thus, in set notation, □ ∩ ▨ = ∅ and □ ∪ ▨ = ▨.

4.1   Costs Entailed by Incidents

Operators' estimates for the three kinds of cost are shown in Fig. 1. As in the NIS reporting forms, the numbers are given in SEK. (10 SEK is roughly one euro or one US dollar.)

A few immediate observations can be made from Fig. 1. First, medians are typically much smaller than averages (arithmetic means), typical for a skewed distribution, where most cost estimates are relatively small, but a single or a few higher values push the average upwards. This is a well-known phenomenon in cyber incident surveys [1,9].

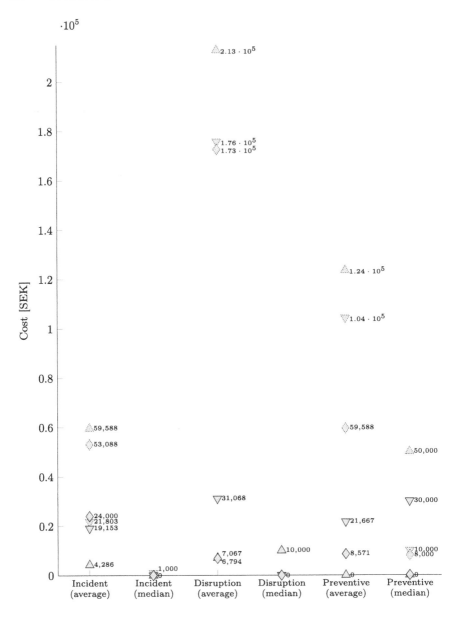

Fig. 1. Operators' estimated costs. Upwards triangles indicate highest possible cost; downwards triangles indicate lowest possible cost; diamonds indicate probable cost. Markers that are circumscribed with a solid line (□) indicate that the estimates being aggregated were marked as certain by the operators; markers that are circumscribed with a dotted line (▦) indicate that the estimates being aggregated include *both* certain and not certain estimates.

Second, the values of highest possible, lowest possible, and most probable costs often seem counterintuitive. For example, for the certain incident costs, both the average and the median of the highest possible cost is smaller than the average and the median, respectively, of the lowest possible and most probable cost. The reason is incomplete data. The estimates being aggregated to form a highest possible cost do not come from (exactly) the same set of operators as the estimates being aggregated to form a lowest possible or most probable costs. In fact, while the operators are supposed to fill out all three (highest possible, lowest possible, and most probable costs), many have only filled out one of them.

Third, the average values based on both certain and uncertain estimates are higher than average values based on certain estimates only. This is particularly evident for the disruption costs, though the tendency is clear also for the incident and preventive costs.

Fourth, the numerical values of costs—while exhibiting large variability—are in the range of tens to hundreds of kSEK per incident. If the annual number of incident at any one operator is reasonably small, this cost range is roughly in line with previous results about annual outage costs in Swedish enterprises [13, Table 1].

4.2 Funding of Costs Entailed by Incidents

Operators were also asked how costs were funded. Responses on funding of the cost of *incidents* are given in Fig. 2. Responding to this question, operators could allocate the cost over six funding sources indicated (including an 'other' option), subject to the constraint that the total cost summed to 100%.

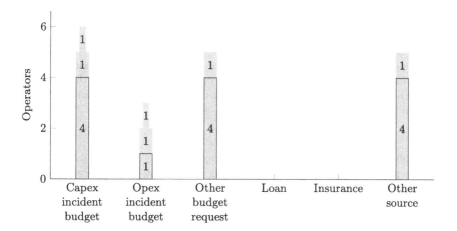

Fig. 2. Operators' funding of *incident* costs. Budget allocations that are circumscribed with a solid line (□) were marked as certain by the operators; budget allocations that are not circumscribed ( ) were marked as not certain. 100% allocations have full width; 50% allocations have half width. $N = 33$

For example, the leftmost bar in Fig. 2 shows the number of operators who took the incident cost from a capex incident budget.[2] There were four operators who certainly took 100% of costs from there, one operator who probably, but not certainly, took 100% of costs from there, and one operator who probably, but not certainly, took 50% of costs from there.

As seen in the figure, no operator used loans or insurance to cover costs. Furthermore, it should be noted that out of 34 operators, only 18 (5.5 capex + 2.5 opex + 5 other budget + 0 loans + 0 insurance + 5 other) have allocated their total cost over the six funding sources given in the question. Only 1 operator did not answer (thus $N = 33$). The remaining 15 *did* answer, but *did not* allocate 100% of costs over the funding sources. This may appear strange, but can be explained by the observation that many of those who incurred a zero cost (understandably) did not bother to distribute this zero cost over different sources.

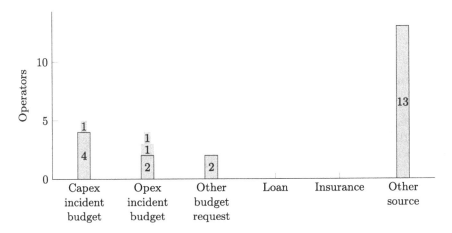

Fig. 3. Operators' funding of *disruption* costs. Budget allocations that are circumscribed with a solid line (□) were marked as certain by the operators; budget allocations that are not circumscribed (▨) were marked as not certain. 100% allocations have full width; 50% allocations have half width. $N = 30$

Responses on funding of the cost of *disruptions* are given in Fig. 3. As before, operators allocated the cost over six funding sources, assigning percentages, and indicating certainty.

Again, no operator used loans or insurance to cover costs.

---

[2] Capital expenses (capex) are one-time costs incurred when buying an asset. Operating expenses (opex) are recurring costs that are incurred for as long as an asset is used.

4.3 Causes of Incidents

The NIS reporting forms also include an assessment of the cause of the incident reported, as shown in Fig. 4.

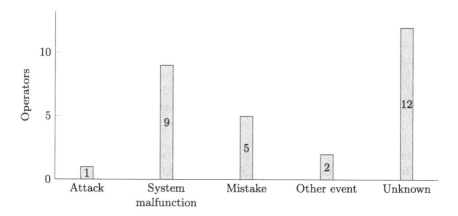

Fig. 4. Causes of incidents. 5 operators did not answer according to the instructions in the form, either by not giving any cause (1) or by giving combinations of two causes (4), resulting in $N = 29$.

Perhaps the most striking feature of Fig. 4 is the large number of unknown causes: between a third and half of reporting operators do not know the causes of the incidents they report. It is also noteworthy that while attacks receive much attention in the media and elsewhere, attacks are not identified as being behind a significant portion of NIS incidents. In this respect, the NIS reports differ considerably from a recent investigation of Swedish manufacturing firms, where 7% of the 649 respondents reported that they had experienced interruptions from intentional attacks in the past 12 months, and 7% reported interruptions from unintentional incidents in the same period [14, Fig. 3].

5 Discussion

In the following, the results from the previous section are discussed from a few different perspectives.

5.1 Characteristics of Operators Incurring High Cost

As mentioned in Sect. 3, the most common cost estimate supplied by the operators was the *lowest possible cost* of incident, disruption, and preventive actions taken, respectively. (Thus, in Fig. 1, the markers representing the most data points are the downwards triangles.)

Considering the *top five* lowest possible *incident* costs, these operators are *not* from any particular sector (such as healthcare). However, what they do have in common is that they have all identified vulnerabilities (in a broad sense, not necessarily particular CVEs) which, had they been addressed before the incident, could have prevented it or at least limited its consequences. In all of these cases, the operators report that they have identified significant preventive measures that they are about to implement, are in the process of implementing, or have already implemented.

Considering the *top five* lowest possible *disruption* costs, four out of five operators are from health and medical services. Again, most of these operators identified vulnerabilities which, had they been addressed before the incident, could have prevented it or at least limited its consequences. When (the lowest possible) preventive costs have been assessed, they are in the 50,000–250,0000 and 400,000–450,000 SEK ranges.

Considering the *top five* lowest possible *preventive* costs, these operators are *not* from any particular sector. All but one of these operators identified vulnerabilities which, had they been addressed before the incident, could have prevented it or at least limited its consequences.

A general observation is that the operators incurring the highest costs for the incident and the disruption, respectively, are operators whose information technology infrastructure does not conform to best practices. For example, the equipment used is old and basic security such as network segmentation, backups, traffic monitoring, etc. are not in place. These technical solutions give the impression that the IT environment for the essential service was set up about a decade ago but has not been maintained since. Thus, once incidents occur, the costs of maintenance and upgrades, previously postponed, suddenly catch up with the operator.

Most of these operators report incidents in *their own infrastructures.* This can be contrasted with the fact that out of the 88 NIS reports received in 2020, 68% (60 reports) concerned incidents occurring in the infrastructure of an external vendor used by the operator. Thus, there is a tendency that while most incidents occur in the infrastructure of external vendors, the *most costly* incidents occur in the infrastructure of the operators themselves. A possible explanation is that, in the two sectors mostly represented in the reporting, incidents in the operators' own infrastructure often entail tangible extra costs for additional manual labor, e.g., using more physicians and nurses to administer appropriate treatment and care despite medical records being unavailable, or sending personnel to inspect water purification on site.

5.2   Cyber Insurance

As seen in Figs. 2 and 3, no operator used insurance to cover costs. From one perspective, this is a bit surprising: Sweden has a relatively high cyber insurance adoption rate. In absolute numbers, it is known that at least some 110,000 Swedish enterprises have cyber insurance [12, p. 24], and a recent survey of cyber security practices of Swedish manufacturing firms indicated that some 30% of companies has cyber insurance [14, Fig. 6].

However, high cyber insurance coverage in manufacturing, or private sector at-large, does not necessarily mean that the, mostly public, operators of essential infrastructure are among the insured. One explanation could thus be that public sector enterprises do not typically have cyber insurance policies. Another explanation could be that the interruptions fall short of the waiting periods, typically some 24, 36, 48, or 72 h, during which no indemnity is paid [10]. A third explanation could be that even though an enterprise has a cyber insurance policy, not all business interruptions are necessarily covered [11]. (The converse is also true; it might be that an insurance policy *not* designed to cover cyber incidents might still unintentionally do so; a phenomenon of great concern to insurers, known as *silent cyber coverage* [29].)

5.3   Validity and Reliability

The validity of the findings is good: All the reports are based on actual incidents entailing actual costs for the operators, and the cost estimates had to be produced within four weeks after the incidents, meaning that circumstances were fresh in the memory of respondents. From this perspective, validity is better than, for instance, if cost estimates had been based on annual summaries collected ex post (as in, e.g., [13]), or based on fictitious scenario estimates (as in, e.g., [20]).

Reliability, on the other hand, is threatened by the difficulty to correctly assess costs. It is very probable that different operators have used different ways to assess costs. This is also reflected in the incompleteness and relative difficulty of interpretation of some of the results reported in Sect. 4 (such as the large number of 'other' responses illustrated in Figs. 2 and 3). Clearly, figures must be interpreted with some caution in light of this.

In contrast, reliability is strengthened by the fact that ideally, there should be no *sampling bias* at all: indeed, this is a not a sample but a *census* of incidents, since all operators are required by law to report. This is a considerable strength, that in theory goes a long way towards rectifying the well-known problems of bias and incomplete data in cyber incident surveys [1,9]. Nevertheless, the results reported in Sect. 4 also illustrate some practical limits to this argument: even though operators are forced to report incidents, it is more difficult to force quality in the reporting.

One possible source of confusion could be that the costs of the incident (such as an outage in the operational technology controlling a water plant) and those of the resulting disruption (such as water needing to be cleaned) might be difficult to distinguish. However, the nature of operations of most respondents in the data set is such that this should not be a problem.

Here, it is also worth reminding that operators could mark estimates as being certain or not certain. Cost estimates marked as certain are often reported when the same error happens over and over again, meaning that the cost is well-known. Examples include recurring incidents in sensor systems run by the operator or in external services run by service providers.

5.4   Generalization to Other Countries

Another aspect of validity and reliability concerns the possibility to general-ize results to other countries. On a general level, the NIS Directive is in place throughout the EU, and the Swedish experiences should be relevant to infer tentative conclusions about other countries as well. On a more particular level, however, it is important to bear in mind that the NIS Directive has been imple-mented in different ways in different countries. Thus, before generalizing to any particular country, it is useful to consult the comparison of implementations compiled by the European Commission [8]. In particular, it is important to bear in mind the distinction between incident cost (as depicted in Fig. 2) and disrup-tion cost (as depicted in Fig. 3) which may not be upheld in reporting from other countries.

Again, it should also be stressed that the NIS definition of incidents may be different from how the 'cyber incident' term is used in other contexts. The NIS definition is broader in that it includes incidents regardless of cause, whereas in other contexts it is common to (implicitly or explicitly) focus on attacks only. At the same time, the NIS definition is narrower in its focus on availability only (as opposed to integrity and confidentiality). As a consequence, any comparisons of costs reported in Sect. 4 with costs reported in other studies should be made with care, and assumptions about comparability should be made as explicit as possible.

5.5   Usefulness of Data from NIS Reporting

In conjunction with the discussion of validity and reliability, it is also appro-priate to discuss the wider usefulness of the cost data that can be obtained from mandatory NIS reporting. As seen in Sect. 4, results are incomplete and sometimes difficult to interpret. This can be contrasted to some of the prior expectations.

For example, since lack of actuarial data on cyber incidents is a known imped-iment to the development cyber insurance [4,6,24, pp. 94–95], it has been pro-posed that the mandatory incident reporting regimes of the GDPR and the NIS Directive could create relevant cyber data for insurers [7,17]. While this idea may indeed have some potential, the data in Sect. 4 clearly illustrates that such data is no panacea.

Even if hurdles relating to security and competition were solved, just making NIS reporting, as-is, available to insurers would not by itself solve the problem of lack of data for cyber insurance. Making the most of the reporting requires additional quality assurance mechanisms. In particular, it seems that in order to make cost estimates from NIS reports more useful, operators might need additional assistance and training in producing such estimates in a reliable and uniform way. With increasing experience of how reporting works in practice, it may also become possible to revise the forms to facilitate better reports, though this should be made with some caution as it makes future longitudinal studies more difficult.

6   Conclusions

Based on data consisting of all the mandatory NIS reports in Sweden in 2020, this paper has investigated economic aspects of the incidents reported. The costs reported exhibit large variability and skewed distributions, where a single or a few higher values push the average upwards. The numerical values are in the range of tens to hundreds of kSEK per incident. Operators were also asked about incident causes. It is noteworthy that the most common incident causes are malfunctions and mistakes, whereas attacks are rare. For many incidents, however, the cause is unknown.

A general observation is that the operators incurring the highest costs have technology infrastructures that do not conform to best practices (e.g., using old equipment lacking basic security).

No operators funded their incident costs using loans or insurance. This is somewhat surprising, since Sweden has a relatively high cyber insurance adoption rate. However, it may be that the cyber insurance coverage is lower among the operators of essential infrastructure.

Apart from the concrete results on incidents costs, the data set also reveals that even though the reporting is mandated by law, operator cost estimates are incomplete and sometimes difficult to interpret. This points towards future work: Operators probably need additional assistance and training in producing cost estimates in a reliable and uniform way, so that the data becomes more useful.

References

1. Anderson, R., et al.: Measuring the cost of cybercrime. In: Böhme, R. (ed.) The Economics of Information Security and Privacy, pp. 265–300. Springer, Heidelberg (2013). https://doi.org/10.1007/978-3-642-39498-0_12
2. Anderson, R., Moore, T.: The economics of information security. Science **314**(5799), 610–613 (2006). https://doi.org/10.1126/science.1130992
3. Bahşi, H., Franke, U., Langfeldt Friberg, E.: The cyber-insurance market in Norway. Inf. Comput. Secur. **28**(1), 54–670 (2019). https://doi.org/10.1108/ICS-01-2019-0012
4. Biener, C., Eling, M., Wirfs, J.H.: Insurability of cyber risk: an empirical analysis. Geneva Pap. Risk Insur. Issues Pract. **40**(1), 131–158 (2015). https://doi.org/10.1057/gpp.2014.19
5. van Eeten, M.: Patching security governance: an empirical view of emergent governance mechanisms for cybersecurity. Digit. Policy Regul. Gov. **19**(6), 429–448 (2017). https://doi.org/10.1108/DPRG-05-2017-0029
6. EIOPA European Insurance and Occupational Pensions Authority: Cyber risk for insurers—challenges and opportunities (2019). https://doi.org/10.2854/305969
7. EIOPA European Insurance and Occupational Pensions Authority: EIOPA strategy on cyber underwriting (2020). https://doi.org/10.2854/793935

8. Report from the Commission to the European Parliament and the Council assessing the consistency of the approaches taken by Member States in the identification of operators of essential services in accordance with Article 23(1) of Directive 2016/1148/EU on security of network and information systems (2019). https://eur-lex.europa.eu/legal-content/EN/TXT/?uri=CELEX:52019DC0546. COM(2019) 546

9. Florêncio, D., Herley, C.: Sex, lies and cyber-crime surveys. In: Schneier, B. (ed.) Economics of Information Security and Privacy III, pp. 35–53. Springer, New York (2013). https://doi.org/10.1007/978-1-4614-1981-5_3

10. Franke, U.: The cyber insurance market in Sweden. Comput. Secur. **68**, 130–144 (2017). https://doi.org/10.1016/j.cose.2017.04.010

11. Franke, U.: Cyber insurance against electronic payment service outages. In: Katsikas, S.K., Alcaraz, C. (eds.) STM 2018. LNCS, vol. 11091, pp. 73–84. Springer, Cham (2018). https://doi.org/10.1007/978-3-030-01141-3_5

12. Franke, U.: Cybersäkerhet för en uppkopplad ekonomi [Cyber security for the online economy]. Entreprenörskapsforum (2020). http://urn.kb.se/resolve?urn=urn:nbn:se:ri:diva-48918

13. Franke, U.: IT service outage cost: case study and implications for cyber insurance. Geneva Pap. Risk Insur. Issues Pract. **45**(4), 760–784 (2020). https://doi.org/10.1057/s41288-020-00177-4

14. Franke, U., Wernberg, J.: A survey of cyber security in the Swedish manufacturing industry. In: 2020 International Conference on Cyber Situational Awareness, Data Analytics And Assessment (Cyber SA). IEEE, June 2020. https://doi.org/10.1109/CyberSA49311.2020.9139673

15. Goldstein, J., Chernobai, A., Benaroch, M.: An event study analysis of the economic impact of IT operational risk and its subcategories. J. Assoc. Inf. Syst. **12**(9), 1 (2011)

16. Ibrahimovic, S., Franke, U.: A probabilistic approach to IT risk management in the Basel regulatory framework: a case study. J. Financ. Regul. Compliance **25**, 176–195 (2016). https://doi.org/10.1108/JFRC-06-2016-0050

17. Insurance Europe: Key messages on EIOPA's cyber underwriting strategy (2020). https://www.insuranceeurope.eu/publications/1718/key-messages-on-eiopa-s-cyber-underwriting-strategy/. Published June 15, 2020

18. Jensen, M.S.: Sector responsibility or sector task? New cyber strategy occasion for rethinking the Danish Sector Responsibility Principle. Scand. J. Mil. Stud. **1**(1), 1–18 (2018)

19. Kassen, M.: Understanding transparency of government from a Nordic perspective: open government and open data movement as a multidimensional collaborative phenomenon in Sweden. J. Glob. Inf. Technol. Manage. **20**(4), 236–275 (2017). https://doi.org/10.1080/1097198X.2017.1388696

20. Cloud Down: Impacts on the US economy. Technical report, Lloyd's of London (2018). https://www.lloyds.com/news-and-risk-insight/risk-reports/library/technology/cloud-down

21. Maglaras, L., Drivas, G., Noou, K., Rallis, S.: NIS directive: the case of Greece. EAI Endorsed Trans. Secur. Saf. **4**(14), 154769–154775 (2018)

22. Markopoulou, D., Papakonstantinou, V., de Hert, P.: The new EU cybersecurity framework: the NIS Directive, ENISA's role and the General Data Protection Regulation. Comput. Law Secur. Rev. **35**(6), 105336 (2019). https://doi.org/10.1016/j.clsr.2019.06.007

23. Directive (EU) 2016/1148 of the European Parliament and of the Council of 6 July 2016 concerning measures for a high common level of security of network and information systems across the Union. Off. J. Eur. Union L **194**, 1–30 (2016). http://data.europa.eu/eli/dir/2016/1148/oj

24. OECD: Enhancing the Role of Insurance in Cyber Risk Management (2017). https://doi.org/10.1787/9789264282148-en

25. Rachev, S.T., Chernobai, A., Menn, C.: Empirical examination of operational loss distributions. In: Perspectives on Operations Research, pp. 379–401. Springer, Cham (2006). https://doi.org/10.1007/978-3-8350-9064-4_21

26. Timmers, P.: The European Union's cybersecurity industrial policy. J. Cyber Policy **3**(3), 363–384 (2018). https://doi.org/10.1080/23738871.2018.1562560

27. Wallis, T., Johnson, C.: Implementing the NIS Directive, driving cybersecurity improvements for Essential Services. In: 2020 International Conference on Cyber Situational Awareness, Data Analytics and Assessment (CyberSA), pp. 1–10 (2020). https://doi.org/10.1109/CyberSA49311.2020.9139641

28. Woods, D.W., Böhme, R.: SoK: quantifying cyber risk. In: 2021 IEEE Symposium on Security and Privacy (SP), Los Alamitos, CA, USA, pp. 211–228. IEEE Computer Society, May 2021. https://doi.org/10.1109/SP40001.2021.00053

29. Wrede, D., Stegen, T., von der Schulenburg, J.M.G.: Affirmative and silent cyber coverage in traditional insurance policies: qualitative content analysis of selected insurance products from the German insurance market. Geneva Pap. Risk Insur. Issues Pract. **45**(4), 657–689 (2020). https://doi.org/10.1057/s41288-020-00183-6

Human Factor, Security Awareness and Crisis Management for C(I)IP and Critical Services

Impact Analysis of PLC Performance When Applying Cyber Security Solutions Using Active Information Gathering

Yeop Chang$^{(\boxtimes)}$ ⓘ, Taeyeon Kim ⓘ, and Woonyon Kim ⓘ

The Affiliated Institute of ETRI, Jeonmin-dong, Yuseong-gu, Daejeon, Korea
{ranivris,tykim,wnkim}@nsr.re.kr

Abstract. ICS Controllers such as the Programmable Logic Controllers (PLC), Intelligent Electronic Devices (IED), and Remote Terminal Units (RTU) are the primary components responsible for the operation of a control system. Dedicated security solutions are required to protect these devices from advanced cyber threats. Security solutions which operate passively are gradually being introduced into the Industrial Control Systems (ICS). However, most utilities are opposed to the installation of security solutions which actively generate requests to the devices owing to maintenance contracts or concerns about device malfunctions. To overcome these issues, it is necessary to quantitatively analyze the impact of the security solutions on the control device. This study proposes a detailed analysis procedure considering the characteristics of the controllers. The experimental results are shared using a CompactLogix PLC to help stakeholders aiming to strengthen the security of their control devices.

Keywords: ICS security · PLC · Performance impact analysis

1 Introduction

Industrial Control Systems (ICS) are used to safely and efficiently control the infrastructure facilities, such as power plants, water treatment, and automated factories. They consist of various component and operate organically to achieve their objectives. ICS controllers such as Programmable Logic Controller (PLC), Intelligent Electronic Devices (IED) and Remote Terminal Units (RTU) are key components for sensor monitoring and physical equipment control. It is natural that cyber campaigns targeting control systems such as Stuxnet [9], BlackEnergy [11], and TRITON [14] target these control devices to cause physical damage. *ICS controllers* operating in the control systems must be protected from these cyber threats.

Over the past decade, various types of security solutions have been proposed and gradually applied to protect the control systems from materialized security threats. Initially, traffic analysis solutions mainly used passive monitoring or

© Springer Nature Switzerland AG 2021
D. Percia David et al. (Eds.): CRITIS 2021, LNCS 13139, pp. 133–151, 2021.
https://doi.org/10.1007/978-3-030-93200-8_8

Bump-in-the-Wire (BitW) method to avoid affecting the operation of the control system. Several studies have been conducted to detect abnormal behavior using network traffic and control system information such as control logic, tag value, and I/O signal. Recently, some security scanners have been developed to check the security status of control devices for efficient management or to detect cyber attacks. In addition, asset management solutions have been developed for detecting illegal changes.

Consequently, various efforts have been made to strengthen the security of the control system, but the introduction of security solutions to the ICS controllers have been avoided. Most operators are strongly opposed to a tool that actively collects information, when compared to a solution which operates passively. The main reasons are worry about the malfunction of the control device which may be caused by the active tools and the maintenance contract problem related to the change in the control system configuration.

To overcome these issues, this study proposes an experimental procedure to determine the impact of security products in advance. As a case study, an impact analysis experiment is conducted using CompactLogix, a medium-sized PLC by Rockwell Automation (RA), one of the major vendors in the world. Firstly, the metrics observed in the control device are identified for impact analysis. This includes the values for the current operational status that can be obtained through the Engineering WorkStation (EWS) or from the externally observable traffic and signals. The candidate services used by the security solutions when acquiring the information are then determined, and load generating programs are developed for each service. After generating a load on the control device for each defined scenario, an impact analysis is performed by analyzing metrics or the values calculated from metrics, Finally, we proposed candidate Key Performance Indicators (KPI) that can be used to analyze the impact of other control devices.

The main contributions of this study are as follows: Firstly, unlike previous studies, the KPIs were selected by considering the unique characteristics of the PLC when introducing a security solution. Secondly, we actually performed an impact analysis on the control device, and suggested a performance impact analysis procedure applicable to other devices.

This paper is organized as follows: Sect. 2 briefly introduces the characteristics of the PLC, which is analyzed in this study among the various other control devices. Section 3 summarizes the status of the research being conducted on the security technology targeting the PLCs and the research related to the performance impact of the control devices. Section 4 comprehensively describes the experimental system structure and the procedures. The results of the performance impact experiment are then analyzed in detail in Sect. 5. This study proposes the KPIs for the PLC and along with a practical experimental procedure that other researchers can use. Lastly, the conclusion presents the possible applications of the research conducted in this study.

2   Background

The PLC is a general-purpose ICS controller used in various industrial areas. It is composed of several modules such as the CPU, I/O, and communication modules according to the diverse demand of the field. The PLC continuously reads signals from the sensor, and controls the field devices based on the current state during a control loop. Low priority tasks are performed between each loop, which include non-RT communications for management or data exchange. PLC also provides IT services such as FTP, Web, and SNMP for convenience. The characteristics of PLC to satisfy real-time performance are as follows.

Task-Based. A task is a time unit to execute an application program. The PLC must have one or more tasks to achieve its objectives. In general, the PLC supports continuous, periodic, and event tasks. A Continuous Task (CT) always runs in the background when a task with a higher priority does not work. A Periodic Task (PT) is used to define a task with high real-time (RT) requirements which operates in specific period (e.g., 20 ms) The event task processes a predetermined action for a predefined event (e.g., first-scan, error, digital signal change, etc.). Figure 1 shows how tasks are scheduled by type. If the PLC needs to perform low priority operation (e.g., non-RT communication), the CT temporarily stops its operation and performs the corresponding communication. The PLCs developed by Siemens or RA allow engineers to control the ratio of the resources used for non-RT communication.

Real-Time (RT) Communication. The PLC generally provides two types of communication methods: RT and non-RT communication. Non-RT communication is usually performed over TCP and is used when communication reliability is required, such as in engineering work. RT communication is used to synchronize I/O information, and is generally performed in a connectionless manner, such as in UDP or link layer control. If more accurate RT communication is required, it is transmitted only in a designated time-slot with the support of network devices. In the past, a time-deterministic fieldbus was used for RT communication. Ethernet-based RT communication such as EtherCAT, EtherNet/IP, and PROFINET RT/IRT have been used recently.

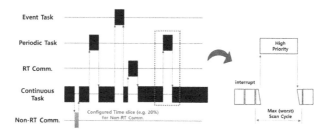

Fig. 1. PLC's task scheduling

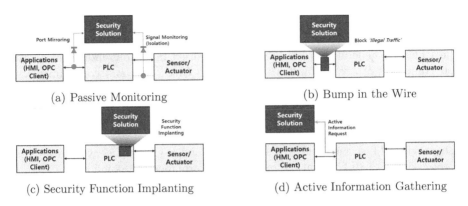

Fig. 2. PLC security solution types according to system structure

Request Per Interval (RPI). To perform RT communication in the control network, the nodes must negotiate a communication cycle beforehand. The setting time of the RT communication period between the devices is Request Per Interval (RPI). Certain devices that can set the RPI in the backplane communication between the CPU module and the I/O modules. For the RA PLC, the CPU module reads signals from the input module or sends commands to the output module at regular intervals. Engineers can change the interval by setting the RPI.

3   Related Works

3.1   Security Solutions for PLC

Various security solutions have been proposed and developed to protect control devices. We divided them into four categories based on the operation method of the security solutions: *passive monitoring, BitW, security function implanting,* and *active information gathering* as shown in Fig. 2. The passive monitoring method detects inappropriate commands to the controller or abnormal behavior through network mirroring and signal line picking [8]. The BitW method generally blocks inappropriate commands [12], or downloads firmware/control-logic to controllers after inspection [5]. Most of the security solutions specialized for controllers operate in the passive monitoring method or the BitW method which does not directly affect the controllers.

Adding new security functions by modifying the control logic or firmware is classified as security function implanting [6,15]. This method is experimental, and the function will only be available after the manufacturer completes verification and implements the function in the controller. Active information gathering involves checking the security status or detecting the evidence of attacks by acquiring information from the controllers. Various security solutions such as PLC tag information collectors [4], log collectors [7,18], and vulnerability scanners [1,17] fall into this category.

As the importance of security management of digital assets in ICSs increases, the introduction of security solutions using active information gathering will be used more and more. The impact of introducing the security solutions in this category must be checked to verify whether it affects the main functions of the controllers. Unfortunately, there has been no systematic research conducted on the analysis of the impact of such security solutions on control devices.

3.2 Impact Analysis of Security Solutions in ICS

The introduction of security solutions to enable the ICSs to respond to cybersecurity threats has been discussed continuously. The National Institute of Standards and Technology (NIST) presents the security profile required for critical infrastructures to satisfy Cyber Security Framework (CSF) [2]. In the process of applying various security solutions to the control system to satisfy the security profile, their impact on the control system was also analyzed. The productivity of the ICS, the CPU utilization of the digital assets, etc. are determined as the KPIs required to analyze the impact. And the NIST published the reports [16, 19] which present the method of designing experiments and measuring the KPIs. KPIs were analyzed by introducing various security solutions applicable to the ICSs one by one. This study is expected to be used as a case study on the analysis of the impact of introducing security solutions to the ICSs. However, the proposed KPIs are insufficient when considering the controllers. This study did not consider how the PLC tasks work, and how the controllers communicate for RT control. Additionally, it is difficult to obtain the metrics suggested in this report from various devices because most PLCs do not disclose their internal status to the testers.

Other studies analyzed the impact of the security solutions on the controllers by providing an excessive communication load. IEC 62443-4-2 [3] stated that communication robustness is crucial for the safe operation of control devices, and that the functions of essential services must not be degraded even under a specific load. Niedermaier et al. [13] analyzed the changes in the scan cycle by giving extreme loads into the controller from the perspective of the attackers. [3], and [13] are focused on the performance degradation of controllers only when receiving excessive communication traffic. Therefore, it is necessary to analyze the impact of a legitimate and appropriate level of communication load.

4 Experimental Design

4.1 Metrics for PLC Performance

The performance indicators of the control device must first be identified to analyze the impact of the security solution. Although the controller does not provide all the information to the testers, it does provide certain necessary information such as the max/last scan cycle time of the tasks and the memory usage of a control logic. This study performs an impact analysis based on the CT and PT

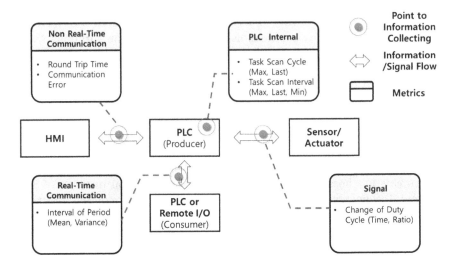

Fig. 3. Metrics for PLC performance

scan cycle-related metrics provided by the PLC. Additionally, the network traffic or control signals are analyzed from outside the PLC to determine its impact. These include delays and jitters in the network traffic and signal output. Figure 3 shows key metrics that can be checked inside and outside the PLC.

4.2   Experimental System Architecture

An experimental system is designed and built to analyze the impact of the information acquisition attempts on the CT/PT and the RT/non-RT communication of a PLC, as shown in Fig. 4. For the RT communication test, a producer/consumer communication setting is configured using two CompactLogix PLCs. The CPU model of CompactLogix is L24ER-QB1B, and the firmware version is 24.011 (released in 2014). For non-RT communication, we implemented a Human-Machine Interface (HMI) application using InGear[1] library. Additionally, *load Generators* has been developed which play the role of virtual security solutions that acquire information from the PLC. Network traffic was collected using the mirroring function of the network switch and analyzed with Wireshark[2] for the RT and non-RT network traffic analysis, and the digital signal out is collected using Saleae Logic Analyzer[3].

The control logic operating in PLC and RT communication settings are as follows: the producer PLC operates two tasks, one CT and one PT. The CT changes one digital output point ($0{\rightarrow}1$, $1{\rightarrow}0$) after approximately 30,000 scans. The PT runs every 50 ms, and one digital output point is changed every 43rd

---

[1] InGear, https://ingeardrivers.com/products/net-products/netlogix/.

[2] Wireshark, https://www.wireshark.org.

[3] Saleae Logic Analyzer, https://www.saleae.com/home2/.

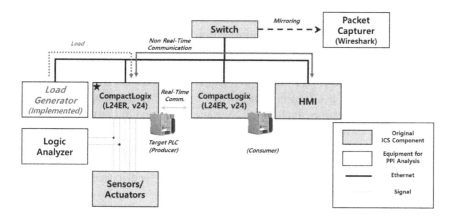

Fig. 4. Experimental system structure for impact analysis of PLC performance

Table 1. RA CompactLogix's network scanning result

Port	Service	Description
TCP 80	HTTP	A PLC provides its status and network diagnostics through web pages
TCP 44818	EtherNet/IP	An encapsulation protocol of CIP. SCADA applications monitor or control by using CIP
UDP 68	DHCP/Bootp	A DHCP/Bootp server assigns an IP address to PLC configured using DHCP/Bootp
UDP 131	SNMP	A PLC provides SNMP service
UDP 319,320	Unknown	PTP (Probably)
UDP 2222	EtherNet/IP	Used for IO (real-time) communication, unconnected CIP message
UDP 44818	EtherNet/IP	EtherNet/IP port. But we cannot find any traffic during experiment

scan cycle. The number of scan cycles for CT and PT was adjusted so that the two output points had similar output patterns. Therefore, there is the number of CT and PT executions does not hold any significance. The producer PLC and the consumer PLC each set the RPI at 20 ms and set the topic to send and receive 20 bytes of data.

4.3   Communication Load Scenarios

In addition to the dedicated services of vendors, the PLCs also provide information acquisition services such as SNMP and HTTP. This study aims to determine the impact of loads occurring through each service. Therefore, the type of information service provided by the target PLC must be verified. Table 1 shows the results of a port scan of CompactLogix using Nmap[4]. The following three services are determined to be suitable for information acquisition: SNMP, HTTP, and Common Industrial Protocol (CIP) over EtherNet/IP. ICMP is added because some security solutions use ICMP to check whether the network node is active.

SNMP, ICMP, and HTTP are representative services that are widely used in the IT field. The CIP is a standard protocol for automation managed by ODVA[5], and various manufacturers, including RA, have developed industrial devices that support the CIP. The controllers produced by other manufacturers also typically provide IT protocols and a dedicated protocol for device management. The security solutions that actively acquire information from controllers must use one or more of these protocols. Therefore, the impact of the security solutions must be analyzed when using each service.

Communication load scenarios are designed in this study, as shown in Table 2 to analyze the impact of the four services that can obtain information from CompactLogix. Each load scenario is divided into two levels: normal (a) and excessive (b). At normal levels, the load generator sends an information retrieval request containing several packets per second, which may be faster than the usual security solutions targeting the control devices. If there is no or insignificant impact even for this level of load, a security solution using the service can be introduced. At excessive levels, the load generator creates multiple (usually 10) processes that perform the same operation as in (a). If the impact is insignificant even in this case, a security solution can be potentially installed for controllers that generate normal loads. The threshold value can be considered when introducing a service if a significant change was confirmed.

Additionally, a *6.RA_Auth* load scenario is proposed. This authentication process has been developed by the RA to protect the PLC from arbitrary attackers, using the value in vendor specific class and service range defined in CIP. CompactLogix performs RSA encryption in this authentication process analyzed in [10]. The security solutions for control devices can also use the information which is obtained only after legitimate authentication process. Since the controller is expected to use a large amount of computational resources, it is selected as an additional load scenario if it directly uses the CPU to perform the RSA calculations without dedicated hardware assistance.

4.4 Load Generator Implementation

Load generators have been implemented for the five types of communication loads selected in the previous section. They are usually implemented using Python scripts. Load scenarios 2 and 3 are implemented by calling ping, or snmpwalk provided the OS. To generate web traffic for load scenario 4, a urllib module of Python 3 is used. In the *5.CIP* scenario, several instances of *Studio 5000*, which uses CIP to manage a CompactLogix, are executed. Lastly, a load generator is developed for a *6.RA_Auth* scenario by analyzing the authentication

---

[4] Nmap, https://nmap.org.
[5] Open DeviceNet Vendor Association, https://www.odva.org/.

Table 2. Load test scenarios for target PLC (RA CompactLogix)

Load test scenario	Level
1. Base	Base scenario. No overload
2. ICMP	– a. 1 ping per second
	– b. 100 threads of '2a'
3. SNMP	– a. 1 request per second
	– b. 10 threads of '3a'
4. Web	– a. 5 web pages request per second
	– b. 10 threads of '4a'
5. CIP	– a. 1 CIP application gathering information from PLC
	– b. 10 CIP applications of '5a'
6. RA_Auth	– a. 1 authentication trial per second
	– b. 10 threads of '6a'

```
def snmp_overload_test():
    while True:
        command = ['snmpwalk -v2c -c public 192.168.0.100']
        subprocess.check_output(command, shell=True)
        time.sleep(1.0)

thread_numbers = 10
for each_thread in range(thread_numbers):
    t = threading.Thread(target=snmp_overload_test)
    t.start()
```

Fig. 5. Python scripts of SNMP load generator (Simplified)

process identified in [10]. The simplified codes of the SNMP load generator are shown in Fig. 5.

5 Experiment, Results, and Discussion

In order to analyze the impact of active cyber security solutions, experiments were conducted on basic load scenarios and excessive load scenarios. Since we wanted measurement results at the millisecond or microsecond level, we conducted the experiment with real devices rather than simulated devices. Simultaneous experiments on the physical devices were not possible with the number of controllers we have, thus experimentation time should be adjusted to an appropriate level.

The experiment was conducted for 4 h for each scenario, which is considered to be reasonable for the following reasons:

– There is no significant statistical difference observed in the mean, standard deviation, and distribution in the data collected for more than 1 day when compared to the data collected for 4 h.
– There is no statistical difference over time in the data collected over 4 h.
– After each load test, the metrics measured in the experiment are restored to the same level as the base scenario. Therefore, it is concluded that there is no permanent effect.

Performance impact analysis experiments were performed for ten types of load scenarios, and except for two cases, the experiments are performed normally. During testing *4b.Web_10* load scenario, the PLC stopped and entered fault mode. The *6b.RA_Auth_10* load scenario cannot be tested because CompactLogix does not support multiple authentication simultaneously. Two exceptional cases are discussed in Sect. 5.2.

5.1   Impact Analysis Results

The results of the performance impact experiment for CompactLogix are shown is Table 3 and the results of analysis of the metrics for each load scenario are described in greater detail.

Maximum of Continuous Task Scan Cycle/Interval. Figure 6 shows the results of the max CT scan cycle and interval for each load scenario. The max scan cycle of the CT ranges from 1.8 ms to 1.97 ms, and the max interval is also approximately equal. The maximum scan cycle is much longer than the average scan cycle of 50 μs. If high-priority interrupts occurred during one scan cycle, CT should be delayed, as described in Fig. 1. Even when comparing scenarios (*5a.CIP_1* and *5b.CIP_10*), in which the load occurred more than 10 times, the difference in the delay due to the interrupts was insignificant.

Maximum of Periodic Task Scan Cycle/Interval. Figure 7 shows the results of the max PT scan cycle and max PT scan interval for each load scenario. The maximum interval of the PT was measured from 50.268 ms to 50.292 ms. It was difficult to check the PT cycle change according to the load scenario. The maximum PT scan cycle was only measured for *3b.SNMP_100* was slightly longer than the others.

It was difficult to determine the influence of the load due to the analysis of the max scan cycle time and max interval of the CT and PT. Furthermore, if the control logic has branches, the maximum scan cycle may not be able to clearly demonstrate the effect of the load. Therefore, the average scan cycle is analyzed rather than the maximum scan cycle. It is difficult to identify all scan cycle times externally, so the average time is calculated by summing the execution times of each scan cycle. When the PLC changes the digital output value after a certain number of logic executions, the digital output signal was measured using a logic analyzer.

Sum of Continuous Task Scan Cycle. The change period of the digital output signal was measured, as shown in Fig. 8. The analysis results are similar to the combined multiple Gaussian distributions rather than a single Gaussian distribution because the output value is passed to the output module based on the RPI setting (20 ms). In both cases (2a.ICMP_1 and 2b.ICMP_100), no changes were found on CT. *3. SNMP, 4. Web and 5. CIP* scenarios, all increase the

Table 3. Impact analysis results of RA CompactLogix's performance

		1.Base	2a.ICMP_1	2b.ICMP_100	3a.SNMP_1	3b.SNMP_10	4a.Web	5a.CIP_1	5b.CIP_10	6a.RA_Auth
CT Scan Cycle Max		1.88800	1.9300 (102.225%)	1.8060 (95.657%)	1.8990 (100.583%)	1.9760 (104.661%)	1.8680 (98.941%)	1.9040 (100.847%)	1.8350 (97.193%)	1.8210 (96.451%)
CT Scan Interval Max		1.83300	1.9040 (103.873%)	1.8760 (102.346%)	1.9150 (104.474%)	1.9050 (103.928%)	1.8700 (102.019%)	1.9450 (106.110%)	1.8480 (100.818%)	1.7900 (97.654%)
PT Scan cycle max		0.37000	0.3520 (95.135%)	0.3520 (95.135%)	0.3660 (98.919%)	0.4600 (124.324%)	0.3440 (92.973%)	0.3620 (97.838%)	0.3370 (91.081%)	0.3610 (97.568%)
PT Scan Interval Max		50.27300	50.2680 (99.990%)	50.2690 (99.992%)	50.2850 (100.024%)	50.2800 (100.014%)	50.2610 (99.976%)	50.2920 (100.038%)	50.2560 (99.966%)	50.2840 (100.022%)
Sum of CT Scan Cycle (sec)	mean	2.11471	2.1163 (100.075%)	2.1147 (99.998%)	2.1283 (100.641%)	2.1529 (101.804%)	2.1409 (101.240%)	2.1188 (100.195%)	2.1583 (102.061%)	2.2226 (105.103%)
	std	0.00328	0.0038 (115.695%)	0.0053 (162.415%)	0.0069 (209.784%)	0.0057 (172.915%)	0.0069 (210.052%)	0.0046 (140.077%)	0.0046 (140.647%)	0.0149 (453.609%)
Sum of PT Scan Cycle (sec)	mean	2.10000	2.1000 (100.000%)	2.1000 (100.000%)	2.1000 (100.000%)	2.1000 (100.000%)	2.1000 (100.000%)	2.1000 (100.000%)	2.1000 (100.000%)	2.1000 (100.000%)
	std	0.00465	0.0046 (98.226%)	0.0046 (99.136%)	0.0042 (90.062%)	0.0042 (89.603%)	0.0043 (92.018%)	0.0044 (94.525%)	0.0037 (80.311%)	0.0034 (73.814%)
Real-Time UDP Traffic Periodicity(ms)	mean	20.00020	20.0002 (100.000%)	20.0002 (100.000%)	20.0002 (100.000%)	20.0002 (100.000%)	20.0002 (100.000%)	20.0002 (100.000%)	20.0002 (100.000%)	20.0002 (100.000%)
	std	0.03570	0.0327 (91.597%)	0.0385 (107.843%)	0.0400 (112.045%)	0.0401 (112.325%)	0.0387 (108.403%)	0.0386 (108.123%)	0.0367 (102.801%)	0.0375 (105.042%)
Real-Time TCP Traffic Periodicity (ms)	mean	3038.98260	3039.1769 (100.006%)	3038.8211 (99.995%)	3037.9378 (99.966%)	3036.5311 (99.919%)	3038.3505 (99.979%)	3040.0165 (100.034%)	3034.7304 (99.860%)	3037.3555 (99.946%)
	std	1.37920	1.3686 (99.231%)	1.4686 (106.482%)	1.3900 (100.783%)	1.3705 (99.369%)	1.4509 (105.199%)	1.4094 (102.190%)	10.5628 (765.864%)	7.9395 (575.660%)
HMI Request RTT (ms)	mean	4.74882	4.6142 (97.165%)	4.6523 (97.966%)	4.7878 (100.820%)	4.7160 (99.308%)	4.6946 (98.858%)	4.5504 (95.821%)	4.6416 (97.742%)	6.4942 (136.755%)
	std	1.33683	1.4186 (106.117%)	1.5697 (117.419%)	1.3099 (97.988%)	1.3940 (104.278%)	1.4339 (107.261%)	1.4320 (107.122%)	1.4789 (110.631%)	4.2569 (318.431%)

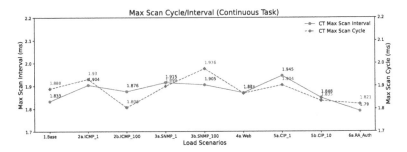

Fig. 6. Maximum continuous task scan cycle/interval

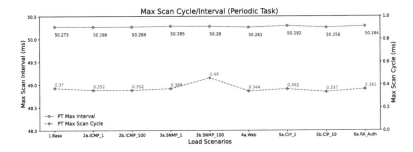

Fig. 7. Maximum periodic task scan cycle/interval

sum_of_scan_cycle_time of the CT, and the increase was greater for scenario b, which produced a greater traffic load than scenario a. The greatest impact was observed in the case of the *6a.RA_Auth* scenario, even though the load genera-tor produces very little network traffic. The average execution time increased by approximately 5.1% when compared to the base scenario, and the standard devi-ation increased up to 4.5 times. Therefore, the execution of the encryption is con-firmed to significantly affect the average execution time of CompactLogix's CT.

Sum of Periodic Task Scan Cycle. The sum of the PT scan cycle time is shown in Fig. 9. Unlike CT, all the load scenarios showed the same average value and slightly different distributions.

Real-Time Communication. Four different connections are identified in CompactLogix's RT communication traffic. It consists of two TCP connections and two UDP connections, as shown in Fig. 10. In the first TCP connection, the consumer requests the producer to transmit the RT data with the topic name, after which only the TCP Keep-Alive messages are transmitted. The producer then opens the second TCP connection to the consumer and periodically sends the CIP's *Forward Open* command periodically (3.04 s). In the third UDP con-nection from the producer, the I/O values are continuously transmitted to the consumer at the RPI cycle (20 ms) set by the producer. The consumer sends a

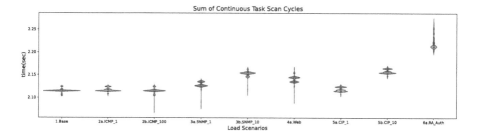

Fig. 8. Sum of continuous task scan cycle

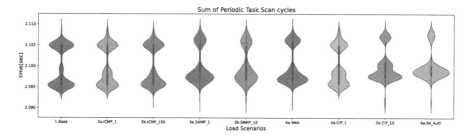

Fig. 9. Sum of periodic task scan cycle

CIP packet over the UDP after every 250 ms through the fourth UDP connection. This may correspond to the status information.

Since this experiment places a load on the producer, the periodicity of the *Forward Open* packet transmission of the second TCP connection and the RT data packet transmission pattern of the third UDP connection were analyzed. Figure 11a shows the measurement results of the third UDP communication pattern, which send every 20 ms for each load. All the averages had the same period values (20 ms). The standard deviation increased only slightly by 12.3% (from 0.0357 to 0.0401 ms) for *4b.SNMP_100*, when compared to the base scenario. Concurrently, the TCP pattern continuously sent by the producer was analyzed, as shown in Fig. 11b. There was no change in the mean, but the standard deviation increased significantly to 7.65 times in *5b.CIP_10*, where more CIP requests were sent during the load test. In the *5b.CIP_10* scenario, which transmits a small amount of CIP communication to the PLC, and *6a.RA_Auth*, which requests encryption to the PLC, the TCP communication pattern fluctuates.

Non-real-time Communication. Fast and stable communication is required between the HMI and the controller for the operator to quickly determine and manage the ICS. Therefore, the round trip time (RTT) between the HMI and the PLC was analyzed for each load scenario, and the result is shown in the violin plot in Fig. 12. In most load scenarios, the RTT duration increased slightly and had a value within 1–8 ms. However, in the *6a.RA_Auth* scenario, the maximum

Fig. 10. Real-time related communication pattern of CompactLogix

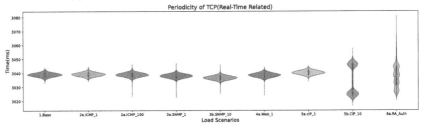

(a) UDP pattern in producer/consumer communication

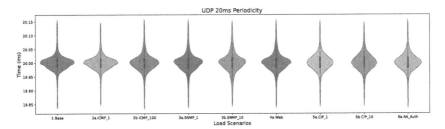

(b) TCP pattern in producer/consumer communication

Fig. 11. Real-time communication analysis result

RTT value increased significantly, reaching 30 ms, and the average increased from 4.748 to 6.494 ms (37.8%). The standard deviation also increased sharply from 1.337 to 4.259 ms (316%). Considering that the traffic is generated at less than 1 Mbps in the 1 Gigabit network during the experiment, it is concluded that most of these delays occurred in the producer PLC. It was reconfirmed that the encryption significantly affects the non-RT communication. Nevertheless, considering the characteristics of the HMI, a delay of approximately 30 ms was considered to be acceptable by the operator.

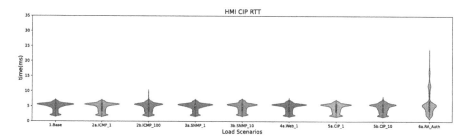

Fig. 12. Round trip time of HMI request

5.2   Discussion

In eight load scenarios where the experiment was normally performed, the periodic task and the RT communication had no significant effect. However, owing to the traffic load, an increase of up to 5.1% can be observed for the average scan cycle time of CT and 36.8% for the RTT of non-RT communication. The impact was not discernible in the normal load scenario (type a), and a significant amount of change was observed only in the extreme scenario (type b) and the *6a.RA_Auth* scenario, where the encryption operation was performed forcibly. Therefore, it is acceptable to deploy a security solution into the ICS which requests information less than once per second.

Additionally, it was observed that CompactLogix does not allocate sufficient resources to non-RT services. For example, in scenario *3a.SNMP_1* took approximately 0.1 s for several SNMP request-response processes when bringing information from the controller, but in scenario *3b.SNMP_10*, this process took up to 8 s. Similarly, in scenario *4b.Web_10*, the time required increased several times as many processes have attempted to acquire the information. Conversely, of course, it was confirmed that resources were provided with high priorities for RT functions. We confirmed that the effect of the load from information acquisition on the RT function of the device was insignificant.

An additional analysis of the two exceptional scenarios presents the following information: In the *4b.Web_10* scenario, the PLC was repeatedly shut down and this phenomenon did not occur in the case of *4a.Web_1*. Finding an exact point lies outside the scope of this experiment. CompactLogix may encounter an implementation error when handling multiple HTTP requests simultaneously. Particularly in the case of DoS attacks, the data stored in the flash memory of the PLC were erased. To continue the experiment, the control logic and configuration had to be downloaded to the PLC once again. In the *6b.RA_Auth_10* scenario, CompactLogix responds with the unknown response code (0xFF) to all the authentication requests. It looks as a protection mechanism that blocks brute force attacks, but it blocks normal access from *Studio 5000* afterwards.

Therefore, the controller is observed to be limited in its ability to respond to simultaneous access and requests. Based on our analysis results, it would be nice to refer to the following guidelines when introducing a security solution for

Table 4. Key performance indicators for PLC

ID	Name	Description
1	Max scan cycle of continuous task	Continuous task's cycle time that took the longest during a load test
2	Max scan cycle of periodic task	Periodic task's cycle time that took the longest during a load test
3	Sum of continuous task's scan cycle time	Measurement of elapsed time after n times execution of continuous task
4	Sum of periodic task's interval	Measurement of elapsed time after n times execution of periodic task
5	Periodicity of RT Communication	Transmission interval of scheduled communication
6	RTT of HMI request/response	Round trip time from sending an HMI request packet to receiving an HMI response packet
7	Error packets in communication	Number of missed or error packets

controllers: If multiple security solutions work for controllers, accumulating the information in one point is better than collecting information individually. If the authentication process is required when connecting to the controller, maintaining the session has a lower impact when compared to creating a new session each time.

6   Performance Impact Analysis Procedure

6.1   Candidate KPIs for PLC

This study proposes KPIs that can be used in the impact analysis as shown in Table 4. These candidate KPIs can be obtained from PLC, measured externally, or derived from other metrics. If the manufacturer additionally provides internal information of the control device such as 'communication usage rate', such information may be added to KPIs. In the future studies, we believe that these performance indicators can help in analyzing the influence of other controllers. Although no significant impact of max scan cycle of the PT and the max scan cycle CT could be determined, they were selected as KPIs because they are important performance goals of the PLCs.

6.2   Proposed Procedure

Based on our impact analysis results, the experimental procedure for analyzing the impact of cyber security solutions on the controller was proposed as shown in Fig. 13. The KPIs of the control device were first identified and can be selected based on the information available from the vendor's manual, and the candidate

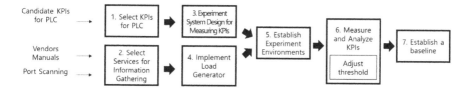

Fig. 13. Procedures of security solutions impact analysis for controllers

KPIs proposed in this study. To measure these KPIs, an experimental environment was constructed using the control system components (controllers, HMI, field devices, and so on) and monitoring tools. By implementing a load generator that can mimic a cyber security solution that sends a request for information, experimenters can see the change in KPIs based on load scenarios. If any performance impact is found from the control device, the frequency of the service requests is adjusted such that the impact does not occur or is at an acceptable level. After the stability is verified through sufficient experimentation, they can present appropriate baseline for security solutions to follow. Utilities or security companies can develop or apply security technologies by referring to these guidelines.

7   Conclusion

This study is the first to analyze the impact of the introduction of the active security solutions on the control devices, to the best of our knowledge. It proposed certain KPIs considering the characteristics of controllers (task and communication type) and an impact analysis process for an active security solution to analyze the impact on the control device. The impact of introducing a security solution that operates actively using CompactLogix developed by RA is analyzed as a case study. From the experiment, it is confirmed that there is no significant effect on the control device when information is obtained from the control device at a normal level. However, when the frequency of the information collection is abnormally high, a slight delay occurs in the average execution time of the CT and the non-RT communication response. Since the use of robust hardware that satisfies the requirements of the industrial environment is essential, it is confirmed that a delay occurs when the encryption operation is forced. However, even in this case, no significant difference was found according to information acquisition in the PT and RT communication because the PLC was designed for real-time control. Considering the performance and the release date of the target CompactLogix, a security solution can be introduced for the current controllers to the ICSs without any problems.

Since the impact analysis experiments performed in this study are not limited to specific devices, it is expected that the KPI candidates and the experimental procedures proposed by this study will be greatly beneficial to other researchers as well in determining the impact of the developed security technology on the controllers. The control system operator can review the introduction of the security solution and ensure that its impact is tolerable by adjusting the information acquisition cycle. Furthermore, the control system developer can specify the effect of each service on the operation of the controller in a 'quantitative' specification. Both the security researchers and the control system operators can actively consider the development and introduction of security technology into the ICSs by referring to the results of these experiments, and the security of the control system can thus be enhanced.

References

1. "Ripple20" Treck IOT/ICS device discovery and exploit detection. https://github.com/corelight/ripple20. Accessed 9 Sept 2021
2. Framework for Improving Critical Infrastructure Cybersecurity v1.1. National Institute of Standards and Technology (2018)
3. IEC 62443-4-2:2019 Security for industrial automation and control systems - Part 4–2: Technical security requirements for IACS components. IEC (2019)
4. Autem: PLC Analyzer Pro. https://www.autem.de/products/plc-analyzer-pro-6/. Accessed 9 Sept 2021
5. Benkraouda, H., Chakkantakath, M.A., Keliris, A., Maniatakos, M.: SNIFU: secure network interception for firmware updates in legacy PLCS. In: 2020 IEEE 38th VLSI Test Symposium (VTS), pp. 1–6 (2020). https://doi.org/10.1109/VTS48691.2020.9107609
6. Chan, C.-F., Chow, K.-P., Yiu, S.-M., Yau, K.: Enhancing the security and forensic capabilities of programmable logic controllers. In: DigitalForensics 2018. IAICT, vol. 532, pp. 351–367. Springer, Cham (2018). https://doi.org/10.1007/978-3-319-99277-8_19
7. Choi, J., Kim, H., Choi, S., Yun, J.H., Min, B.G., Kim, H.: Vendor-independent monitoring on programmable logic controller status for ICS security log management. In: Proceedings of the 2019 ACM Asia Conference on Computer and Communications Security, pp. 682–684 (2019)
8. Cruz, T., et al.: Improving network security monitoring for industrial control systems. In: 2015 IFIP/IEEE International Symposium on Integrated Network Management (IM), pp. 878–881 (2015). https://doi.org/10.1109/INM.2015.7140399
9. Falliere, N., Murchu, L.O., Chien, E.: W32.Stuxnet dossier. In: White Paper, Symantec Corp., Security Response, vol. 5(6), p. 29 (2011)
10. Grandgenett, R., Mahoney, W., Gandhi, R.: Authentication bypass and remote escalated I/O command attacks. In: Proceedings of the 10th Annual Cyber and Information Security Research Conference, pp. 1–7 (2015)
11. Khan, R., Maynard, P., McLaughlin, K., Laverty, D., Sezer, S.: Threat analysis of blackenergy malware for synchrophasor based real-time control and monitoring in smart grid. In: 4th International Symposium for ICS and SCADA Cyber Security Research (ICS-CSR), pp. 53–63 (2016)
12. Li, D., Guo, H., Zhou, J., Zhou, L., Wong, J.W.: SCADAWall: a CPI-enabled firewall model for SCADA security. Comput. Secur. **80**, 134–154 (2019)
13. Niedermaier, M., et al.: You snooze, you lose: measuring plc cycle times under attacks. In: 12th USENIX Workshop on Offensive Technologies (WOOT 2018) (2018)

14. Pinto, A.D., Dragoni, Y., Carcano, A.: TRITON: the first ICS cyber attack on safety instrument systems. In: Proceedings of Black Hat USA (2018)
15. Son, J., Noh, S., Choi, J., Yoon, H.: A practical challenge-response authentication mechanism for a programmable logic controller control system with one-time password in nuclear power plants. Nucl. Eng. Technol. **51**(7), 1791–1798 (2019)
16. Stouffer, K., Zimmerman, T., Tang, C., Chchonsik, J., McCarthy, J.: NISTIR 8183 Cybersecurity Framework Manufacturing Profile. US Department of Commerce, National Institute of Standards and Technology (2017)
17. Tenable: Nessus SCADA plugin. https://www.tenable.com/plugins/nessus/families/SCADA. Accessed 9 Sept 2021
18. Yau, K., Chow, K.P.: PLC forensics based on control program logic change detection. J. Digit. Forensics Secur. Law **10**(4), 5 (2015)
19. Zimmerman, T.A.: NISTIR 8177 Metrics and Key Performance Indicators for Robotic Cybersecurity Performance Analysis. US Department of Commerce, National Institute of Standards and Technology (2017)

Multi-categorical Risk Assessment for Urban Critical Infrastructures

Sandra König[1](✉) , Stefan Schauer[4] , and Stefan Rass[2,3]

[1] Center for Digital Safety and Security, Austrian Institute of Technology, Vienna, Austria
sandra.koenig@ait.ac.at
[2] LIT Secure and Correct Systems Lab, Johannes Kepler University Linz, Linz, Austria
stefan.rass@jku.at
[3] Institute for Artificial Intelligence and Cybersecurity, Universitaet Klagenfurt, Klagenfurt, Austria
stefan.rass@aau.at
[4] Center for Digital Safety and Security, Austrian Institute of Technology, Klagenfurt, Austria
stefan.schauer@ait.ac.at

Abstract. Measuring risk in multiple dimensions is vital for a comprehensive understanding and for risk analysis. Therefore, we here propose to use multiple impact categories. This yield generalized multi-categorical risk measures, depending on how the likelihood of occurrence is measured. For the one-dimensional case, risk is measured through a vector, while in the multi-dimensional case an entire matrix of risk scores arises. This multidimensional view is supposed to increase the understanding of relevant risks and provides valuable input to risk treatment.

Keywords: Critical infrastructures · Risk assessment · Cascading effects

1 Introduction

Traditionally, risk is measured as the product of impact and likelihood of occurrence, where both quantities are real numbers. However, the consequences of an incident are usually very complex and affect a system in many different ways, so that it is inadequate to measure this with only one number. Rather, multiple aspects of the impact should be considered, e.g., by choosing several impact categories. In this paper, we propose a method to assess risk in situations where the expected loss is rated in multiple categories and illustrate its use for urban critical infrastructures (CIs). The proposed method is generic and can therefore also be applied to other networks, e.g., for interdependent CIs from different states. The complexity of nowadays interdependent critical infrastructures makes it hard to predict the impact of an incident which promotes the use of qualitative scales. Still, such a qualitative assessment should be done regarding multiple factors. The

© Springer Nature Switzerland AG 2021
D. Percia David et al. (Eds.): CRITIS 2021, LNCS 13139, pp. 152–167, 2021.
https://doi.org/10.1007/978-3-030-93200-8_9

likelihood of occurrence is commonly estimated as a scalar, but we also sketch a multi-categorical approach and how this affects the risk assessment. Risk assessment of CIs faces numerous challenges. Interdependencies between CIs as well as the use of information and communication technologies yields new threats. Cyberattacks such as the Wannacry ransomware [7] and the NotPetya malware [22] (both in 2017) had significant effects on CIs such as power grids and hospitals [9]. In urban areas where CIs are in close geographic proximity interdependencies are even stronger. Further, the aftermaths of an incident are growing in complexity. Cascading effects make it hard to measure the impact, but also the likelihood of occurrence. A convenient way to deal with this issue is the use of qualitative assessments, as, e.g., proposed by the German BSI [27]. While this approach is adequate to represent the intrinsic uncertainty about consequences, a single categorical assessment is not able to capture complex manifold impacts that affect more than one aspect of relevance. Therefore, we propose the use of *multiple* impact categories to describe several forms of impact in Sect. 3. A change in the impact measurement requires an adaption of the risk assessment. Section 4 describes a way to deal with multiple impact categories based on a risk matrix. It also sketches an approach where the likelihood of occurrence is measured in multiple categories. Section 5 describes how such a generalized risk assessment can be transferred from single CI to an entire network of CIs. The approach is illustrated with an example in Sect. 6. Related work is provided in Sect. 2 and concluding remarks on the use of such multi-dimensional risk assessment are given in Sect. 7.

2   Related Work

Multi-criteria risk management usually applies multi-criteria decision-making [29], which relates most of multi-objective optimization naturally to our work as a theoretical underpinning. A non-exhaustive selection of work relevant for matters of decision making is [28], who present an early survey and discussion about different approaches. In the specific context of investments, [18,39] discuss optimal allocations of resources w.r.t. multiple dimensions of interest. On a more generic level, [17,19,31,34,35,43,44] discuss the problem of optimal defense in multiple dimensions, all reducing the multi-criteria optimization to a conventional optimization of a scalarized aggregate goal, thus making the whole theory of optimization applicable to the multi-criteria setting. The alternative route of ordering risks along explicit priorities, i.e., lexicographically, has received less but noticeable attention by [8,11,36,41,48] up to software implementations [46]. This direction is to be distinguished from the scalarization approach, since the lexicographic order does not lend itself to a numeric representation by a utility function, such as is usually presumed in decision making [50].

Risk management, on the contrary, has seen the majority of efforts on improving the assessment itself, using multiple dimensions to compute a risk score from, but not primarily also making decisions using multiple scores itself. Sophisticated techniques for risk assessment have come as entire frameworks such as CORAS [10], ENISA's MEHARI methodology [12], SAHARA [38] or specific methods of risk assessment like [4,20,25,30,33] to specify or quantify risks. These have also been widely applied at national level by different countries (e.g., [40,42]) and the European Union [14,15]. More domain-specific proposals complement these, addressing the particularities of risk assessment for the cyber domain [3,26,49], the automotive domain [53], supply chains [23], critical infrastructures [5,24,47,51], water supply [21,52], but also threat-specific like for natural disasters [13,16].

Our work is further complementary to these efforts in proposing a method on how to use these assessments into a bigger and unified picture and multi-dimensional risk management strategy, targeting practitioners and aiming at ease of *explainable* decision making.

3   Impact Assessment

The impact assessment of a scenario depends on the point of view of the expert who conducts the assessment. It depends on what needs to be protected, but also on interests and values of the organization. For example, a water provider is interested in the water quality, but CIs depending on it (such as a hospital) may be more concerned about the availability of cooling water than drinking water. Common to various CI operators is the fact that the impact of an incident is not sufficiently well described through a single quantity. Rather, the assessment should consider multiple factors. High-level categories that are used in the context of CIs are the following [6]:

(A) Humans affected
(B) Property damage
(C) Economic damage
(D) Environmental damage
(E) Political-social effects

Category A is not only concerned about deaths, but also includes, e.g., injured or psychologically affected people. These categories may be extended or refined for more specific assessment, depending on the context of the analysis.

It is recommended to measure the actual impact on a qualitative scale to take into consideration that precise predictions of the impact are not possible due to the high complexity and resulting uncertainty. The Austrian Ministry of

Table 1. General qualitative impact scale

Score	Meaning	Description
1	Minimal	Insignificant impact
2	Minor	Reversible impact
3	Moderate	Slight effect
4	Major	Irreversible effect
5	Massive	Extensive irreversible effect

the Interior uses a 5-tier scale [6], while the Federal Department of Home Affairs in Switzerland uses a 8-tier scale [2]. Table 1 provides a common description of such scales as, e.g., used in [37].

A more precise description of the scores depends on the specific CI. Table 2 shows an interpretation of the scale for a hospital.

Table 2. Qualitative impact scale for a hospital

Score	Description
1	Normal
2	Slight impairment, e.g., reduced availability of experts
3	Some impairment, but all patients get treatment
4	Reduced availability of resources, less urgent treatment postponed
5	Intensive care is limited or not available

The impact of an incident is assessed according to each category on the same scale, so that the resulting impact assessment can be described through a tuple $I = (I_A, I_B, I_C, I_D, I_E)$ and can be represented through a histogram. The impact assessment is done by experts and may be supported through simulation tools such as [1]. Simulations prove especially helpful in more complex situations where cascading effects come into play. The results of the simulation should in any case again be discussed with experts.

In Austria, an earthquake typically has a higher effect on property than on humans, economy as well as the environment [54]. Political-social impacts are generally not expected after a single event. This results in the impact $(I_A, I_B, I_C, I_D, I_E) = (1, 4, 2, 2, 1)$. Figure 1 visualizes this assessment.

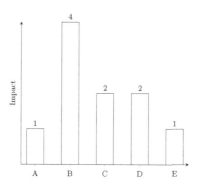

Fig. 1. Loss for each category in case of an earthquake

4   Local Risk Assessment

A multi-categorical impact assessment requires an adaption of the corresponding risk assessment. The classical approach for combining qualitative impact and likelihood assessments to a risk measure is using a risk matrix. This approach can be generalized for multiple impact categories. In this section we show how to determine a *Risk Score*, depending on how likelihood is measured. This risk assessment is local in the sense that it only considers the risk for a single part in a network of CIs. A global risk assessment based on this local assessment is described in the next section.

4.1   One-Dimensional Likelihood Assessment

The likelihood of occurrence of an event is often estimated through the relative frequency. However, the required historical data is usually sparse in risk management such that the corresponding estimates are not reliable. Therefore, a qualitative likelihood assessment is typically used in practice. Table 3 provides a common description of a 5-tier scale for the likelihood (see, e.g., [37]).

Table 3. Qualitative likelihood scale

	Meaning	Description
1	Very unlikely	Only in exceptional circumstances
2	Unlikely	Not expected under normal conditions
3	Possible	Equally likely or unlikely
4	Likely	Probable to occur
5	Very likely	Expected to occur

In the case where likelihood is measured through a single value (whether numeric or a category, potentially aggregated from several values), we follow the common approach of using a risk matrix to deduce the risk level from likelihood and impact. More explicitly, we consider a risk matrix as shown in Table 4 where each combination of likelihood (column) and impact (row) corresponds to the cell. The color of the cell represents the risk assigned to this combination, where green corresponds to the situation where the risk is lowest (lower-left part of matrix) and red corresponds to the highest risk (upper-right part of the matrix). Intermediate levels are colored in yellow and orange, representing increasing risk levels. We map this colors to a *Risk Score* ranging from 1 (green, best case) to 4 (red, worst case). A scenario which is very unlikely ($L = 1$) but causes massive impact ($I = 5$) is in the uppermost left cell (as illustrated in Table 4) which is yellow, therefore its corresponding risk level is 2. The form of the risk matrix, i.e., the coloring of the cells, is up to the user. The color scale shown in Table 4 is often used, but may be modified depending on the considered situation and risk appetite.

Table 4. Risk matrix example

Likelihood/ Impact	Very un- likely	Unlikely	Possible	Likely	Very likely
Massive	$R(1,5)$				
Major					
Moderate					
Minor					
Minimal					

When considering multiple impact categories, this mapping from a pair (L, I_j) of likelihood L and impact I_j in category j (where $j \in \{A, B, C, D, E\}$ with the categories defined in Sect. 3) to a risk score R_j needs to be applied for each category, resulting in a vector of risk scores

$$R = (R_A, R_B, R_C, R_D, R_E),$$

where R_j is the risk score in category j ($j \in \{A, B, C, D, E\}$). Note that the risk matrices used for the mappings do *not* need to be equal, but its structure may depend on the impact category.

Reconsider the earthquake example from above and assume the likelihood of occurrence is unlikely. Then the corresponding column (second from the left) in each of the five risk matrices determine the five risk scores. For illustration assume that all risk matrices have the structure shown in Fig. 4. Then the impact assessment $I = (1, 4, 2, 2, 1)$ yields a risk score $R = (1, 2, 1, 1, 1)$ since only the cell corresponding to a "major impact" (second row from above) is yellow and therefore yields a risk score of $R_B = 2$ while the cells corresponding to the other categorical impact are green and therefore the risk score is 1. In this assessment it is assumed that category A is most important to the user (first entry in the risk score vector) and category E is least important for the users (last entry in the risk score vector). This can, in fact should, be adapted to the application context.

Risk management requires comparison of risk assessment of different scenarios. Vector-valued risk scores can be compared according to a lexicographic ordering, that is, the values of the first entry are compared first, followed by the entries of the second entries etc. If lexicographic ordering is used, the impact categories must be sorted according to the preferences of the user, such that the values of more important categories are compared before less important ones. For example, human lives count more than economic damage (like in the Corona crisis). The ordering used here represents our own preferences and may be adapted by the user.

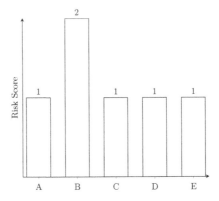

Fig. 2. Risk score for each category in case of an earthquake

4.2   Multi-dimensional Likelihood Assessment

Similar as for the impact, it is not always sufficient to measure the likelihood of a scenario according to just one criterion. Besides the (estimated) relative frequency, further aspects may be relevant, such as

– Vulnerability of the affected component
– Environmental conditions (climate change, geographic conditions)
– Capabilities of the attacker
– Motivation of the attacker

For multiple likelihood categories the identification of the risk score needs to be adapted even further. The basic procedure is as in the case of a one-dimensional likelihood assignment, i.e., it is based on a risk matrix. With 5 impact categories as proposed in Sect. 3 and ℓ likelihood categories, the risk assessment requires 5ℓ risk matrices, namely one for each combination of impact and likelihood category.

While the resulting risk scores are collected in a vector in the one-dimensional case, the additional dimensions in the likelihood assessment now yield a matrix of risk scores

$$R_{ij} = R(L_i, I_j)$$

depending on the likelihood value L_i in category i, and on the impact value I_j in category j. Comparing such matrices of risk scores is less clear than the comparison of vectors of risk score. We recommend prioritizing both impact and likelihood categories such that the corresponding matrix can be interpreted as a classical risk matrix: risk scores for the most relevant impact and the most relevant likelihood category (uppermost right) has first priority and the corresponding entry in the matrix can be colored red. Risk scores corresponding to less relevant categories (lowermost left) are colored in green and considered last. The actual coloring of the combination of categories is up to the user.

Table 5 illustrates the result of this risk assessment for a risk matrix as shown in Table 4 with $\ell = 3$ likelihood categories C_1, C_2, C_3, each measured on the 5-tier scale. Consider the earthquake example with impact values $I = (1, 4, 2, 2, 1)$ and likelihood values $L = (2, 1, 2)$ and use for simplicity the risk matrix shown in Table 4 to determine the corresponding values. Note that the arguments correspond to the *score* in each category, not to the category itself. In particular, it is possible that the entry in a red area is low, i.e., the risk for the most important impact and likelihood category is low since the expected impact and likelihood are low. The color of the risk value in the cell in Table 5 corresponds to the criticality according to the priorities of the various categories, where impact category D has been considered less important than category E.

Table 5. Risk matrix for 3 likelihood categories

Likelihood/Impact	C_1	C_2	C_3
A	$R(1,1) = 1$	$R(2,2) = 1$	$R(1,1) = 1$
B	$R(1,2) = 1$	$R(1,5) = 2$	$R(1,4) = 2$
C	$R(4,1) = 2$	$R(1,1) = 1$	$R(3,2) = 2$
D	$R(2,1) = 1$	$R(2,2) = 1$	$R(1,2) = 1$
E	$R(1,1) = 1$	$R(1,1) = 1$	$R(1,1) = 1$

5   Global Risk Assessment

Risk assessment of a network of interdependent CIs, should incorporate the risk assessment of components to include this knowledge about the local behavior. For consistency, the global risk assessment should be of the same form as the local risk assessment, i.e., the same categories and the same scale should be used.

A convenient way to aggregate the local risk assessments is by assigning different weights to the components and compute an average assessment in each category according to these weights. The weights of the components are interpreted as prioritization, i.e., the most important parts get the highest weight. In case such a weighting is not possible or not desired, an average value can be determined (i.e., choosing equal weights for all components). Depending on how the local assessments are combined, the global assessment may not always return values on the same scale as the local assessments. If this is desired (e.g., for comparison purposes), it is possible to round up to the next integer (conservative approach) or to the integer closest to the average. For example, assume that three assets, abstractly just called 1, 2 and 3, will be affected by an incident according and the local risk assessment in the categories A to E is

$$R^1 = (4, 3, 2, 1, 2), \quad R^2 = (4, 2, 2, 2, 1), \quad R^3 = (2, 2, 1, 1, 1)$$

Putting weights $\alpha_1 = 0.4, \alpha_2 = 0.3, \alpha_3 = 0.3$ on the assets (such that the sum is 1) yields a global risk of $\sum_{i=1}^{3} \alpha_i R^i$, so

$$R_{global} = (3.4, 2.4, 1.7, 1.3, 1.4)$$

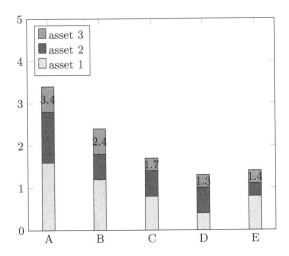

Fig. 3. Loss for each category in case of an earthquake

Figure 3 illustrates this assessment where different colors represent the partition of each asset to the global risk. The proposed methodology explicitly avoids a worst-case perspective where the maximum local risk score is chosen as the global risk score because this view is very pessimistic and often causes an information loss.

6   Example

In order to illustrate the application of the described impact and risk assessment, we consider a part of an urban CI network. This network consists of critical assets from different sectors, some of which are depending on each other (cf. Fig. 4). In this example, the focus is on the water domain (depicted in blue) with specifically important assets such as several pumps and the control room. Additionally, the admin of the control room is explicitly modelled since his actions may influence the impact of an incident (including humans in the model becomes crucial when considering cyber-attacks, including ransomware).

The water plant is closely interacting with other CIs. Operation of the pumps requires reliable power support, and control systems require a stable Internet connection. On the other hand, the provided drinking and cooling water is essential for many other CIs, such as hospitals. Due to its high importance, the electric power supply (depicted in red) is modelled in some more detail, including a

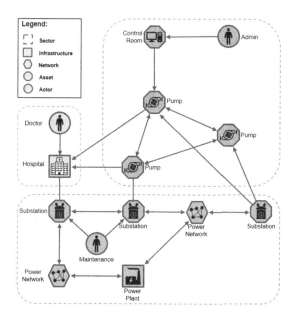

Fig. 4. Simplified example of an CI interdependency graph.

power plant, several substations as well as a maintenance worker (representing an entire maintenance crew in reality). The health sector (depicted in violet) is only considered at a very high level since it does not directly influence the operation of the water provider in the considered scenario (things would be different if we considered, e.g., a pandemic, where limited capacity of a hospital may yield a shortage of personal at other CIs). Power networks themselves are highly complex entities but are represented in this example as single nodes since the focus is on availability of power rather than on reasons of failure. For their assessment no deep functional details about the behavior are needed, and a high-level description is sufficient. The health sector is only consisting of one hospital and one doctor, representing the entirety of medical stuff to keep the analysis comprehensible. In a practical use case, the model has to be more detailed to capture the dependencies of interest.

Edges among the critical infrastructures and entities represent the dependencies among them. These dependencies can be either physical, i.e., a service or product is exchanged between two entities, logical, i.e., for maintenance of components, or informational, i.e., data or information is exchanged between them. Further, the three pumps in the water sector are depending on each other to keep the pressure required for maintaining the water supply. If one of them shuts down, the other two will shut down accordingly. Similarly, in the electrical power sector the power plant generates the power, which is then distributed via the network to the substations. If the substations are cut off the network or go offline due to maintenance reasons, the pumps or the hospital will be cut off the power supply as well. Finally, the hospital needs to be supplied with electrical power as well as water and is also depending on the medical staff to provide health care services.

We consider again the scenario of an earthquake and describe its effect on the CI network. Recent statistics show that on average earthquakes with minor damage happen every 2 to 3 years while moderate damage to buildings is expected every 75 years in Austria [54]. According to the likelihoods scale in Table 3, this corresponds to a likelihood score of 2. Regarding the impact assessment it is important to take into account direct and indirect consequences of the incident. Let us assume that the earthquake affects the substation on the right-hand side of the power sector diagram. If this fails, it will affect the power network as well as the two pumps directly depending on it. In a next step, this affects the third pump in the water supply network which in turn may cause limited water availability at the hospital. The power supplier faces moderate property damage and minor (short term) economic damage due to the disruption, further the environment is affected at the premises. The water supplier is assumed to be well prepared against reduced availability of power (as long as it does not exceed a certain duration), the local interruption does not affect the water supply network itself. Most importantly, water quality is not significantly affected by the considered incident. A water shortage at the hospital affects humans and may have some social effects (e.g., cause awareness that smooth operation cannot be taken for granted). Some interruption in the usual operation will occur but this is expected to last only for a short time. These effects are represented through the impact assessments for power, water and health, I_P, I_W and I_H given below.

$$I_P = (1, 3, 2, 3, 1)$$
$$I_W = (1, 1, 2, 1, 1)$$
$$I_H = (2, 1, 2, 1, 2)$$

This assessment is in line with discussion held during the ODYSSEUS project.

For the global risk, we assign a weight of 0.6 to the water supplier, which is in the focus of our analysis, and 0.2 to power and health, correspondingly. Figure 5 illustrates the resulting global risk assessment.

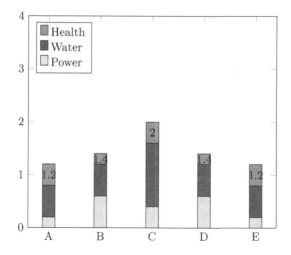

Fig. 5. Loss for each category in case of an earthquake

7   Discussion and Conclusion

A multi-categorical risk assessment captures more information about a risk scenario than a classical scalar assessment and is therefore recommended in a comprehensive risk analysis. However, this more general approach comes with a certain cost. First and foremost, this is due to expert knowledge that is needed to do the numerous assessments ($i \times \ell$ assessments for i impact categories and ℓ likelihood categories). Besides, the used framework should be discussed. Which categories are relevant? What scale should be used (even or odd number of categories) and how should the values be interpreted for each category? How do the risk matrices look that are used to decide which risks are worst? While such discussions take time, we think the time is spent well since it contributes to a common understanding of risk management in general and the specific risks in particular.

A multidimensional impact assessment is relevant to better understand consequences of an incident. Such a comprehensive view is important input for risk treatment, as it helps identifying actions that prevent any kind of severe damage from the considered system. It is important to keep this comprehensive view throughout the entire risk management process. Current approaches extend classical risk management processes, that work with real-valued risk measures, to the case of multi-categorical risk measures (which are a special case of probabilistic risk measures) [45]. Validation of the new methods through discussion with experts and stakeholder workshops is recommended and anticipated in the near future. Additional future work focuses on simultaneous treatment of risk and resilience, where both quantities are assessed according to multiple categories [32].

Acknowledgement. This work was supported by the research Project ODYSSEUS ("Simulation und Analyse kritischer Netzwerk-Infrastrukturen in Städten") funded by the Austrian Research Promotion Agency under Grant No.873539.

References

1. AIT: SAURON propagation engine (2020). https://atlas.ait.ac.at/sauron/
2. BABS: Katastrophen und notlagen schweiz - methode zur risikoanalyse methode zur risikoanalyse von katastrophen und notlagen für die schweiz (2013)
3. Beck, A., Rass, S.: Using neural networks to aid CVSS risk aggregation - an empirically validated approach. J. Innov. Digit. Ecosyst. **3**(2), 148–154 (2016). https://doi.org/10.1016/j.jides.2016.10.002
4. Bier, V.M., Cox, L.A.: Probabilistic risk analysis for engineered systems. In: Edwards, W. (ed.) Advances in Decision Analysis, pp. 279–301. Cambridge University Press (2007)
5. Bloomfield, R.E., Popov, P., Salako, K., Stankovic, V., Wright, D.: Preliminary interdependency analysis: An approach to support critical-infrastructure risk-assessment. Reliab. Eng. Syst. Saf. **167**, 198–217 (20117). https://doi.org/10.1016/j.ress.2017.05.030, https://linkinghub.elsevier.com/retrieve/pii/S0951832017305963
6. Bundesministerium für Inneres: Risikomanagement im katastrophenmanagement (2018)
7. Cimpanu, C.: WannaCry ransomware infects actual medical devices, not just computers (2017). https://www.bleepingcomputer.com/news/security/wannacry-ransomware-infects-actual-medical-devices-not-just-computers/
8. Cococcioni, M., Pappalardo, M., Sergeyev, Y.D.: Lexicographic multi-objective linear programming using grossone methodology: theory and algorithm. Appl. Math. Comput. **318**, 298–311 (2018). https://doi.org/10.1016/j.amc.2017.05.058, https://linkinghub.elsevier.com/retrieve/pii/S0096300317303703
9. Department of Health: Investigation: wannacry cyber attack and the NHS (2018). https://www.nao.org.uk/wp-content/uploads/2017/10/Investigation-WannaCry-cyber-attack-and-the-NHS.pdf
10. Dimitrakos, T., Bicarregui, J., Stølen, K.: CORAS - a framework for risk analysis of security critical systems. ERCIM News, April 2002
11. Ehrgott, M.: Discrete decision problems, multiple criteria optimization classes and lexicographic max-ordering. In: Fandel, G., Trockel, W., Stewart, T.J., van den Honert, R.C. (eds.) Trends in Multicriteria Decision Making. Lecture Notes in Economics and Mathematical Systems, vol. 465, pp. 31–44. Springer, Heidelberg (1998). https://doi.org/10.1007/978-3-642-45772-2_3
12. ENISA: Mehari (2019). https://www.enisa.europa.eu/topics/threat-risk-management/risk-management/current-risk/risk-management-inventory/rm-ra-methods/m_mehari.html
13. Espinoza, S., Poulos, A., Rudnick, H., de la Llera, J.C., Panteli, M., Mancarella, P.: Risk and resilience assessment with component criticality ranking of electric power systems subject to earthquakes. IEEE Syst. J. **14**(2), 2837–2848 (2020). https://doi.org/10.1109/JSYST.2019.2961356, https://ieeexplore.ieee.org/document/8999572/
14. European Commission: Council conclusions on further developing risk assessment for disaster management within the European Union. https://www.consilium.europa.eu/uedocs/cms_data/docs/pressdata/en/jha/121462.pdf (2011)

15. European Parliament, European Council: Directive (EU) 2016/ 1148 of 6 July 2016 - concerning measures for a high common level of security of network and information systems across the union, 06 July 2016. http://eur-lex.europa.eu/legal-content/EN/TXT/PDF/?uri=CELEX:32016L1148&from=EN

16. Fekete, A.: Critical infrastructure cascading effects. disaster resilience assessment for floods affecting city of Cologne and Rhein-Erft-Kreis. J. Flood Risk Manage. **13**(2), e312600 (2020). https://doi.org/10.1111/jfr3.12600

17. Fernandez, F.R., Monroy, L., Puerto, J.: Multicriteria goal games. J. Optim. Theory Appl. **99**(2), 403–421 (1998). `C:\Users\stefan\Documents\Citavi5\Proj ects\Literaturdatenbank\CitaviAttachments\Houmb,Franqueira2009-Estimat ingToERiskLevelusing.pdf`

18. Fielder, A., Konig, S., Panaousis, E., Schauer, S., Rass, S.: Uncertainty in cyber security investments. arXiv preprint arXiv:1712.05893 (2017)

19. Ghose, D.: A necessary and sufficient condition for Pareto-optimal security strategies in multicriteria matrix games. J. Optim. Theory Appl. **68**(3), 463–481 (1991), https://doi.org/10.1007/BF00940065

20. Goerlandt, F., Reniers, G.: On the assessment of uncertainty in risk diagrams. Saf. Sci. **84**, 67–77 (2016). https://doi.org/10.1016/j.ssci.2015.12.001, https://linkinghub.elsevier.com/retrieve/pii/S0925753515003215

21. Gouglidis, A., König, S., Green, B., Rossegger, K., Hutchison, D.: Protecting water utility networks from advanced persistent threats: a case study. In: Rass, S., Schauer, S. (eds.) Game Theory for Security and Risk Management. SDGTFA, pp. 313–333. Springer, Cham (2018). https://doi.org/10.1007/978-3-319-75268-6_13

22. Greenerg, A.: The untold story of NotPetya, the most devastating cyberattck in history (2018). https://www.wired.com/story/notpetya-cyberattack-ukraine-russia-code-crashed-the-world/

23. Göllner, J., Peer, A., Gronalt, M., Quirchmayr, G.: Risk analysis for supply chain networks. In: I3M: The 11th International Multidisciplinary Modelling & Simulation Multiconference - HMS-track: Intermodal transportation systems and services. University of Bordeaux, France, , 10 September 2014

24. Haimes, Y., Santos, J., Crowther, K., Henry, M., Lian, C., Yan, Z.: Risk analysis in interdependent infrastructures. In: Goetz, E., Shenoi, S. (eds.) ICCIP 2007. IIFIP, vol. 253, pp. 297–310. Springer, Boston, MA (2008). https://doi.org/10.1007/978-0-387-75462-8_21

25. Hogganvik, I.: A graphical approach to security risk analysis. Ph.D. thesis, University of Oslo - Faculty of Mathematics and Natural Sciences (2007)

26. Houmb, S.H., Franqueira, V.N.L.: Estimating toe risk level using CVSS. In: International Conference on Availability, Reliability and Security, pp. 718–725. IEEE Computer Society Press (2009)

27. Informationstechnik, B.f.S.i.d.: BSI-Standard 100–2: IT-grundschutz methodology (2008). https://www.bsi.bund.de/SharedDocs/Downloads/EN/BSI/Publications/BSIStandards/standard_100-2_e_pdf.pdf?__blob=publicationFile&v=1

28. Karpak, B., Zionts, S. (eds.): Multiple Criteria Decision Making and Risk Analysis Using Microcomputers. NATO ASI Series, Series F, vol. 56. Springer, Heidelberg (1989)

29. Keeney, R.L., Raiffa, H.: Decisions with Multiple Objectives: Preferences and Value Tradeoffs. Wiley Series in Probability and Mathematical Statistics, Wiley (1976)

30. Kelly, D., Smith, C.: Bayesian Inference for Probabilistic Risk Assessment: A Practitioner's Guidebook. Springer, Reliability Engineering, London (2011). https://doi.org/10.1007/978-1-84996-187-5

31. König, S.: Improving risk assessment for interdependent urban critical infrastructures. In: Proceedings of the Hamburg International Conference of Logistics (HICL), Institut für Logistik und Unternehmensführung, Technische Universität, Epubli, Hamburg 23 September 2020. https://doi.org/10.15480/882.3123, https://tore.tuhh.de/handle/11420/8013

32. König, S.: Simultaneous treatment of risk and resilience (2021)

33. König, S., Gouglidis, A.: Random damage in interconnected networks. In: Rass, S., Schauer, S. (eds.) Game Theory for Security and Risk Management. SDGTFA, pp. 185–201. Springer, Cham (2018). https://doi.org/10.1007/978-3-319-75268-6_8

34. König, S., Gouglidis, A., Green, B., Solar, A.: Assessing the impact of malware attacks in utility networks. In: Rass, S., Schauer, S. (eds.) Game Theory for Security and Risk Management. SDGTFA, pp. 335–351. Springer, Cham (2018). https://doi.org/10.1007/978-3-319-75268-6_14

35. König, S., Grafenauer, T., Rass, S., Schauer, S.: Practical risk analysis in interdependent critical infrastructures - a how-to. In: SECURWARE 2018, The Twelfth International Conference on Emerging Security Information, Systems and Technologies, Venice, Italypp, pp. 150–157 (2018). http://www.thinkmind.org/download.php?articleid=securware_2017_6_30_38023

36. Konnov, I.: On lexicographic vector equilibrium problems. J. Optim. Theory Appl. **118**(3), 681–688 (2003). https://doi.org/10.1023/B:JOTA.0000004877.39408.80

37. van Lenteren, J., et al.: Environmental risk assessment of exotic natural enemies used in inundative biological control. BioControl **48**(1), 3–38 (2003). https://doi.org/10.1023/a:1021262931608

38. Macher, G., Sporer, H., Berlach, R., Armengaud, E., Kreiner, C.: SAHARA: a security-aware hazard and risk analysis method. In: Design, Automation & Test in Europe Conference & Exhibition (DATE), pp. 621–624. IEEE Conference Publications (2015). https://doi.org/10.7873/DATE.2015.0622, http://ieeexplore.ieee.org/xpl/articleDetails.jsp?arnumber=7092463

39. Mainik, G., Rüschendorf, L.: Ordering of multivariate risk models with respect to extreme portfolio losses. In: Rüschendorf, L. (ed.) Mathematical Risk Analysis. Dependence, Risk Bounds, Optimal Allocations and Portfolios, Springer Series in Operations Research and Financial Engineering, pp. 353–383. Springer, Heidelberg (2013). https://doi.org/10.1007/978-3-642-33590-7_14

40. MSB, Lindstedt, U.: National risk assessment 2011–2013 - the swedish experience (2014). https://www.msb.se/RibData/Filer/pdf/26621.pdf

41. Ogryczak, W., Śliwiński, T.: On direct methods for lexicographic min-max optimization. In: Gavrilova, M., et al. (eds.) ICCSA 2006. LNCS, vol. 3982, pp. 802–811. Springer, Heidelberg (2006). https://doi.org/10.1007/11751595_85

42. Pruyt, E., Wijnmalen, D., Bökkerink, M.: What can we learn from he evaluation of the dutch national risk assessment?. Risk Anal. **33**(8), 1385–1388 (2013)

43. Rass, S., Rainer, B.: Numerical computation of multi-goal security strategies. In: Poovendran, R., Saad, W. (eds.) GameSec 2014. LNCS, vol. 8840, pp. 118–133. Springer, Cham (2014). https://doi.org/10.1007/978-3-319-12601-2_7

44. Rass, Stefan: Security strategies and multi-criteria decision making. In: Rass, Stefan, Schauer, Stefan (eds.) Game Theory for Security and Risk Management. SDGTFA, pp. 47–74. Springer, Cham (2018). https://doi.org/10.1007/978-3-319-75268-6_3

45. Rass, S., König, S.: HyRiM: multicriteria risk management using zero-sum games with vector-valued payoffs that are probability distributions (2018). https://cran.r-project.org/package=HyRiM

46. Rass, S., König, S., Alshawish, A.: R package 'HyRiM': multicriteria risk management using zero-sum games with vector-valued payoffs that are probability distributions, version 2.0.0 (2020). https://CRAN.R-project.org/package=HyRiM
47. Rass, S., Schauer, S., König, S., Zhu, Q.: Cyber-Security in Critical Infrastructures: A Game-Theoretic Approach. SpringerNature, Cham (2020)
48. Rass, S., Wiegele, A., König, S.: Security games over lexicographic orders. In: GameSec 2020. LNCS, vol. 12513, pp. 422–441. Springer, Cham (2020). https://doi.org/10.1007/978-3-030-64793-3_23
49. Rios Insua, D., Couce-Vieira, A., Rubio, J.A., Pieters, W., Labunets, K., G. Rasines, D.: An adversarial risk analysis framework for cybersecurity. Risk Anal. **41**, 16–36 (2019). https://doi.org/10.1111/risa.13331
50. Robert, C.P.: The Bayesian Choice. Springer, Cham (2001)
51. Schaberreiter, T., Kittilä, K., Halunen, K., Röning, J., Khadraoui, D.: Risk assessment in critical infrastructure security modelling based on dependency analysis. In: Bologna, S., Hämmerli, B., Gritzalis, D., Wolthusen, S. (eds.) CRITIS 2011. LNCS, vol. 6983, pp. 213–217. Springer, Heidelberg (2013). https://doi.org/10.1007/978-3-642-41476-3_20
52. Slovic, P., Fischhoff, B., Lichtenstein, S.: Rating the risks. In: Risk/Benefit Analysis in Water Resources Planning and Management, pp. 193–217. Springer, Boston (1981). https://doi.org/10.1007/978-1-4899-2168-0_17
53. Weiss, N., Schrötter, M., Hackenberg, R.: On threat analysis and risk estimation of automotive ransomware. In: ACM Computer Science in Cars Symposium on - CSCS 2019. pp. 1–9. ACM Press (2019). https://doi.org/10.1145/3359999.3360492, http://dl.acm.org/citation.cfm?doid=3359999.3360492
54. Zentralanstalt für Meteorologie und Geodynamik: Erdbeben in Österreich - Übersicht (2021). https://www.zamg.ac.at/cms/de/geophysik/erdbeben/erdbeben-in-oesterreich/uebersicht_neu

Use-Case Informed Task Analysis for Secure and Usable Design Solutions in Rail

Amna Altaf[1](✉), Shamal Faily[2], Huseyin Dogan[1], Alexios Mylonas[3], and Eylem Thron[4]

[1] Bournemouth University, Poole, UK
{aaltaf,hdogan}@bournemouth.ac.uk
[2] Robert Gordon University, Aberdeen, UK
s.faily@rgu.ac.uk
[3] University of Hertfordshire, Hatfield, UK
a.mylonas@herts.ac.uk
[4] CCD Design and Ergonomics Ltd., London, UK
eylem.thron@designbyccd.com

Abstract. Meeting secure and usable design goals needs the combined effort of safety, security and human factors experts. Human factors experts rely on a combination of cognitive and hierarchical task analysis techniques to support their work. We present an approach where use-case specifications are used to support task analysis, and human failure levels help identify design challenges leading to errors or mistakes. We illustrate this approach by prototyping the role of the European Railway Traffic Management System (ERTMS) - Signaller, which provides human factors experts a chance to work in collaboration with safety and security design experts.

Keywords: Use-case · Task analysis · Cognitive task analysis · Hierarchical task analysis · Human factors · Security-by-design

1 Introduction

Traditionally, the rail infrastructure is built around safety and human factors. However, as the rail information infrastructure becomes integrated with operational technology, especially with the implementation of European Railway Traffic Management System (ERTMS), new vulnerabilities are introduced leading to new threats that exploit them. As such attacks are directly or indirectly responsible for compromising safety, cyber security as well has become a new concern for rail safety engineers. This emphasises the growing need for achievement of usable security and safety for system efficiency within critical infrastructure of rail [19].

Security risks might originate from hidden vulnerabilities within design of system [5]. Integrated tools would help experts by considering and visualising security risks, safety hazards, and human failures - particularly as security mishaps can result from the latter [27]. These human failures stem from errors,

D. Percia David et al. (Eds.): CRITIS 2021, LNCS 13139, pp. 168–185, 2021.
https://doi.org/10.1007/978-3-030-93200-8_10

mistakes or lapses which are also the determining factors for human performance [23]. As such safety engineers, focus on identifying all potential hazards as a result of security risks and human failures [5].

The open-source Computer Aided Integration of Requirements and Information Security (CAIRIS) platform has previously been used in conjunction with Human Factors Analysis and Classification System (HFACS) to determine safety hazards and human factors issues [3]. This tool-support aids efficient and systematic analysis, leading to better design decisions. Human factors experts typically rely on Task Analysis (TA) as one of the many approaches for making design decisions based on human performance [1]. The application of appropriate TA tool to ensure automation and efficiency is crucial for design analysis that accounts for human factors.

In this paper, we present an approach where User Experience (UX) techniques are used to conduct TA with CAIRIS, using a combination of Cognitive Task Analysis (CTA) and Hierarchical Task Analysis (HTA). CTA identifies different types and values of cognitive reactions, which influence human performance during completion of tasks. HTA helps identify task dependencies and sequences as a hierarchy, where high-level use cases are refined into low-level use cases. Using the use-case specifications format, relevant cognitive reactions i.e., vigilance, situation awareness, workload, stress, and risk awareness, are scored and used to visualise HTA models. Different levels of human failures are then identified. By using use case exceptions and the HFACS framework, the use cases with highest level of human failures can be categorised and used to identify associated safety and security design solutions in the form of risk analysis. To demonstrate our approach, we have prototyped the role of Signaller using ERTMS.

The rest of the paper is structured as follows. Section 2 describes the related work and Sect. 3 describes our approach. Our approach is demonstrated by using ERTMS specifications in Sect. 4. This is followed by discussion and conclusion for future directions of our work in Sects. 5 and 6.

2   Related Work

2.1   Task Analysis Processes and Tools

Tasks are performed by users to achieve goals. These are assumptions made about the behavioural specifications of users involved and how they are supposed to interact with the system [14]. Task Analysis (TA) is used to determine the set of tasks to be performed by users under observation. The TA is conducted by identifying the task for analysis, determining the associated sub-tasks and writing a step-by-step narrative for sequence of actions to be performed [1].

There are two main types of TA: hierarchical and cognitive task analysis [14]. The Hierarchical Task Analysis (HTA) is conducted to determine the hierarchy of tasks by decomposing high-level into low-level tasks [11]. The Cognitive Task Analysis (CTA) focuses on the cognitive load put by tasks on users depending on their cognitive abilities [25]. The most notable techniques used for eliciting data for TA are: interviews, focus group discussions, surveys, workshops and questionnaires.

The decisions about design, training needs, human error analysis, stress and workload management are dependent on TA [15]. The human factors experts aim to identify human error sources for resolving human factors issues. As these human error sources are considered determining factors for risk and safety analysis during accident investigations [16]. A Training Needs Analysis (TNA) and mental workload behind tasks can also be used to identify the training gaps to train operators interacting with a system.

The TA approaches are used by human factors experts to identify the system design and engineering requirements. Software tools to support TA include Human Factors Workbench (HFW), Predictive Human Error Analysis (PHEA), and Performance Influencing Factors Analysis [16]. The Human Factors Risk Manager (HFRM) also supports risk scoring, failure modes, and the capture of error descriptions [16].

Table 1. Methods and tools for task analysis with applications

Task analysis method	Tool-support	Application
Hierarchical Task Analysis (HTA) [16]	Human Factors Risk Manager (HFRM), Human Factors Workbench (HFW)	Risk scoring, failure mode, error description
Cognitive Task Analysis (CTA) [29]	Applied Cognitive Task Analysis (ACTA)	Cognitive demand & skill, training recommendation, interface improvement
Ecological Task Analysis (ETA) [13]	–	Control theory, cognitive psychology
Operator Action Event Tree (OAET) [15]	Event tree (success & failure)	Human reliability assessment
Flow diagram [15]	Flow chart	Binary decision logic
Influence Modelling and Assessment System (IMAS) [15]	Cause-consequence model	Skills diagnostic, mental model
Critical Action and Decision Evaluation Technique (CADET) [15]	Critical Action or Decision (CAD)	Potential cognitive error, failure scenario

Computer Aided Software Engineering (CASE) tools and components are typically used for modelling, e.g. the Unified Modelling Language (UML), scenario-based design and Concur Task Trees (CTT) [14]. The UML pre-defined specification formats in the form of use cases are used to describe actor/s, specific conditions, steps and exceptions for TA, but is limited to data representation. CTT helps in the comprehension of hierarchical task breakdown, representation of activities using graphical syntax, and task allocation including attributes, but it lacks in understanding the cognitive attributes (i.e. mental workload) needed to complete tasks.

A brief summary of TA approaches and methodologies as supported by available software tools along with their applications is provided in Table 1. Different methods are appropriate for different applications. For example, CTA is applied for determining cognitive demand and skill, whereas HTA is more suitable for risk scoring and error description.

2.2 Evaluating Performance and Potential Human Error

The security of a system is directly or indirectly dependent on human interaction [34,36]. Thus, defining security as a socio-technical work system in progress, where humans are threat to the system. The human-centered security concerns include procedures to complete a task, authentication required in case of multiples systems, and the theft of physical systems (laptops, hard-drives etc.).

The Generic Error Modelling System (GEMS) is a reference model that accounts for the socio-technical nature of work [34]. The model explains the slips (failure to complete action), lapses (forgetting something) and mistakes (unintentional violation of rules) as *Active Failures* which are caused by humans. Violations made by humans are categorised as active failures. *Latent Failures* are explained as the resident pathogens; they are the insiders who made the breaches. The system defects inherited due to poor design, faulty maintenance and poor management decisions impose a great security and safety threat to system [5].

The cognitive attributes and models are used to identify the human factors concerns and issues, as this is one of the determining factors for human performance and reliability [23]. For instance, the study in [25] offers a practicable tool for determining the cognitive attributes responsible for human performance for critical infrastructure of rail.

Previous work defines *vigilance* as the ability to remain alert for a defined period of time. Memory, attention, visual information processing abilities, auditory and visual display are identified as vigilance increment factors, as compared to multi-tasking and reading texts which are vigilance decrement factors [2]. A decision-making process that allows a user to choose best option during a given scenario is termed as *situation awareness* [17]. During task operation, the critical thinking abilities combined with workload are necessary for better situation assessment [24]. Usually, the models for human performance tend to focus on cognitive aspects of *workload* rather than physical [6], where this cognitive attribute is dependent on skills, Human Machine Interface (HMI) design, rules and guidelines [25]. On the other hand, lack of control and fear of task failure are considered *stress* inducing factors [9]. In addition, the *risk awareness* is also considered as one of the cognitive attributes and this culture is promoted by expertise, technical abilities, better communication skills and knowledge [26].

Based on Reason's error taxonomy of cognitive, behavioural, personal and organizational factors, the Human Factors Analysis and Classification System (HFACS) framework represents four levels of failures and error sources [40]. HFACS has been used by critical infrastructure stakeholders to determine the human error sources behind accidents and incidents [41]. Human factors experts use this framework to investigate the accidents by identifying and classifying the human causes in the form of errors, mistakes or violations. Ultimately, it is the job of the system design to ensure safe acts, by making certain that there is no room for any human mistakes or errors.

2.3   Usable Security and Requirements Engineering

The threat to a system in an environment is usually caused by an attacker which is the human element responsible for compromising the security [36]. Therefore, the human factors approaches are necessary but not sufficient, and need specific usable security consideration. Security engineers now give importance to human dimension of system during design phases by considering the usability attributes during asset identification, threat scenario, misuse case, task duration, responsibility modelling etc. [21].

Therefore, the concept of effective information security revolves around the idea of HCI-security of the system. The HCI-security expertise takes the form of design principles and user-centered approaches for designing usable security [37]. In the following sub-sections, the secure and usable modelling techniques along with available tool-support options are discussed:

Assured Personas. The term *Personas* explains the archetypical behaviour of users. This is based on ground information collected from similar environments, where the user is expected to act [10]. According to [31], the system design can be understood from an assumptive perspective. For personas, the data sources and information obtained are backed up by imagining a variety of roles in which the personas are likely to be categorised [32].

In addition to roles, personas can also be supported by stories and scenarios. A better and refined system view can be obtained by generating personas within relevant narrative scenarios and real-life situations [30]. The story-based personas have better chances of explaining the user behaviours [32]. A persona built from a user-centered design approach has better chances of being used for various analysis purposes [21] for example, threat modelling and risk analysis.

The argumentation models within personas are based on Toulmin's model of argumentation, such that each characteristic is justified by one or more *grounds* that evidence the validity, *warrants* that act as inference rules connecting the grounds to the characteristic, and *rebuttals* that act as counterarguments for the characteristic. A model qualifier is also used to describe the confidence in the validity of the characteristic [39].

These argumentation models are used to act as the source of confirmation, for data sources used as document references for designing security approaches like roles and personas definition. The document references in the form of factoids (arguments) are elicited by carefully reading the data sources, which are used to do the affinity diagramming. For this purpose, a *Trello*[1] board can be used to organise the factoids into different groups. The assumption data is organised into clusters of similar characteristics in several sessions and discussions with relevant stakeholders.

---

[1] https://trello.com.

Use-Case. The inclusion of goal and responsibility in single structural format is represented as a use-case [8]. Usually, use-case is written in the form of scenario where an actor is associated with goal leading to fulfilment of responsibility. A general template comprises of use-case name, scope, level, pre and post conditions, actions, and other characteristics enabling to consider functional requirements and scope of project [7]. The traditional use-case approach is used to write narratives for misuse cases, for identifying security requirements [38]. However, the lack of appropriate principles and guidelines for writing a use-case, makes it an approach with open-end results and solutions.

KAOS Goal Modelling Language. Goal and task models can help the security engineers to better understand the system threat model. The Knowledge Acquisition in autOmated Specification (KAOS) is a method for analysing, specifying, and structuring goals required for a system [12]. The goals and tasks modelled using UML-class diagrams, may indicate security requirements that need to be fulfilled, along with possible obstacles that model obstructions to system goals.

IRIS and CAIRIS. The Integrating Requirements and Information Security (IRIS) process framework [20] was devised to understand how design concepts associated with security, usability, and software engineering could be aligned. It is complemented by the Computer Aided Integration of Requirements and Information Security (CAIRIS) platform. CAIRIS acts as an exemplar for tool-support to manage and analyse design data collected when applying an IRIS process. IRIS and CAIRIS have been used in several real-world case studies, including the development of security policies for critical infrastructure systems [22].

Vulnerabilities and threats contribute to potential risks, and threats are contingent on attacker's intent. This intent helps analysts identify the tasks and goals they carry out or exploit, which can help determine human factors issues in the form of human errors (active failures). Also, the roles present personas which help stakeholders to determine the task scenarios in more detail [3]. These task scenarios can be used by human factors engineers to inform hierarchical and cognitive task analysis which can predict the reliability of systems in different environments. Also, the identification of threats/vulnerabilities/risks (risk analysis) can be orthogonal to things like TA. Consequently, although not explicitly designed with safety in mind, IRIS provides a foundation for integrating security, safety and human factors.

3   Approach

We have devised an approach based on personas for task elicitation and use-case specifications informed Task Analysis (TA). The concepts associated within this approach are shown in UML class diagram in Fig. 1. The personas narrative elaborates the task performed by a role, which helps to identify tasks for analysis. Second, TA is conducted using a use-case specification pre-defined format.

Finally, for each use-case specification Cognitive Task Analysis (CTA) and Hierarchical Task Analysis (HTA) is performed. CTA is conducted by scoring relevant cognitive reactions. This leads to identification of different levels of human failures with the use of *Algorithm* 1. During HTA, associations between use cases are identified. After colour coding of the use cases, graphical models are generated based on *Algorithm* 2.

The use case models with specified level of human failures help security and safety engineers better make sense of the associated risk modelling and safety analysis elements, like vulnerabilities, threats and potential hazards. Use cases with the highest level of human failures are categorised using Human Factors Analysis and Classification System (HFACS) framework to inform specific human error sources.

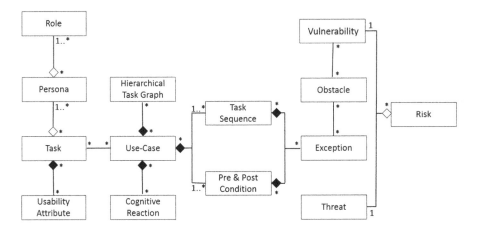

Fig. 1. Use-case specifications informed task analysis concepts

3.1   Personas for Task Elicitation

Personas are based on the Toulmin's Argumentation Models (Grounds, Warrants and Rebuttals), which aim at providing proper structure and assurance for qualitative data analysis [4]. This approach is automated by using tool-support at different stages, such as *Trello* board for organising factoids into clusters and CAIRIS for importing factoids and establishing persona characteristics by generating argumentations models [20]. Using these argumentation models, the personas characteristics are identified, and scenario-based narrative is written.

These personas narratives are used to elicit tasks for TA. After task elicitation, the relevant stakeholders are presented with organised information in rough tabular forms and their feedback is used to validate data for writing proper use-case specifications for conducting TA.

3.2   Use-Case Specifications Informed Task Analysis

TA is conducted for the elicited tasks. For this purpose, use-case specifications are used as data gathering, representation and analysis tool. Use cases allow both the user and functional characteristics of system to be presented, simultaneously.

As human factor engineers commonly use spreadsheets to support their workflow, we propose using Microsoft Excel (or a similar application) for managing TA data. We developed a script in Python to convert the spreadsheet data to the CAIRIS XML model format, so subsequent import into CAIRIS. A set of attributes are defined for the preparation of use-case specifications, including use case title, abbreviated title, use case id, actor/s, objective, pre and post condition/s, task sequence and exception/s. The choice for these attributes is based on two components of the system: *user* and *function*. These selected attributes simplify complexity, by making it easier for stakeholders to read, understand and analyse use cases. Finally, the use case specifications are presented to human factors experts for validation through feedback. Afterwards, these use case specifications are imported into CAIRIS.

3.3   Cognitive Task Analysis

Cognitive Task Analysis (CTA) is conducted to evaluate cognitive reactions against each use case. Previous work has shown that five cognitive reactions have an influence on human performance based on Performance Shaping Factors (PSFs), such as tiredness, emotional tension, skills, Human Machine Interface (HMI) design, rules, guidelines, and safety awareness [25]. Therefore, we use these following five cognitive reactions to evaluate human failures: i) vigilance, ii) situation awareness, iii) workload, iv) stress, and v) risk awareness. These are further described in Table 2.

Table 2. Cognitive reactions and performance shaping factors

Cognitive reaction	Performance shaping factors
Vigilance	Tiredness, emotional stress, tension and fatigue
Situation awareness	Skill-set of an individual and Human Machine Interface (HMI) design
Workload	Skills, HMI design, rules and guidelines
Stress	HMI design, rules and guidelines
Risk awareness	Safety awareness, rules and guidelines

For each use case, *Low, Medium, High or None* values are assigned to these cognitive reactions based on expert rationale. To collect the values and rationale, open-ended semi-structured interviews are held with relevant stakeholders. There is no mandatory list of questions, but the intent is to elicit knowledge through on open discussion. The stakeholders are presented with the proposed use case specifications, where they are asked to select different values for cognitive reactions, and document and justify their rationale.

Using values of cognitive reactions stored in CAIRIS, *Algorithm* 1 determines different levels of human failures. Each use case is taken as an input, and provides level of human failure for that specific use case as output. For each use case, *cognitive_reaction[n]* returns an array of 5 values of cognitive reactions where n ranges from 1 to 5. The values of *cognitive_reaction[n]* vary from *High, Medium, Low or Null*. The values are also associated with numbers such as, *(0 for Null, 1 for Low, 2 for Medium and 3 for High)*. The mean (ranging from 0 to 3) of these cognitive reactions is calculated to determine different levels of human failures. Mean is a suitable measure of central tendency, as median only points out the middle value while ignoring the individual value behind each cognitive reaction, and mode determines extreme values either too high or too low. There are three levels of human failures against mean, *0 or 1 for Low, 2 for Medium and 3 for High*, where *Low* being the use-case with less chances of human failure and *High* being the use-case with extreme chances of human failure.

Algorithm 1: Level of Human Failure for each Use-Case

Data: u - the use-case specification
Result: l - the level of human failure for u

1 **Function** *failurelevel(u)* **is**
2      $sum = 0$;
3   **for** $n \leftarrow 1$ *to* 5 **do**
4          $sum \mathrel{+}= cognitive\_reaction[n]$;
5      $mean \leftarrow \text{round}(sum/5)$;
6   **if** $mean <= 1$ **then**
7          $l \leftarrow$ Low;
8   break;
9   **if** $mean == 2$ **then**
10         $l \leftarrow$ Medium;
11   break;
12   **if** $mean == 3$ **then**
13         $l \leftarrow$ High;
14   break;

3.4 Hierarchical Task Analysis

The task hierarchy is drawn from the task sequences as stated in use case specifications. The high-level use cases and tasks are divided into low-level use cases and tasks, where each use case is filled in with a particular colour depending on level of human failure assigned to it. The colour mapping is *dark blue, blue and light blue* for *High, Medium and Low* level of human failure, respectively. Using these colour codes, the different levels of human failures are better illustrated with HTA graphs using *Algorithm* 2. These different levels of human failures highlight use cases and tasks requiring more attention by human factors, safety and security experts for design analysis.

The *Algorithm* 2 takes no input instead its output is a set of quadruples i.e., (h, h_fl, t, t_fl) in which h is the head task name, h_fl is the head task failure level, t is the tail task name, and t_fl is the tail task failure level. The empty sets are defined for the quadruples *hta*, and task node/failure level pairs *visited* while enumerating the set (lines 2 & 3). The *buildTaskGraph* is a function that generates a set of tuples from the CAIRIS model. Using this function, the algorithm retrieves a set of tuples (h, t) in which h is the head task name and t is the tail task name. Each tuple in *buildTaskGraph* is enumerated, if h intersects with the first element in visited set then the task node/failure level from the set is retrieved (lines 6 & 7), otherwise the *failurelevel* using *Algorithm* 1 is calculated for the task node and *union* of task node/failure level with *visited* set is done (lines 9 & 10). These steps are repeated for t (lines 12–17). Once we have tuples for h and t then quadruple is constructed by performing *union* with quadruple set *hta* (line 18). On completion of the algorithm, quadruple set is returned (line 20).

Algorithm 2: Build HTA Graph

    Input   : None
    Data: tg - set where each element is a tuple (h,t) in which h is the head task name and t is the tail task name, tt - tuple drawn from tg, $visited$ - set where each element is a tuple (t,fl) in which t is the task name, and fl is the task failure level, h_fl - tuple (h, fl) where h is the head task name and fl is the head task failure level, t_fl - tuple (t,fl) where t is the tail task name and fl is the tail task failure level.
    Output: hta - set where each element is quadruple (h, h_fl, t, t_fl) in which h is the head task name, h_fl is the head task failure level, t is the tail task name, and t_fl is the tail task failure level.

```
 1  Function buildHTAModel is
 2  │    hta ← ∅;
 3  │    visited ← ∅;
 4  │    tg ← buildTaskGraph;
 5  │    while tt ← tg do
 6  │    │    if tt[0] ∈ visited then
 7  │    │    │    (h, fl) ← visited tt[0];
 8  │    │    else
 9  │    │    │    (h, fl) ← failurelevel (tt[0]);
10  │    │    │    visited ← visited ∪ (h,fl);
11  │    │    end
12  │    │    if tt[1] ∈ visited then
13  │    │    │    (t,fl) ← visited tt[1];
14  │    │    else
15  │    │    │    (t,fl) ← failurelevel (tt[1]);
16  │    │    │    visited ← visited ∪ (t,fl);
17  │    │    end
18  │    │    hta ← hta ∪ (h, h_fl, t, t_fl);
19  │    end
20  │    return hta;
21  end
```

3.5 Risk Analysis

Within the use case specification, an exception is an undesirable situation where the task sequence is disturbed. The security and safety experts are given the opportunity to analyse exceptions in detail for the possibility of potential vulnerabilities, threats, risks and hazards during tasks within system. As with the exploitation of vulnerability, the risk of occurrence of threat may lead to catastrophic accident due to potential hazard. Therefore, by using the human factors approach of task analysis, the identified exceptions within use case specifications help to achieve safe and secure design solutions by risk analysis.

3.6   Implementation in CAIRIS

For demonstrate how this approach can be tool-supported, we have forked the GitHub repository of CAIRIS and implemented *Algorithm* 1 and 2. The forked GitHub repository is available at link: https://github.com/s5121191/cairis and can be reviewed for implementation details.

4   Preliminary Evaluation: Identifying Tasks for Human Error Potential

Due to technological advancements in rail infrastructure, many operational tasks are becoming more centred around mental (cognitive) abilities rather than physical. Following the deployment of the European Railway Traffic Management System (ERTMS), working relationships are more dependent than ever on team coordination capabilities. For example, the driver and signaller work in conjunction with each other to ensure safe and efficient operations. Mindful of this, we used the ERTMS specifications [35] to conduct a Task Analysis (TA) of the role of *Train Signaller*.[2] We have sketched a rough profile of *A Day in the Life of a Train Signaller*, which consisted of task breakdown in a time-line from 0030 to 2350 h.

Table 3. Documentation and Literature used for Train Signaller Personas

Ser.	Article title	Author	Publisher
1	A day in the life of a train - operational concept [18]	ERTMS	Operational Principles and Rules - Technical Document
2	Network Rail - signalling control centers [33]	Network Rail	Published and Issued by Network Rail - Module A5-5
3	Operational concept for the European Railway Traffic Management System [35]	Rail Safety and Standards Board	RSSB-ERTMS-OC Issue 2
4	Understanding railway signaller tasks and operations [28]	Ex-Signalman and Human Factors Consultant	Interview Notes

4.1   Personas for Task Elicitation

The ERTMS Operational Concept was used to develop an understanding of the job of Train Signaller. The open-source documentation and literature specified in Table 3 was used to ground our knowledge. We supplemented this knowledge by interviewing a number of other relevant rail stakeholders. A total of 4 interviews were conducted, one from human factors expert with focus on TA methodologies,

---

[2] The complete CAIRIS model of this analysis is available at https://github.com/s5121191/CRITIS-21.

one from safety engineer for potential hazard analysis using human-error sources and two from train signallers for collecting data about ERTMS signalling tasks performed in routine.

We defined models associated with the role of rail *Signaller*. From our knowledge base, we elicited 73 factoids, which grounded 11 argumentation models for the persona of a train signaller (*Daniel*). These argumentation models contributed towards the narrative of Daniel, explaining his activities, attitudes and aptitudes. Using personas narrative for *Daniel*, 16 major tasks were elicited for the role of train signaller. For example, the task of *Combine Workstation* is found from persona characteristic of activities for *Daniel* as shown by highlighted text.

*Daniel is performing the job of railway signaller. Daniel working from his signaller's workstation is responsible for monitoring and controlling train movements after **combining workstations**.*

These tasks were organised in rough tabular form and fed back to stakeholders for validation.

Use Case Title	Conflict Prediction and Resolution	
Abbreviated Title	Conflict and Resolution	
Use Case ID	UC_9	
Actors	Signaller	
Objective: User desires to predict capacity of traffic management of the ERTMS, using conflict and resolution functionality.		
Pre-Conditions: User points out failures indicated via alarm systems. For example, an over-crowded terminal station etc.		
Task Sequence: 1. Use case starts when user wants to predict operation conflicts. 2. User monitors centralised traffic control system. 3. User detects potential operation conflicts. 4. User suggests optimal scheduling strategies for delays and deviations from timetables. 5. Use case ends.		**Exceptions:** User fails to make timely predictions due to heavy work load and stress.
Post-Conditions: User provides advance plat-forming/ routing options to minimise delay using Automatic Route Setting (ARS).		

Fig. 2. Use-case specification for 'conflict prediction and resolution'

4.2 Use Case Specifications Informed Task Analysis

Use cases were identified and specified, using a pre-defined format. Using *Microsoft Excel*, points were scribbled down along-side data collection. This was an iterative process, where each use case specification went through series of transformations. There were three major parts for each use-case: actor (performing the task), steps (task sequence) and conditions (identifying constraints/ exceptions). After careful consideration, a total of 16 use case specifications were specified. For example, Fig. 2 specifies a use case for *Conflict Prediction and Resolution*. Following validation from stakeholders, these use case specifications were imported into CAIRIS.

4.3 Cognitive Task Analysis

After specifying the use cases, CTA was conducted by scoring each use case against cognitive reactions. For example, in the use-case of *Conflict Prediction and Resolution*, the values assigned were as follows: vigilance was *High*, situation awareness was *Medium*, workload was *High*, stress was *High* and risk awareness was *Medium*, with a defined rationale where *under manual control train movements or alterations in timetable may cause additional workload*. These values of cognitive reactions were fed into the *Algorithm* 1, where the mean was evaluated as *3*. This indicated that the *Conflict Prediction and Resolution* use case was associated with a *High* level of human failure.

Table 4. Cognitive task analysis for use-case specifications

Use-case ID	Use-case name	Vigilance	Situation awareness	Workload	Stress	Risk awareness	Level of human failure
UC-1	Combine workstation	Low	High	Medium	Null	High	Medium
UC-2	Grant possessions and isolation	Medium	Medium	Low	Null	Medium	Low
UC-3	Maintain operations Log	Low	Medium	Low	Low	Low	Low
UC-4	Ensure normal service delivery	Low	Medium	Medium	Low	Low	Low
UC-5	Monitor regulator intervention	Low	Low	Medium	Medium	Low	Low
UC-6	Conduct manual routing	High	Low	Medium	Low	High	Medium
UC-7	Plan stock positioning	Low	Low	Medium	Low	Low	Low
UC-8	Grant off-peak blockage	High	Medium	Medium	High	High	High
UC-9	Conflict predict and resolution	High	Medium	High	High	Medium	High
UC-10	Issue temporary timetable	Medium	Medium	Medium	Low	High	Medium
UC-11	Identify broken rail	High	Low	Low	Medium	Medium	Medium
UC-12	Test back-up facilities	Medium	Medium	Low	Low	Low	Low
UC-13	Map operational planning	High	Medium	Medium	Low	High	Medium
UC-14	Run route availability	High	High	Medium	High	Low	Medium
UC-15	Run sectional time	Low	Low	Low	Low	Low	Low
UC-16	Order of implementation	Medium	Medium	Low	Low	Low	Low

Consequently, the design analysis of this use case lead to situations where there is a strong tendency towards mistakes or errors. The different values of cognitive reactions for the use cases is shown in Table 4, together with with mean calculation from *Algorithm* 1.

4.4 Hierarchical Task Analysis

With the help of *Algorithm* 2, the colour coded HTA graph was generated with use cases of Low, Medium or High level of human failures, as shown in Fig. 3.

Here, in the HTA graph, 9 use cases and tasks can be seen impacting each other. Based on the full HTA graph, 3 use cases – *Combine Workstations, Grant Off-Peak Blockage* and *Conflict Prediction and Resolution* – correspond with *High* levels of human failure.

By conducting TA as a combination of CTA and HTA tools, the cognitive load on humans parallel to hierarchy of tasks is better understood. For example,the use case *Map Operational Planning* depends on *Run Route Availability* and *Run Sectional Time*, where cognitive reactions like *vigilance, situation awareness and workload* are important. This breakdown highlights tasks dependency and logic behind goals, whereas resources, time and expertise are evaluated using cognitive reactions. Both of equip human factors experts with sufficient knowledge when making design decisions.

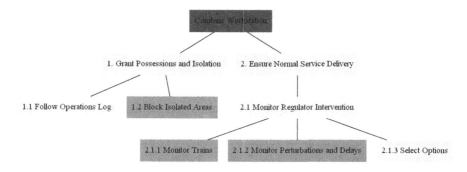

Fig. 3. HTA graph with levels of human failure

4.5   Risk Analysis

During the specification of *Conflict Prediction and Resolution*, an exception was identified where a user fails to make timely predictions due to heavy workload and stress. This might occur due to the vulnerability of *Lack of Independent Check*, where the user should update checklists with timely prediction data. This vulnerability affords two threats: *Delays during Routing* and *Operational Conflicts*. These threats contribute to the risk *Failure of Automatic Route Settings*, and this failure leads to hazard *Collision between Trains*, with severe consequences.

5   Discussion

The approach entails TA as the human factors technique for determining potential human error sources. These human error sources highlight possible security risk elements in the form of vulnerability, threat, risk and hazard. The intent and effort are recognised using CTA, where attributes like vigilance, situation awareness, workload, stress and risk awareness are contributing factors. However, the task and use case hierarchical breakdown using HTA contributes to an understanding the division of effort between these tasks.

This is an area where human factors experts can provide important feedback. When presented with human error sources behind tasks performed, they can benefit from a graphical visualisation to show the tasks requiring more attention. By collaborating with security and safety engineers, the potential hazards arising from these tasks are also visualised using threat modelling and risk analysis in CAIRIS. Here, CAIRIS developed the link between tasks identified for TA and vulnerabilities resulting from these tasks.

With the occurrence of exceptions, possible exploitation opportunities were identified. For example, in our case study, the major exceptions found in the use cases are *power failure, equipment failure, conflicts and delays, track circuit failure*, etc. These exceptions link to KAOS goal models, which give security and safety experts an idea about possible vulnerabilities leading to threats, risks and hazards (i.e. risk analysis). Similarly, the cognitive reactions defined against each use case could determine the potential human error sources using HFACS framework. Using HFACS, each use case with the highest level of human failure is labelled against the closest possible description of human error. For example, the use case *Conflict Prediction and Resolution* corresponds to a high level of human failure, where vigilance, workload and stress are important. Hence, the chances of occurrence of *Skill-based Error* and *Violation* are high, requiring scrutiny from human factors experts. Vigilance and workload may lead to the identification of *Decision Error*, but this is unlikely because this type of error results from a wrong judgement during emergency situations, rather than during routine operations.

6   Conclusion

In this paper, we present an approach where use cases drive TA for designing and evaluating safe and secure rail infrastructures. We catalogue the rail infrastructure for design analysis and, through a preliminary evaluation on regular tasks performed by an ERTMS Signaller, highlight human error sources behind these tasks. In doing so, we show how these human error sources contribute towards design solutions by identifying safety hazards and security risks.

In presenting our approach, we have made three contributions. First, we have derived a TA approach from the security and requirements engineering IRIS framework using concepts such as roles and personas, task and goal-obstacle modelling. Second, we have shown how CTA and HTA can be combined as single, tool-support TA approach to highlight the importance of mental load with a detailed task breakdown. Finally, we have shown how use case specifications assist with task sequencing and exception identification. These exceptions help security and safety experts to conduct risk and hazards analysis by identifying potential vulnerabilities and threats hidden beneath system design.

TA with CAIRIS as tool-support facilitates other kinds of analysis, including asset, goal-obstacle, responsibility, threat and risk modelling, and even hazard investigation using safety analysis techniques. Thus, by using this approach the human factors experts are given a chance to work in collaboration with security and safety experts to analyse and make collective design decisions in critical infrastructure. As future work, we build on our approach by integrating further human factor techniques and methods to further facilitate the design of safe, secure, and usable rail solutions.

Acknowledgements. The work described in this paper was funded by the BU studentship *Integrating Safety, Security, and Human Factors Engineering in Rail Infrastructure Design & Evaluation.* We are also grateful to Ricardo for their support.

References

1. Affairs, A.S.F.P.: Task Analysis, September 2013. /how-to-and-tools/methods/task-analysis.html
2. Al-Shargie, F., Tariq, U., Mir, H., Alawar, H., Babiloni, F., Al-Nashash, H.: Vigilance decrement and enhancement techniques: a review. Brain Sci. **9**(8), 178 (2019). https://doi.org/10.3390/brainsci9080178
3. Altaf, A., Faily, S., Dogan, H., Mylonas, A., Thron, E.: Identifying safety and human factors issues in rail using IRIS and CAIRIS. In: Katsikas, S., et al. (eds.) CyberICPS/SECPRE/SPOSE/ADIoT -2019. LNCS, vol. 11980, pp. 98–107. Springer, Cham (2020). https://doi.org/10.1007/978-3-030-42048-2_7
4. Atzeni, A., Cameroni, C., Faily, S., Lyle, J., Flechais, I.: Here's Johnny: a methodology for developing attacker personas. In: 2011 Sixth International Conference on Availability, Reliability and Security, Vienna, Austria, pp. 722–727. IEEE, August 2011. https://doi.org/10.1109/ARES.2011.115
5. Brostoff, S., Sasse, A.: Safe and sound: a safety-critical approach to security, p. 10 (2001)
6. Cao, S., Liu, Y.: Modelling workload in cognitive and concurrent tasks with time stress using an integrated cognitive architecture. Int. J. Hum. Factors Model. Simul. **5**, 113 (2015). https://doi.org/10.1504/IJHFMS.2015.075360
7. Cockburn, A.: Basic use case template vol. 8, no. 2, October 1998
8. Cockburn, A., Bank, N.: Structuring use cases with goals, December 1997
9. Conway, D., Dick, I., Li, Z., Wang, Y., Chen, F.: The effect of stress on cognitive load measurement. In: Kotzé, P., Marsden, G., Lindgaard, G., Wesson, J., Winckler, M. (eds.) INTERACT 2013. LNCS, vol. 8120, pp. 659–666. Springer, Heidelberg (2013). https://doi.org/10.1007/978-3-642-40498-6_58
10. Cooper, A.: The Inmates Are Running the Asylum. Macmillan Publishing Co., London (1999)
11. Crandall, B., Klein, G., Hoffman, R.R.: Working Minds: A Practitioner's Guide to Cognitive Task Analysis. MIT Press, Cambridge (2006)
12. Dardenne, A., van Lamsweerde, A., Fickas, S.: Goal-directed requirements acquisition. Sci. Comput. Program. **20**(1), 3–50 (1993). https://doi.org/10.1016/0167-6423(93)90021-G
13. Davis, W., Burton, A.: Ecological task analysis: translating movement behavior theory into practice. Adapt. Phys. Activ. Q. **8**, 154–177 (1991). https://doi.org/10.1123/apaq.8.2.154
14. Diaper, D., Stanton, N.: The Handbook of Task Analysis for Human-Computer Interaction. CRC Press, Mahwah (2004)
15. Embrey, D.: Task analysis techniques, p. 14 (2000)

16. Embrey, D.D., Zaed, S.: A set of computer based tools identifying and preventing human error in plant operations, p. 11 (2021)
17. Erbacher, R.F., Frincke, D.A., Wong, P.C., Moody, S., Fink, G.: A multi-phase network situational awareness cognitive task analysis. Inf. Vis. **9**(3), 204–219 (2012). https://doi.org/10.1057/ivs.2010.5
18. ERTMS: A day in the life of a train - operational concept, April 2019
19. European Network and Information Security Agency: Railway Cybersecurity: Security Measures in the Railway Transport Sector. Publications Office, LU (2020)
20. Faily, S.: Designing Usable and Secure Software with IRIS and CAIRIS. Springer, Cham (2018). https://doi.org/10.1007/978-3-319-75493-2
21. Faily, S., Fléchais, I.: Barry is not the weakest link: eliciting secure system requirements with personas, p. 8, September 2010
22. Faily, S., Flechais, I.: User-centered information security policy development in a Post-Stuxnet world. In: 2011 Sixth International Conference on Availability, Reliability and Security, Vienna, Austria, pp. 716–721. IEEE, August 2011. https://doi.org/10.1109/ARES.2011.111
23. Felice, F.D., Petrillo, A.: Methodological approach for performing human reliability and error analysis in railway transportation system. Int. J. Eng. Technol. **3**(5), 341–353 (2011)
24. Golightly, D., Balfe, N., Sharples, S., Lowe, E.: Measuring situation awareness in rail signaling. In: Rail Human Factors Around the World: Impacts on and of People for Successful Rail Operations, pp. 361–369, April 2009. https://doi.org/10.1201/b12742-43
25. Hammerl, M., Vanderhaegen, F.: Human factors in the railway system safety analysis process. In: 3rd International Rail Human Factors Conference, p. 9 (2009)
26. Jen, R.: How to increase risk awareness. In: PMI® Global Congress 2012. PA: Project Management Institute, Vancouver, British Columbia, Canada, North America (2012)
27. Jonsson, E., Olovsson, T.: On the integration of security and dependability in computer systems, p. 6 (1998)
28. Martin, K.: Understanding railway signaller tasks and operations, February 2020
29. Militello, L., Hutton, R.: Applied Cognitive Task Analysis (ACTA): a practitioner's toolkit for understanding cognitive task demands. Ergonomics **41**, 1618–41 (1998). https://doi.org/10.1080/001401398186108
30. Nielsen, L.: Personas - User Focused Design. Human–Computer Interaction Series. Springer, London (2013). https://doi.org/10.1007/978-1-4471-4084-9
31. Norman, D.: Emotional design: why we love (or hate) everyday things. J. Am. Cult. **27**(2), 234 (2004)
32. Pruitt, J., Grudin, J.: Personas: practice and theory. In: Proceedings of the 2003 Conference on Designing for User Experiences, DUX'03, pp. 1–15. ACM, New York (2003). https://doi.org/10.1145/997078.997089
33. Rail, N.: Network rail - signalling control centers, June 2018
34. Reason, J.: Human Error (1990). https://doi.org/10.1017/CBO9781139062367
35. RSSB: Operational Concept for ERTMS, June 2014
36. Schneier, B.: Secrets and Lies: Digital Security in a Networked World. Wiley, Hoboken (2000)
37. Shostack, A.: Threat Modeling: Designing for Security. Wiley, Indianapolis (2014)
38. Sindre, G., Opdahl, A.L.: Eliciting security requirements with misuse cases. Requir. Eng. **10**(1), 34–44 (2005). https://doi.org/10.1007/s00766-004-0194-4
39. Toulmin, S.E.: The Uses of Argument, p. 259 (2003)

40. Wiegmann, D.A., Shappell, S.A.: A Human Error Approach to Aviation Accident Analysis: The Human Factors Analysis and Classification System, 1 edn. Routledge, Aldershot, Burlington, July 2003
41. Zhou, J.L., Lei, Y.: Paths between latent and active errors: analysis of 407 railway accidents/incidents' causes in China. Saf. Sci. **110**, 47–58 (2018). https://doi.org/10.1016/j.ssci.2017.12.027

Studying Neutrality in Cyber-Space: a Comparative Geographical Analysis of Honeypot Responses

Martin Strohmeier[1(✉)], James Pavur[2(✉)], Ivan Martinovic[2], and Vincent Lenders[1]

[1] Armasuisse Science + Technology, Thun, Switzerland
{martin.strohmeier,vincent.lenders}@armasuisse.ch
[2] Department of Computer Science, University of Oxford, Oxford, UK
{james.pavur,ivan.martinovic}@cs.ox.ac.uk

Abstract. Neutrality has long played a central role in the political and strategic stances of many small states. The impact of neutrality on matters of national security and sovereignty have thus been subject to significant academic interest. With the recent emergence of cyber as a fifth dimension of interstate competition, the impact of permanent state neutrality in this domain has not yet been well characterized.

We examine the reality of this concept using countries with a long-standing history and tradition of neutrality in matters of warfare and foreign policy. A theoretical analysis of the complexities of neutrality and cyber-crime is used to motivate a novel data-driven experimental assessment of real-world outcomes for neutral states.

This experimental study leverages low-interaction honeypots distributed across 13 countries. Delving into more than 1.5 billion network sessions made from these honeypots over an 80-day period reveals more than one million malicious attacks originating from information systems in 177 different countries. Through statistical analysis of these attacks, we find little evidence that low-sophistication adversaries target their attacks with consideration of victim location or state neutrality. Beyond the immediate implications of these findings, we believe the method presented in this paper represents a unique data-driven approach to comparative international study of cyber-neutrality and the global dynamics of cyber-security more broadly.

Keywords: Cyber-neutrality · Cyber-sovereignty · Honeypots

1 Introduction

The strategic value of a national policy of neutrality in the modern era is an oft-debated topic. While much of this discussion has focused on conventional security and diplomatic practice, the intersection between cyber-space and state

---

M. Strohmeier and J. Pavur—Both authors contributed equally to this work.

D. Percia David et al. (Eds.): CRITIS 2021, LNCS 13139, pp. 186–203, 2021.
https://doi.org/10.1007/978-3-030-93200-8_11

neutrality is not well understood. Given that cyber-aggression often occurs far below traditional thresholds for interstate conflict, lacks reliable attribution, and exhibits aterritorial properties, it remains an open question as to whether small-state neutrality has any practical effect on a nation's overall information security.

A natural baseline assumption for this hypothesis on neutrality effects may be that low-effort actors are looking for attack infrastructure or opportunistic targets and, hence, agnostic preferences to location seem intuitive. This is clearly in contrast to high-sophistication attacks using zero-day knowledge against high-value targets, which are all but apolitical. However, practitioners have long noted clear preferences among even low-level cyber-crime actors and their customers to avoid certain locations and countries depending on geopolitical allegiances, enforced for example via policies [22] or by checking undesirable locale characteristics of the target platforms [23].

We examine the reality of this concept using the example of Switzerland, a country with a long-standing history and tradition of neutrality. A theoretical analysis of the complexities of neutrality and cyber-crime is used to motivate a data-driven experimental assessment of real-world outcomes for formally neutral states including Switzerland and Singapore.

This assessment consists of a large-scale comparative study using purpose-built low-interaction honeypot installations deployed in 13 countries. The resultant dataset encapsulates more than 1.5 billion connections over a period of about two months. Analyzing the more than one million malicious attacks found within this dataset shows that there is little difference in low-level cyber-attacker behavior with regards to target geography or stance on neutrality. These findings present broader insights into the effect that neutrality may have on exposure to transnational cyber-crime.

The remainder of this work is organised as follows. First, we briefly introduce the literature on the general topic of neutrality in Sect. 2, before moving on to its application in cyber-space. Section 4 covers both aspects for our case study of Switzerland. Section 5 introduces our experimental setup, which is followed by the results, discussion and conclusion.

2   Background and Related Work

The role and relevance of permanent neutrality is a complex topic which has been subject to centuries of debate and interpretation [1]. A complete analysis thus lies well beyond the scope of this research. Nevertheless, it is worth considering those aspects of traditional neutrality theory which are particularly relevant to cyber-defense.

In this paper, we define neutrality simply as a permanent and public legal position which eschews warfighting as an instrument of foreign policy. This is distinct from the related concepts of non-alignment, and neutralism - which relate to diplomatic practices in multipolar systems and ad-hoc decisions regarding particular conflicts [20]. This narrow definition implies certain obligations and constraints under international law not only for the neutral state, but also for belligerents [3, 20]. Often, neutrality in practice incorporates aspects of non-alignment and diplomatic restraint, but this is not treated as an absolute requirement.

In practice, only a handful of modern states meet this definition. Even within this subset, specific cases are complex. For example, membership in the European Union challenges the ultimate neutrality of states like Austria and Sweden. Similarly, some states have only recently declared neutrality, such as Ghana (in 2012), Mongolia (in 2015), and Rwanda (in 2009). In such instances, these stances may not have accrued meaningful credibility with belligerents.

Historically, territorial sovereignty has been a vital lens for determining the operation of state neutrality. For example, a neutral state invaded by foreign military forces has an absolute right to defend itself and would not lose its neutral status in doing so. On the other hand, an invasion by a neutral state into the territory of another state would jeopardize its status, at which point retaliation by both the invaded state and its allies would be justifiable [3]. These principles extend beyond direct military invasion into even non-violent activities. For example, a neutral state could not permit the establishment of a foreign military base within its borders or sell arms to conflict participants [3, 20]. In return, belligerent parties are obligated to respect the sovereignty of the neutral state by, for example, avoiding incursions into their territorial waters and airspace.

In practice, complex variations on neutrality principles have emerged. Often, these tensions result from changes to the nature of warfighting. For example, military technologies required for effective Cold War deterrence surpassed the production capabilities of most neutrals. In order to sustain armed neutrality, these states paradoxically had to compromise on some of its principles for access to arms. This dynamic ultimately leads to Swiss and Swedish adherence to US-led sanctions regimes in exchange for the ability to import radar systems and other military technologies [26]. Similar compromises may be required in the cyber-context for access to privileged threat intelligence or technical assistance.

Moreover, modern conflict now incorporates non-state actors whose obligations to permanent neutrals is unclear. Recently, Swiss courts ruled that a private Swiss citizen leading a Christian militia in Syria had nevertheless violated the national principle of neutrality [31]. Similar cases have involved Swiss nationals suspected of joining ISIL-affiliated insurgent groups [10]. States seeking to maintain neutrality may be legally obligated to prevent such instances [24]. Moreover, non-neutral states may have a reciprocal obligation to ensure that their own citizens respect the rights of neutrals. Ad-hoc neutrals already justify foreign military operations on the failure of states to exercise this control over domestic radicals. For permanent neutrals, acceptable recourse is less clear. The analogy to the cyber-criminal context is intuitive. Traditional neutrality norms provide little guidance on the degree to which states are obligated to prevent their own citizens from attacking information systems abroad. While it is clear that all states still have an obligation to prevent harm emanating from a state's territory due to the due diligence principle, the specific impact of neutrality on this concept in cyber-space remains unclear both in theory and in practice.

3   Dynamics of Neutrality in Cyber-Space

In short, the meaning of permanent neutrality is not static. Neutrality and its challenges have given rise to a long history of exception and revision. These redefinitions are often political and normative, but they originate in response to positive effects. For example, in the Cold War, neutrality's side effect of technological weakness motivated the political decision to accept sanctions-linked arms deals in Switzerland and Sweden. The focus of this paper is not to answer the normative question as to how neutral states should respond to international cyber-crime. Rather, it is to identify the impact that neutrality has on exposure to international cyber-crime. While it is intuitive that cyber-threats will pose new challenges to neutrality, the form these will take is less clear. In this section, we propose some prominent factors which may impact neutral state cyber-security. Broadly, we consider three possible reasons that neutrality may increase a state's vulnerability to international cyber-crime. These are the difficulty of deterrence by denial, political barriers to deterrence by punishment, and challenges in intelligence sharing and targeted regulation. For realists, permanent neutrality is credible only if backed by significant defensive military force. This is not a universally accepted viewpoint [12,17]. However, the link between neutrality and denial remains central to the professed foreign policy of many neutrals [6]. In the Swiss context, the combination of terrain, military spending, and mandatory conscription serve to dissuade territorial violations. It is not clear that Swiss efforts to defend domestic computer systems can achieve an equivalent effect. While effective denial is difficult in any domain, it is near insurmountable in cyber-space [5]. This suggests that credible armed neutrality in cyber-space cannot rest on the foundation of absolute defense. One alternative to deterrence by denial in cyber-space is the use of counterattacks and deterrence by punishment. States are increasingly asserting a legal right to retaliate in response to both state and non-state actors [21]. Even individual businesses have voiced interest in "hacking back" as a means to discourage cyber-criminal attacks [19,25]. This retaliation may occur in cyber-space, but also via conventional or diplomatic channels. However, many domain features of cyber-space, such as attribution difficulties and unclear proportionality metrics, complicate deterrence by punishment [21,33]. For permanent neutrals, deterrence by punishment is more complex. While neutrals have an indisputable right to self-defense, in conventional contexts designating a legitimate target or proportionate retaliation is much simpler than in cyber-space. Were a neutral to retaliate to a cyber-attack without absolute attribution and credibility, and especially if they were to do so via conventional means, it is unclear if the international community would view this as legitimate. Moreover, as indicated by aforementioned Swiss case law regarding private citizen involvement in the Syrian conflict, "hacking back" operations by corporate entities may similarly threaten the credibility of the state's neutrality [31]. These dynamics may embolden adversaries, and, to the extent that deterrence by punishment works, neutrals may be unwilling or unable to avail themselves of its benefits. A third constraint for neutrals in cyber-space is political non-alignment. While not a definitional requirement, permanent neutrality frequently comes with some degree of non-alignment in foreign policy. This may impair certain functions of cyber-defense, such as reducing political willingness to engage in foreign intelligence collection [44]. Similarly, absent membership in collective security bodies (e.g. NATO) or alliances with major intelligence powers, access to shared cyber-threat intelligence may be limited. Finally, non-alignment may limit the defensive options available to a state. For example, several states have decided for a mix of political and technical reasons, to ban the use of 5G networking equipment from the Chinese telecommunications company Huawei [15]. Putting aside the specific merits of this action, it is unclear if political neutrals could engage in similar targeted trade actions without threatening the credibility of their overall non-alignment. Even with these constraints, state neutrality may nevertheless decrease exposure to international cyber-crime. We present three reasons that this might be the case. First, neutral states may make less attractive targets. Second, they may focus more effectively on defensive technologies. And third, neutral states may benefit from greater judicial reach in criminal prosecutions. While realists contend that neutrality is only as credible as the army which supports it, neutrality may impart strong cultural and political norms that insulate permanent neutrals from external threats. For example, neutral states often act as mediator in disputes between belligerents, accruing diplomatic capital and insulation from both sides of conflicts [27]. This mediator position may even bolster neutral states access to threat intelligence beyond that which is available within any single alignment-bloc [44]. The strong legal norms around neutrality may further disincentivize state-sponsored cyber-crime. Even non-state actors may be affected by the intangible "soft power" effects of permanent neutrality - especially those adversaries motivated by political objectives. Indeed, the long-standing reputation of Swiss neutrality has been characterized as a one of myriad factors potentially explaining the relatively low incidence of international terrorism within Swiss borders [43]. The realist requirement of credible self-defense is also not necessarily impossible for a neutral state. While defense is challenging in cyber-space, absolute defense is not always required. Criminals seek out the path of least resistance and having even marginally better security than peer states can discourage many attacks. As permanent neutrals have historically prioritized defensive military technology, policymakers may find significant investment in defensive cyber-technology more palatable. Indeed, as the role of great-power militaries shifts back towards territorial disputes rather than crisis management, this neutral advantage has been observed in conventional domains. Permanent neutrals are finding their relative expertise from focused investment in modern territorial defense much sought-after on the international stage [27]. Paradoxically, the very constraints imposed by permanent neutrality may be what enables effective focus on cyber-defense. Finally, in the context of transnational cyber-crime, neutral states may be better able to dissuade attacks with the threat of judicial punishment. One of the principle challenges in combatting cyber-crime is limited avenues for extradition and prosecution of foreign nationals [29]. Often, willingness to cooperate in transnational cases hinges on broader diplomatic relations between two states. In the case of a permanent neutral, these relations are less likely to be hostile. Of course, international extradition is a complex legal topic and difficult to generalize. However, in the Swiss case, law enforcement authorities have had limited success with extraditions to and from a wide array of countries crossing political and strategic blocs [4,38]. As case law develops, neutrals may find a deterrence effect from greater judicial reach in transnational cyber-criminal prosecutions. Of course, it may also be the case that state neutrality has little to no effect on exposure to international cyber-crime. Cyber-criminals may not be aware of, or concerned with, the political stances of the countries they target. Far from a banal observation, this outcome would raise critical questions for the behavior of neutral states. If the appearance of neutrality in cyber-space, for example, did not cause any damage to the nation's defensive capabilities but bolstered the overall credibility of its neutrality, policymakers may prioritize actions which preserve this appearance. Conversely, if neutrality offers little benefit, but imposes costs on other functions, policymakers may decide that the appearance of neutrality in cyber-space is not an important priority. This brief analysis suggests that theoretical reasoning alone is unlikely to reveal clear answers as to the effect permanent neutrality has on state exposure to transnational cyber-crime. While we have suggested several factors for consideration, these represent only a small portion of the myriad challenges at the intersection of cyber-space and neutrality, many of which are well characterized elsewhere [14,16,42]. To bring new information to this debate, the remainder of this paper presents a comparative experimental case-study looking at data from real-world transnational cyber-attacks with a focus on the impact of Swiss neutrality.

4   Switzerland and Cyber-Sovereignty: A Brief Review

In the following, we will briefly review the public discussion around the topics of cyber-defense, cyber-sovereignty and neutrality in Switzerland. As acknowledged by most Swiss citizens and academic onlookers (e.g., [36,37]), the Swiss stance on neutrality is both a key operating principle in Swiss diplomacy and holds a significant place in the country's identity. Paired with Swiss direct democracy, any development that has the potential to touch upon this neutrality can spark major debate within the legislature, media and the general public.

4.1   the Swiss Notion of Neutrality

Stolz [36] provides a brief history of neutrality in the Swiss context, which in the eyes of some historians reaches as far back as 1515. In the following 300 years, the states, which made up the Swiss confederation managed to avoid armed conflicts outside Swiss territory. As discussed by Suter [37], this state of affairs was made permanent after the events of the Vienna Congress and the Treaty of Paris in 1815. Switzerland's geographic placement at the heart of Europe and the interests of the European Great Powers at the time manifested this situation for the following centuries. Over time, in particular in the lead up towards the World Wars, the notion of neutrality in Switzerland changed towards a concept of "armed neutrality", whereby a substantial army is required in lieu of strong alliances to successfully deter attacks and preserve territorial integrity. While Swiss neutrality in World War 2 is sometimes viewed as far from perfect as secret consultations and forced economic collaborations happened [36], it is held that the concept is in part responsible for the relative peace Switzerland enjoyed during this time [37]. After World War 2, Switzerland continued on this path, notably forgoing UN membership during the Cold War (and until 2002) and not participating in economic sanctions. More recently, there has been the development of a notion of "active neutrality", whereby the Switzerland of the 21st century acts as a trusted broker and mediator between parties and countries, building on its credible image of impartiality. A vast majority of Swiss citizens supports the policy of neutrality, ensuring that its implementation will continue for the foreseeable future [36].

4.2 The National Strategy for the Protection of Switzerland Against Cyber-Risks

In 2018, the Federal Council of Switzerland published the second version of its National Strategy for the protection of Switzerland against Cyber-Risks (NCS) [39]. This document discusses at a high level the Swiss strategy to "secure and expand welfare [..] for the long term" in the face of digitalization. It takes into account several threat actors, including state actors, which are considered in the areas of cyber-espionage, cyber-sabotage or disinformation and propaganda. Beyond these, the NCS discusses the possibility of cyber-attacks in conflicts, which are acts just short of an all-out cyber war between state actors. Here, it is clearly stated that "Switzerland must therefore include cyber-defense and cyber-diplomacy in its preparations for potential conflict" [39]. In light of this, it is notable that there is explicitly no reference towards neutrality, neither in this context nor in the complete NCS document. It remains speculative whether this is intentional and a direct instantiation of "active neutrality" applied in cyber-space or instead a reflection of the fact that Switzerland's official position on neutrality is still in its infancy when it comes to non-conventional diplomacy. In April 2021, the Swiss Department of Defense announced the continued implementation of the NCS with regards to cyber-defense, the Cyber-Strategy for 2021–2024 [7]. In it, the concept of neutrality is not mentioned specifically, however it is noted that Switzerland has not been a target of attacks on its critical infrastructures yet. Potentially in light of political reality including neutrality, the Cyber-Strategy regards collateral damage as more likely than direct attacks targeting Swiss infrastructure specifically.

4.3   Early Public Debate on Cyber-Sovereignty in Switzerland

While the public debate around the topics of cyber-neutrality and cyber-sovereignty is in very early stages, there have been several events that have shaped the discussion in the past two years. The main discussion on this topic happened around Switzerland's accession as a contributing nation to the NATO Cooperative Cyber-Defence Centre of Excellence in 2018. In acknowledgment of the sensitivity of both engaging with a NATO-led centre of excellence in general and the cooperation with other states on cyber-defense in particular, the Swiss Federal Council argues that cooperation with the CCDCOE is non-problematic with regards the legal and political dimensions of Swiss neutrality [40]. More concretely, it is stated that the CCDCOE was not part of NATO's chain of command nor that it had an operational mandate. No rights or duties under international law could further be derived from participation and the scope of participation remains firmly in Switzerland's hands. This cautious stance has been reflected in Swiss media reports, for example regarding the visit of the 13th Secretary General of NATO, Jens Stoltenberg in 2017 or in the preceding process about participation in the Locked Shields exercise. Here, commentators note the difficult relationship of Switzerland and NATO but that cooperation in the cyber-domain could possibly be strengthened further [28]. Besides the application of the Swiss notion of neutrality towards cyber-space, the concept of "cyber-sovereignty" has seen increased uptake in Swiss government circles. The Federal Council's delegate for Cyber-Security stated that Switzerland must consider focusing on "security, education and neutrality" in order to be successful in the digital world, which would include an increase in security start-ups to protect Swiss ability to act in cyber-space [18,28]. Likewise, the head of the Federal IT Steering Unit considers a retreat towards the national arena an infeasible position, but that well-chosen international cooperation is required, which in turn needs to be adaptive to the situation [32]. The Swiss Federal Council's formal point of view on questions of international law and cyber-space is strongly informed by the Tallinn Manual [34]. In a parliamentary statement, the Department of Foreign Affairs takes the position that neutrality is a fundamentally applicable concept in cyber-conflicts. It is further stated that, while Swiss military law allows offensive responses against any networks where attacks originate from, this requires approval by the Federal Council and needs to be both permissible under international law and compatible with Switzerland's neutrality [8]. More recently, academics have begun considering the issue of Swiss neutrality specifically on cyber-operations. Stolz discusses a major challenge in this area, the "clash between national interest and the self-restrictions of neutrality" [36]. Among other points, this dichotomy affects the national capacity of cyber-defense, which requires strong international collaboration and knowledge exchange, which is potentially at odds with the requirements of traditional neutrality.

Indeed, despite its state neutrality, Switzerland is not only a member of the CCDCOE but has been a founding member of Interpol, is party to the Council of Europe's Budapest Convention on Cybercrime, and even an active member of the Joint Cybercrime Action Taskforce (J-CAT) within Europol's European Cybercrime Centre (EC3). Finally, it is clear that both public opinion and government policy are constantly developing under the impression of current events.

5   Design of a Cyber-Neutrality Experiment

We will now describe the experimental design that we chose in order to test whether neutrality has an impact on largely automated attacks in modern cyberspace. First, we discuss the concept of Honeynet, a system developed to measure the number of attacks an ordinary Internet end point has to endure. Then we elaborate on the global deployment and distribution of Honeynet installations used to study neutrality's effects and the processing of the collected data.

5.1   Honeynet

Honeynet is a Docker-based collection of technologies that mimic the appearance of common, potentially insecure, web services. In this experimental scenario, Honeynet was configured to appear like an IoT device to attackers and simulate realistic targets for both automated and human cyber-attacks. Concretely, this involved deploying the embedded Linux toolkit BusyBox on each honeypot instance. The main attractive feature for potential attackers of our low-interaction honeypot is a telnet client with weak default credentials. Through exploiting this weakness, it is possible to enter the server and install software of the attacker's choosing. To enable good internet citizenship, all honeypot Docker-images were wiped and redeployed every 3 min, at which point the collected network data was transferred and stored at a central processing server in Switzerland in the free and open PCAP format. This was done to prevent any potential of real exploitation by attackers and misuse of the servers against further targets. This approach also ensures that all attempted connections were principally conducted by automated bots looking for easy targets.

5.2   Deployment

Our Honeynet sensors were deployed in 13 different countries around the globe. Besides Switzerland, four were deployed in Western Europe, three each in North America and Asia, two in Eastern Europe and one in the Middle East. Table 1 illustrates the deployment in more detail.

We deployed our Docker-based images on virtual machines (VMs) running Debian 8, 9 and 10. There are several notable insights to be reported from our deployment experiences. First, there is a notable absence of South America, Sub-Saharan Africa, and China. Throughout these regions, there are often stronger identification requirements for renting VMs. Proof of passport and residency requirements made it infeasible to deploy Honeynet in these regions for our initial study, but a more concerted effort in future work may prove beneficial.

Table 1. Deployment of the Honeynet test environment.

City	Country	Region	OS	IP4 range
Amsterdam	Netherlands	Western Europe	Debian 10	142.93.*
Bangalore	India	Asia	Debian 10	165.22.*
Chişinău	Moldova	Eastern Europe	Debian 9	192.121.*
Frankfurt	Germany	Western Europe	Debian 10	206.189.*
Gravelines	France	Western Europe	Debian 10	137.74.*
London	United Kingdom	Western Europe	Debian 10	134.209.*
New York	United States	North America	Debian 10	165.227.*
San Francisco	United States	North America	Debian 10	157.230.*
Singapore	Singapore	Asia	Debian 10	134.209.*
St. Petersburg	Russia	Eastern Europe	Debian 9	213.183.*
Tel Aviv	Israel	Middle East	Debian 9	193.182.*
Thun	Switzerland	Western Europe	Debian 10	194.209.*
Tokyo	Japan	Asia	Debian 9	194.68.*
Toronto	Canada	North America	Debian 10	68.183.*

The second notable event was the attempt to deploy Honeynet on a commercial provider in Switzerland itself. Within a short time frame, MELANI, the Swiss government's reporting and analysis centre for information assurance, contacted the provider we utilized about the deployed server and the appearance of the IP address in international botnet structures. Thus, to not affect our study, we informed MELANI about our experiments. No other provider/country notified us about any similar issues.

5.3   Comparative Traffic Analysis

In total, the honeypots observed around 300 GB of unsolicited traffic from more than 1.5 billion sessions over an 80-day period. The open source tool Arkime (previously Moloch) was used to identify sessions and extract metadata from this traffic [2]. However, not all unsolicited internet connections are necessarily malicious. For example, many legitimate services perform whole-internet scans of active hosts for the purpose of research. To extract the most relevant data, we employed the Suricata network monitoring engine and several heuristic and signature-based intrusion detection rules to tag malicious traffic [9,11,30,41]. This process enabled us to identify approximately 1.1 million malicious sessions originating from more than 100,000 unique attacker IP addresses in 177 countries. For those countries with multiple honeypots in the study, a random sample of data was taken in proportion to the total number of alerts observed. It is worth noting that attacker IP address does not provide a perfect indication of attacker location. Attackers may choose to purchase overseas cloud services or compromise vulnerable computers anywhere from which they can launch subsequent attacks. Nevertheless, servers located in a particular region may still demonstrate geographic effects either due to preference from local attackers or regulatory differences which impact attacker capabilities.

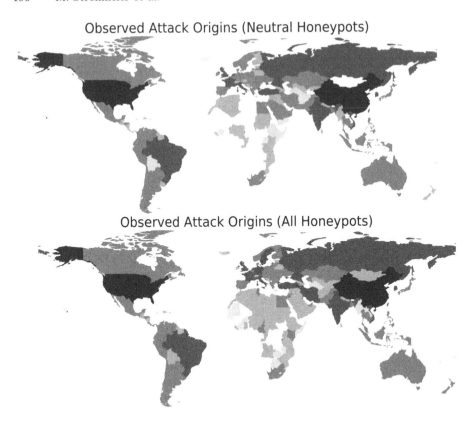

Fig. 1. Comparative mappings of observed attacker origins.

6   Results

Across all honeypots, the distribution of attacker origins was roughly the same, suggesting that observed attacks were largely automated and agnostic to target location. The United States and China represented the principle locations associated with attacker IP address, accounting for roughly half of all observed attacks (Fig. 1). At a macro level, only slight differences could be observed between the distribution of attackers targeting honeypots in the three formally neutral countries (Switzerland, Singapore, and Moldova) compared to the non-neutral honeypots (Fig. 2).

A clearer sense of the relationship between attack quantity and geography can be achieved through correspondence analysis (Fig. 3). The correspondence analysis was implemented using the open-source Python factor analysis library Prince [13]. In Fig. 3, the distance between points on the chart is representative of the chi-squared distances between rows in the normalized contingency table associating attacker country to honeypot country. As a result, proximity between labels in the same dimension (e.g. attacker countries) suggests similarity in observations. Points which are further from the origin are generally more

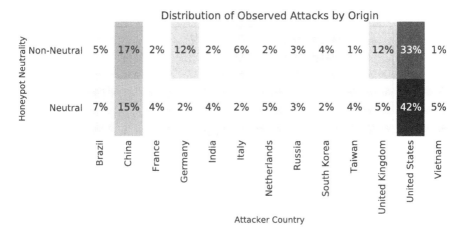

Fig. 2. Comparative distribution of attack origins in neutral vs. non-neutral countries for most observed attackers.

discriminating/distinct from those which are closer. In this case, the sum of the inertia values for components 0 and 1 is high (89.97) suggesting that the correspondence analysis captures much of the variance in observed frequencies. See [35] for more information on interpreting correspondence analysis.

The clustering suggests that attackers from certain countries (e.g. China, Iran, and Russia) are relatively similar in terms of the honeypots which they targeted, while attackers from other countries (e.g. the United States and Vietnam) selected targets quite differently. Likewise, observed attackers for the Russian, Swiss, French, Israeli and Moldovan honeypots were similar, as were the origins for the cluster containing Canadian, British, and Dutch honeypots. More broadly, this analysis suggests that many attackers (those in the cluster towards the lower-left quadrant of Fig. 3), behave similarly regardless of origin IP.

By calculating the uncertainty coefficient on a random sample of 500,000 observations from those attack origins which constituted a meaningful proportion of observed traffic (>0.1%), it is possible to better determine the strength of these relationships (Fig. 4). This suggests that, while a bi-directional association between attacker origin and honeypot location exists, this association is quite weak ($U_1 = 0.17$ & $U_2 = 0.13$). The uncertainty coefficient, or Thiel's U, presented in Fig. 4 is a measure of nominal association between two variables observed in our dataset. The value ranges from 0 (indicating no association) to 1 (indicating perfect association). For this paper, we consider values above 0.2 as moderately associated and values above 0.5 as highly associated. Unlike other metrics (e.g. Cramer's V), this value is asymmetric. So, for example knowing the attacker_country provides a very high degree of information as to the attacker_language ($U = 1$). However, knowing the *attacker_language* provides a slightly less (but still significant) degree of information as to the attacker_country ($U = 0.8$). This makes sense as each country is keyed as having only one dominant language in our dataset, but many countries may share the same dominant language.

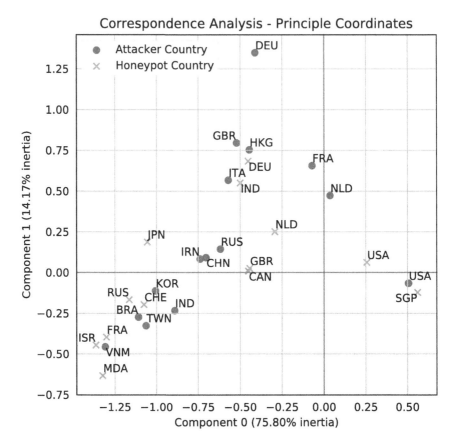

Fig. 3. Correspondence analysis of the contingency table associating attacker country to honeypot country frequencies.

A moderate association between attacker origin and state neutrality is observed but the inverse association is almost non-existent ($U_1 = 0.20$ & $U_2 = 0.06$). That is, knowing a state is neutral does not provide much information about where its attackers come from, but knowing the origin of attackers may provide information as to whether they attack the neutral honeypots. This suggests that only a subset of attackers consider state neutrality (or some unconsidered third factor) in determining. Given the small number of neutral states both in our dataset (and globally) it is possible that a portion of this effect may be explained by the more general weak association between attackers and targeted countries.

It is also worth considering the dynamics involved in specific attack types. Here we find that the specific Suricata signature detected demonstrates a moderate degree of association with the target geography ($U_1 = 0.26$ & $U_2 = 0.16$). A similar association is observed for neutral honeypots, but it is difficult to distinguish these two relationships. This suggests that attackers demonstrate a slight

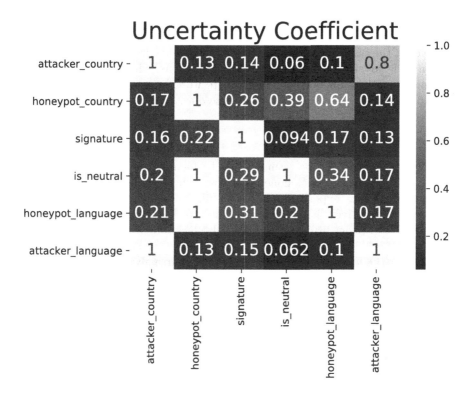

Fig. 4. Uncertainty coefficients.

preference for certain attack types depending on their own locations and the IP of their targets.

While the focus of this analysis is state neutrality, the method may prove useful for understanding other policy interactions with cyber-attack activity. For example, we found no correlation between attacker GDP per capita and the quantity of attacks ($\rho = 0.12$), a potentially surprising outcome as one might expect strong relationships between GDP per capita and availability of IT infrastructure from which to launch attacks. Inversely, honeypots in relatively wealthy countries were not significantly more likely to experience cyber-attacks ($\rho = 0.19$). Deeper research, especially with honeypots in the developing world, may bolster these insights.

7 Discussion

Reflecting on our experimental analysis, we find little evidence that low-level cyber-criminals using largely automated attacks have meaningful sensitivity to the national policies of their victim's countries - much less to national policies on neutrality. Indeed, the experimental data collected in this study most clearly supports the case that attackers are unaware or unconcerned with the geographic location of their targets altogether.

However, the case presented here is a simplified and cursory look at a complex problem and our methodology has several limitations, which we discuss in the following. We follow up by suggesting future work based on our methodology that can potentially shed more light on these questions.

7.1   Limitations

Most importantly, it must be assumed that by focusing on network traffic from attacks against generic telnet honeypots hosted by commercial virtual private server providers, this experimental data is inherently biased towards low-level threat actors. Intuitively it makes sense that attacks which are rudimentary in their means (e.g. telnet brute-force logins) also lack finesse with respect to their targeting.

While not the focus of this paper, there is of course always significant doubt about the true origin of an attacker. Attribution in cyber-space is hard and compromised machines similar to honeypots are typically used as a jump host for further attacks in order to obscure the true origin (not to mention the options of Tor, proxies or virtual private networks).

Finally, we appreciate that state neutrality as technically defined by international law applies to traditional armed conflict. With Cyber being defined as the 5th domain of warfare nowadays, this definition is notionally being broadened. More importantly, however, location preferences along the lines of state allegiances are commonly seen in the wild. One example is given by Brian Krebs, who cites a malware developer forbidding use of their ransomware tool against targets in the Commonwealth of Independent States (CIS) [22].

7.2   Future Work

Future work would benefit from increasing the study size on all dimensions. Of particular value would be geographical broadening to include non-represented countries (which may require the circumvention of several restrictions on overseas VM deployment) and an increased sample of neutral states. Additionally, a multi-year time horizon could provide deeper insights into the relationships considered here and related dynamics tied to political and economic changes. Addressing the issue of low-level threat actors would require much greater technical and logistical effort in future work. Sophisticated high-interaction, dynamic deception honeypots targeted at advanced persistent threats could show lateral movements of human (rather than automated) attackers and their targeting priorities for sensitive data and systems. This would provide clearer insights into the approaches of nation state actors towards neutral states in cyber-space. As such attacks are rarer than the threats considered in this paper, finding relevant activity at statistically meaningful scale would require a coordinated long-term effort. In the short term, it may be more effective to supplement the method presented here with a comprehensive data analysis of global attack reports describing the signatures of complex advanced persistent threats, such as Stuxnet.

8   Conclusion

For many countries, formal neutrality has defined their approach to diplomacy and warfare. Whereas a long history informs our understanding of neutrality's dynamics on land, air and sea, the picture is much less clear for emergent domains like cyber-space. In the process of developing an understanding of the links between state neutrality and transnational cyber-crime, this work also presents a novel experimental approach for testing general hypothesis at the intersection of cyber-space and national policy. By monitoring more than 1.5 billion connections to a research honeypot network spanning 13 countries over a two-month period, we isolated more than a million malicious cyber-attacks from more than 177 counties. Statistical analysis of this dataset suggests that low-sophistication attackers take little stock in victim state neutrality or geography more generally when executing their attacks. While this finding raises significant questions for policymakers seeking to deter cyber-attacks through political and legal means, it also suggests avenues for future experimental research considering more sophisticated cyber-attack dynamics.

Acknowledgments. The authors want to thank Dr. Luca Gambazzi for his invaluable support.

The views and opinions expressed in this article are those of the authors and do not necessarily reflect the official policy or position of any agency of the Swiss government.

References

1. Agius, C., Devine, K.: 'Neutrality: a really dead concept?' A reprise. Coop. Conflict **46**(3), 265–284 (2011)
2. Arkime: Arkime, April 2021. https://github.com/arkime/arkime
3. Bothe, M.: Neutrality, concept and general rules. Max Planck Encyclopedia of Public International Law (2011). http://opil.ouplaw.com/view/10.1093/law:epil/9780199231690/law-9780199231690-e349
4. Bradley, S.: Swiss back extradition with assurances. Swissinfo, January 2008. https://www.swissinfo.ch/eng/swiss-back-extradition-with-assurances/6376598
5. Brantly, A.F.: The cyber deterrence problem. In: 2018 10th International Conference on Cyber Conflict (CyCon), pp. 31–54. IEEE (2018)
6. Dalsjö, R.: 5 Sweden and its deterrence deficit. In: Deterring Russia in Europe: Defence Strategies for Neighbouring States, p. 2010 (2018)
7. Federal Department of Defence, Civil Protection and Sport: Strategie cyber VBS (2021). https://www.vbs.admin.ch/de/verteidigung/schutz-vor-cyber-angriffen.html
8. Dobler, M.: Interpellation 18.3335: cyberespace et droit international, March 2019. https://www.parlament.ch/en/ratsbetrieb/suche-curia-vista/geschaeft?AffairId=20183335

9. Open Information Security Foundation: Suricata, April 2021. https://suricata-ids.org

10. Glaus, D., Vidino, L.: Swiss foreign fighters active in Syria. CTC Sentinel **7**(7), 8–11 (2014)

11. Green, T.: Tgreen/hunting ruleset, April 2021. https://github.com/travisbgreen/hunting-rules

12. Guo, Y., Woo, J.J.: Singapore and Switzerland: Secrets to Small State Success. World Scientific, Singapore (2016)

13. Halford, M.: Prince, April 2021. https://github.com/MaxHalford/prince

14. Healey, J.: When "not my problem" isn't enough: political neutrality and national responsibility in cyber conflict. In: 2012 4th International Conference on Cyber Conflict (CYCON 2012), pp. 1–13. IEEE (2012)

15. Inkster, N.: The Huawei affair and China's technology ambitions. Survival **61**(1), 105–111 (2019)

16. Jensen, E.T.: Sovereignty and neutrality in cyber conflict. Fordham Int. Law J. **35**, 815 (2011)

17. Jesse, N.G.: Choosing to go it alone: Irish neutrality in theoretical and comparative perspective. Int. Polit. Sci. Rev. **27**(1), 7–28 (2006)

18. Kaat, C.: Mr. cyber sagt, warum die schweiz mehr security-start-ups braucht. Netzwoche, October 2019. https://www.netzwoche.ch/storys/2019-10-14/mr-cyber-sagt-warum-die-schweiz-mehr-security-start-ups-braucht

19. Kallberg, J.: A right to cybercounter strikes: the risks of legalizing hack backs. IT Prof. **17**(1), 30–35 (2015)

20. Karsh, E.: Neutrality and Small States. Routledge, London (2012)

21. Kesan, J.P., Hayes, C.M.: Mitigative counterstriking: self-defense and deterrence in cyberspace. Harv. J. Law Technol. **25**, 429 (2011)

22. Krebs, B.: Is 'REvil' the New GandCrab Ransomware? July 2019. https://krebsonsecurity.com/2019/07/is-revil-the-new-gandcrab-ransomware/

23. Krebs, B.: Try This One Weird Trick Russian Hackers Hate, May 2021. https://krebsonsecurity.com/2021/05/try-this-one-weird-trick-russian-hackers-hate/

24. Lloydd, M.: Retrieving neutrality law to consider 'other' foreign fighters under international law. In: European Society of International Law (ESIL) 2017 Research Forum (Granada) (2017)

25. McLaughlin, K.L.: Cyber attack! Is a counter attack warranted? Inf. Secur. J. Glob. Perspect. **20**(1), 58–64 (2011)

26. Nilsson, M., Wyss, M.: The armed neutrality paradox: Sweden and Switzerland in us cold war armaments policy. J. Contemp. Hist. **51**(2), 335–363 (2016)

27. Nünlist, C.: Neutrality for peace: Switzerland's independent foreign policy. In: Engaged Neutrality: An Evolved Approach to the Cold War, pp. 161–187. Lexington Books (2017)

28. Nuspliger, N.: Die bedeutung von neutralität wandelt sich. Neue Zürcher Zeitung, February 2017. https://www.nzz.ch/schweiz/nato-generalsekretaer-stoltenberg-besucht-die-schweiz-die-bedeutung-von-neutralitaet-wandelt-sich-ld.148152?reduced=true

29. Perloff-Giles, A.: Transnational cyber offenses: overcoming jurisdictional challenges. Yale J. Int. Law **43**, 191 (2018)

30. PT Research: Suricata PT open ruleset, April 2021. https://github.com/ptresearch/AttackDetection

31. Reuters: Ex-soldier is convicted of violating swiss neutrality by fighting ISIS. The New York Times, February 2019. https://www.nytimes.com/2019/02/24/world/europe/switzerland-soldier-isis.html

32. Rickenbacher, F.: Der bund will eine deutlich aktivere rolle übernehmen. Netzwoche, October 2019. https://www.netzwoche.ch/news/2019-10-16/der-bund-will-eine-deutlich-aktivere-rolle-uebernehmen
33. Ryan, N.: Five kinds of cyber deterrence. Philos. Technol. **31**(3), 331–338 (2018)
34. Schmitt, M.N.: Tallinn Manual 2.0 on the International Law Applicable to Cyber Operations. Cambridge University Press, Cambridge (2017)
35. Sourial, N., et al.: Correspondence analysis is a useful tool to uncover the relationships among categorical variables. J. Clin. Epidemiol. **63**(6), 638–646 (2010)
36. Stolz, M.: On neutrality and cyber defence. In: European Conference on Cyber Warfare and Security, pp. 484–XIX. Academic Conferences International Limited (2019)
37. Suter, A.: Neutralität. praxis, prinzip und geschichtsbewusstsein. In: Hettling, M., Schaffner, M., König, M., Suter, A., Jakob, T. (eds.) Eine kleine Geschichte der Schweiz. Suhrkamp, Berlin (1998)
38. Attorney General of Switzerland: Coordinated operation in a cybercrime case, July 2019. https://www.nytimes.com/2019/02/24/world/europe/switzerland-soldier-isis.html
39. Federal Council of Switzerland: National strategy for the protection of Switzerland against cyber risks (NCS) 2018–2022 (2018). https://www.swissinfo.ch/eng/swiss-back-extradition-with-assurances/6376598
40. Federal Council of Switzerland: Teilnahme der Schweiz am "cooperative cyber defence centre of excellence", May 2019. https://www.admin.ch/gov/de/start/dokumentation/medienmitteilungen.msg-id-75145.html
41. Proofpoint Inc.: Emerging threats open ruleset, April 2021. https://rules.emergingthreats.net/
42. Turns, D.: Cyber war and the law of neutrality. In: Research Handbook on International Law and Cyberspace. Edward Elgar Publishing (2015)
43. Vidino, L.: Jihadist radicalization in Switzerland. Technical report, ETH Zurich (2013)
44. Wylie, N.: 'The importance of being honest': Switzerland, neutrality and the problems of intelligence collection and liaison. Intell. Natl. Secur. **21**(5), 782–808 (2006)

Future, TechWatch & Forecast for C(I)IP and Critical Services

TABLEAU: Future-Proof Zoning for OT Networks

Piet De Vaere[1(✉)], Claude Hähni[1], Franco Monti[2], and Adrian Perrig[1]

[1] ETH Zürich, Zürich, Switzerland
`{piet.de.vaere,claude.haehni,adrian.perrig}@inf.ethz.ch`
[2] Monti Stampa Furrer & Partners AG, Zürich, Switzerland
`franco.monti@msfpartners.com`

Abstract. For over two decades, hierarchical zoning models have dominated operational technology (OT) network design. However, ongoing changes to industrial network technologies and workloads, together with rising threat levels, are now challenging this design pattern. To address these issues, this paper introduces TABLEAU, a new zoning architecture for OT networks. TABLEAU increases network flexibility by flattening the zone structure and by allowing the seamless integration of plant, edge, corporate, and cloud networks. Simultaneously, TABLEAU facilitates modern security practices and is IEC 62443 compatible, ensuring the continued secure operation of OT infrastructure.

Keywords: OT networking · Network zoning · Industrial IoT · IEC 62443

1 Introduction

Since the introduction of computerized control systems to industrial automation, operational technology (OT) networks have had a strong hierarchical structure. One of the most prominent drivers behind this design is the Purdue Reference Model [4,26], which is widely considered to be the gold standard for designing and securing OT networks; especially in critical infrastructures such as utilities.

More broadly, the hierarchical structure of OT networks has historically been motivated by two reasons. First, industrial processes tend to exhibit natural hierarchy, as is commonly illustrated using the automation pyramid (see Sect. 2). Because control systems are usually placed close to the processes they control, it is natural for them to inherit the hierarchical structure of these processes. Second, using a hierarchical structure allows network designers to place security checkpoints between network levels, incrementally increasing the security level as the hierarchy descends.

For over two decades, OT network designers have successfully followed this approach. However, in recent years, the relevance of the hierarchical model is increasingly being questioned, as the model is struggling to adapt to new realities in the automation space [6,7,12,17,18,25], and because of the increasing

© Springer Nature Switzerland AG 2021
D. Percia David et al. (Eds.): CRITIS 2021, LNCS 13139, pp. 207–227, 2021.
https://doi.org/10.1007/978-3-030-93200-8_12

convergence between information technology (IT) and OT systems. In most networks, network designers already had to give up the strict air gap between IT and OT infrastructure in order to support remote management of automation systems, and new trends are further challenging the hierarchical model. Concretely, these trends can be classified as changes (i) to the network, (ii) to the automation infrastructure, (iii) to information flows, (iv) to threat models, and (v) to operation models. For example, cloud-based predictive maintenance requires raw information to flow directly from sensors on the lowest levels of the network to the cloud, crossing all traditional network levels. This contradicts the hierarchical design principle that individual network flows should not cross more than one network level at once. We further discuss the challenges created by new OT trends in Sect. 3.

Even though the trends introduced above do not render the current network model unusable, they do render it increasingly impractical. Even worse, they incrementally erode the security properties of hierarchical network design. Therefore, it is time to reconsider how we organize OT networks by introducing modern network management techniques to the OT environment. This will allow us to satisfy the contemporary demands placed on our networks, while achieving a high level of security.

To that end, this paper introduces TABLEAU, a modern zoning model for OT networks. TABLEAU builds on Mondrian [13], a recently developed zoning architecture for IT networks (see Sect. 4), and makes it suitable for operation on OT networks by defining a new Mondrian deployment model. By doing so, TABLEAU enables highly flexible network management in OT settings. Particularly, TABLEAU facilitates the seamless and secure integration of networked resources on the plant floor, at the edge, in the corporate network, and even in the cloud. Moreover, TABLEAU makes supplier access to OT infrastructures such as PLC, SCADA or HMI systems easier to configure, and reduces the impact of supply chain attacks by facilitating the creation of more, and smaller, network zones. In addition, TABLEAU accomplishes all of this while remaining compatible with IEC 62443, the leading standard for security in industrial networks [11].

Because of the large number of legacy systems typically present in OT networks, TABLEAU was designed to be brownfield-compatible. Concretely, TABLEAU provides the following two backward compatibility properties. First, TABLEAU can be incrementally deployed on subsections of the network while maintaining full network functionality. Second, it is possible to instantiate a hierarchical network structure on top of a TABLEAU network. Doing so enables network operators to gradually transition their network policies from the hierarchical to the TABLEAU model. We present the TABLEAU zoning architecture in Sect. 5, and we illustrate its features using examples based on a typical critical infrastructure network.

TABLEAU represents a significant break from the established, hierarchy-based security mindset in OT networks. We discuss the implications of this change in Sect. 6. Concretely, we argue that (i) by leveraging modern security mechanisms, and (ii) considering the changes that have occurred to OT networks since the hierarchical security models were established, TABLEAU not only provides much more flexibility to network administrators, but also *increases* the security of the networks in which it is deployed.

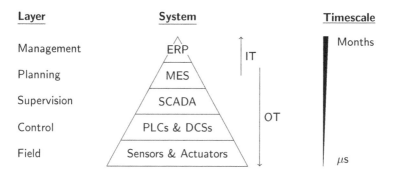

Fig. 1. The automation pyramid.

2   Current OT Networks

Industrial processes are often modeled using the automation pyramid [22]. This model, shown in Fig. 1, is used to capture the hierarchical structure found in industrial organizations, and applies to a broad range of industries. The lowest level of the automation pyramid contains the systems that directly interact with the physical processes that are controlled, i.e., sensors and actuators. Traversing the pyramid upwards, each consecutive level adds a layer of abstraction and aggregation until finally the top level, containing the organization's management, is reached. Two common observations can be made throughout the pyramid. First, process feedback always flows upwards between the levels, while commands flow downwards; there is no direct lateral information flow. Second, the further the distance from the process, the larger the decision timescales become. Traditionally, the lower levels of the automation pyramid are part of the OT network, and the top part of the IT network, but, as we discuss in Sect. 3, this line is blurring.

For communication networks, the hierarchical structure of the automation pyramid is translated to what is commonly referred to as a *Purdue Network*, referencing the *Purdue Model for Control Hierarchy* [26]. We illustrate a Purdue Model-based network in Fig. 2, which shows a network as would typically be found in critical infrastructure. In a Purdue network, network zones are organized in hierarchical levels. Further, zones are organized in such a way that all communication between zones on the same level must traverse a zone of a higher level, and firewalls enforce security policies at each zone transition. For technical reasons, communication on the lowest Purdue layers usually use specialized

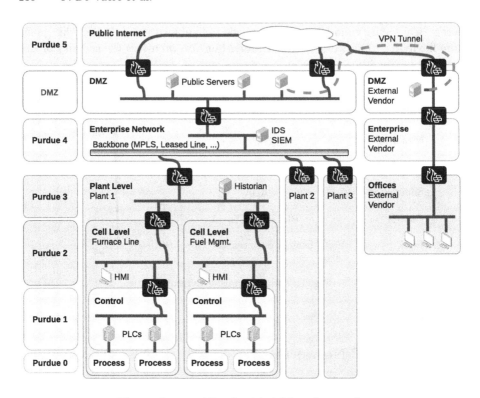

Fig. 2. A typical Purdue Model-based network.

fieldbus networks, further segregating devices deployed in the field from higher layers.

The principal ideas behind this network architecture are that (i) each lower network level has stronger security properties than the one above it, and that (ii) an attacker needs to breach many security boundaries before being able to access the organization's most critical assets (i.e., obtain control over the physical processes). In order for these properties to hold, it is important to design network flows to cross as few zone boundaries as possible. After all, each permitted network flow can be used as a conduit for an attack. Thus, if a single flow crosses multiple security boundaries at once, an attacker can use this flow to bypass Purdue levels.

3   Challenges to OT Networks

The Purdue-based network design discussed in Sect. 2 has successfully served OT operators for over two decades. However, with the advent of the Industrial Internet of Things (IIoT) and the "fourth industrial revolution", the requirements placed on the network are rapidly changing, putting pressure on the Purdue design. We discuss the most significant drivers for these changes in this section.

Changes to the Network. In the last decade, software-defined networking (SDN) has transformed how IT networks are being operated. So far this change has not yet significantly affected OT networks, but the ongoing convergence of IT and OT systems [3] suggests that it is only a matter of time before this will change. Moreover, recent work from the IEEE Time-Sensitive Networking (TSN) working group [8], including the specification of a TSN profile for industrial automation [9], will allow even the lowest levels of automation networks to use standard Ethernet [15,27]. This will likely lead to a replacement of the current fieldbus protocols, and will more closely integrate field devices with higher levels of the automation system, in turn making it harder to maintain the strict separation of Purdue levels and easier for an attacker to cross from the higher levels to secondary technologies deployed in the lower levels.

Further, new networking technologies, such as TSN and SDN, are increasingly centrally managed, which decreases both the relevance and robustness of distributed security enforcement. For example, when an SDN controller is compromised, the adversary can redefine the network fabric to route packets around firewalls, effectively disabling them [23].

Evolution of the Automation Infrastructure. It is common that as the technological capabilities of a system start to exceed the requirements placed on that system by its users, more and more components of that system are replaced by general-purpose components. We have clearly witnessed this in the data center industry with the advent of virtualization technologies (both for end-hosts and for network functions), and also IT/OT convergence is a manifestation of this phenomenon.

Another manifestation of this phenomenon is the rise of *virtualized automation functions*, such as soft-PLC, soft-SCADA, and soft-HMI systems. Contrary to their physical counterparts, virtualized automation functions do not need to be placed physically close to the processes they control. New network technologies (such as TSN) facilitate this further. Concretely, these virtualized computation resources can be placed at the edge (for functions in lower levels of the automation pyramid), or even in the cloud (for functions in the middle to higher levels of the pyramid). This is problematic as current industrial networks are not designed to place physically distant devices logically nearby in the network.

Changes to Information Flows. In traditional automation networks, information does not travel across more than one level of the Purdue Model without being proxied or aggregated. However, the advent of cloud-based big-data analytics for applications such as predictive maintenance has disrupted this. In order to obtain the most accurate predictions, as much raw data from the lower levels of the automation pyramid as possible is now being collected and directly uploaded to the cloud. Supporting such data flows in current networks leads to high management overhead and violates the security principles of the Purdue Model.

Changes to Threat Models. The security of the Purdue Model is primarily based on the assumption that attackers enter the network at the top levels of the model, and have to work their way down into the lower levels with higher security. However, (i) the increased number of network flows that cross multiple Purdue levels at once, (ii) the increased complexity—and thus vulnerability—of automation devices, and (iii) the increased use of wireless and portable technologies are making it increasingly more likely for an attacker to enter the network directly at a lower Purdue level. This breaks the assumption that the security level of the network increases as one descends through the levels of the Purdue Model.

Changes in the Industrial Target Operation Model. Cost pressure and operational efficiency are leading to the regional cluster model, in which several geographically dispersed plants are remotely managed from a single regional node plant. This allows companies to reduce the personnel required to run plants, and to increase remote operations, sometimes even cross-border. However, such a topology of plants, besides building on an increased level of digitalization, adds complexity into the overall configuration when a Purdue-based configuration is maintained. Moreover, traffic flows between a regional node plant and its cluster plants might traverse public networks. This exposes the traffic to man-in-the-middle and spoofing attacks, which in turn can lead to a loss of control over the remotely managed plants. Hence, additional measures need to be taken to assure the integrity and availability of industrial traffic flows.

4   Mondrian Network Zoning

Mondrian [13] is a recent zoning architecture for enterprise networks that was motivated by the need for modern network models which is arising in cloud and hybrid-cloud deployments. These new deployment scenarios are posing additional demands on IT security in large corporate networks. Traditionally, information was processed within a single domain. Today, IT infrastructures are distributed across several heterogeneous systems that all need to communicate with each other. This has lead to increased complexity in the structure of IT networks, with a myriad of systems and policies that need to be managed, kept synchronized, and kept consistent. This is similar to what we are currently experiencing in OT networks. Mondrian offers a secure, flexible, and scalable network zoning architecture that alleviates these issues. One notable property of Mondrian is its capability to securely bridge geographically distributed, heterogeneous networks over untrusted infrastructure. As a result, Mondrian opens the door for many interesting deployment scenarios in which a highly secure and easy to manage zoning architecture is required. In this section, we provide a brief introduction to Mondrian and highlight the properties relevant for TABLEAU.

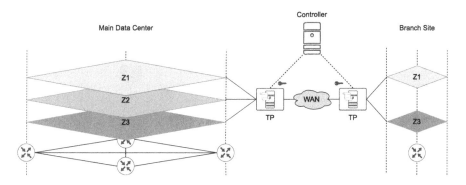

Fig. 3. Mondrian architecture overview. The TPs deployed at each site span the inter-domain transit zone across the wide area network (WAN). The central controller periodically distributes policy updates to the TPs at each branch site. TPs enforce the zone transition policy received from the controller by filtering packets at the local network perimeter. The same logical zone can be distributed across different branch sites (e.g., zones Z1 and Z3).

4.1 Mondrian Overview

Network Zoning with Mondrian. In contrast to current, highly-complex organization of network zones, Mondrian partitions the network into a collection of flat zones. As illustrated in Fig. 3, each of these zones is connected to a designated security gateway called the transition point (TP). Placing zones adjacent to each other, only separated by the TP, simplifies today's network architectures in which traffic often needs to traverse multiple layers to reach its destination. A logically centralized controller provides a comprehensive management interface for operators to orchestrate the network. Common tasks, such as zone migration and zone initialization become much easier, as the network configuration is centralized on a single system. TPs ensure source authentication, zone access authorization, and ingress/egress filtering for all connected network zones. Using the concept of an *inter-domain transit zone*, Mondrian enables network zoning across the boundaries of local networks. This is particularly useful for enterprises that operate geographically distributed branch sites or leverage the cloud as part of their infrastructure.

Flexibility and Scalability. The brain of Mondrian is the logically centralized controller, presenting a single interface with which network operators manage their network. Sites, zones and transition policies can all be centrally managed through this interface. The controller then takes care of distributing these policies to the TPs, which enforce the policies at the individual premises.

Supporting fine-grained zone transition policies offers great flexibility for operators to cover a diverse set of use cases. The centralized interface simplifies

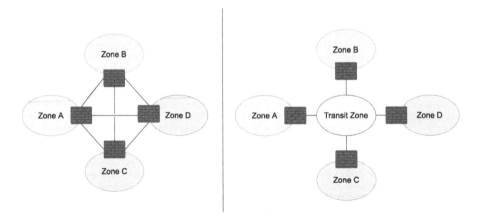

Fig. 4. On the left: a network topology using dedicated links to connect each pair of zones. On the right: The same network organized in a hub-spoke configuration using a transit zone as central element.

today's complex infrastructure with potentially many systems and their respective configurations that need to be updated for every change to the network. As a result, Mondrian is less susceptible to configuration errors and makes policy reviews more efficient. In concert, these properties significantly enhance management scalability.

Deployability. Mondrian supports multiple deployment methods that can be used in conjunction with each other. The primary method uses TPs in the form of all-in-one gateways which perform routing, packet authorization, and tunneling, all without requiring any changes to end hosts. This method reduces the number of security middleboxes that need to be maintained in networks. When using this method, Mondrian can also assume a supportive role in which traffic is pre-filtered before it gets handled by security middleboxes.

Alternatively, Mondrian can be deployed purely in software on commodity computing devices. Similar to a VPN, this allows individuals to remotely access network assets from their personal devices in a secure and authenticated manner. When using this method, a TP runs as virtual gateway on a computer and tunnels packets from the device to a remote TP in the enterprise. In contrast to a traditional VPN, a software TP is part of the regular Mondrian deployment and seamlessly integrates with the rest of the architecture.

4.2 Mondrian in Detail

Inter-domain Transit Zone. One of the main building blocks that allows Mondrian to achieve the properties introduced above is the concept of the inter-domain transit zone. Transit zones are commonly used within local networks to facilitate zone transitions. Concretely, they are special zones that do not contain any end hosts, but merely exist to interconnect other zones. Put differently,

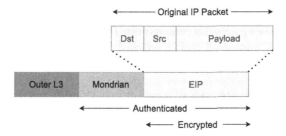

Fig. 5. A depiction of the Mondrian encapsulation. For packets traversing the inter-domain transit zone, a Mondrian header including a zone authenticator is attached to the encrypted original IP packet (EIP). Finally, the Mondrian packet is wrapped in an outer Layer-3 header.

a transit zone is the hub in a hub-spoke network topology, providing connectivity between all the other zones. Hub-spoke configurations allow physically separated network zones to access shared services without the need for dedicated links between each pair of zones (see Fig. 4). Mondrian scales transit zones to inter-domain networks. The inter-domain transit zone spans across a WAN, connecting the branch sites of enterprises. At every site, local zones are directly attached to the inter-domain transit zone, thus creating a collection of disjoint, parallel network zones. Such a network requires packets to traverse fewer security middleboxes as all zone transitions can be checked already at the border of the inter-domain transit zone. Inside the transit zone, the Mondrian protocol is used to transport zone information across the inter-domain transit zone, allowing remote destinations to easily verify zone transitions, even if the underlying network is untrusted. Additionally, the Mondrian protocol is independent from the internal protocols used at each site, which means it is able to bridge networks that operate on otherwise incompatible internal protocols.

Transition Points and Controller. At each network site, Mondrian deploys a dedicated security gateway, called the transition point (TP). Network zones (subnets) at every branch site are directly connected to the TP, creating a flat network structure (see Fig. 3). This means that all inter-zone traffic needs to pass at least one TP. Together, TPs span the inter-domain transit zone. The main task of a TP is twofold: (i) it ensures that traffic does not violate the zone transition policy. For that, TPs check all zone transitions against a policy they receive from a logically centralized controller. On an abstract level, this transition policy is a matrix which defines for each ordered pair of zones (A, B) which traffic is allowed to flow from zone A to zone B. The controller has the full view over the entire distributed network and makes sure that all sites operate with the latest security policy. (ii) For zone transitions that cross the inter-domain transit zone, the second task of TPs is to attach cryptographically secured zone information to each packet before encrypting and forwarding the packet over the WAN. This way, Mondrian achieves integrity and confidentiality of information being sent over a potentially untrusted network. Because the complete original packet, including headers, is encrypted, internal addresses are prevented from leaking. Upon receiving a packet, the remote TP can verify the zone information, decrypt the packet and, if all checks succeed, forward the packet into the local network. The latency overhead introduced by each TP is less than 5 μs [13].

Packet Life-Cycle. The life-cycle of a packet in a Mondrian network is as follows.

1. An end host in a source zone Z_S sends an IP packet towards an end host in a destination zone Z_D by creating a regular IP packet with the usual source and destination addresses.
   (a) If $Z_S = Z_D$, the packet is delivered directly by the Layer-2 protocol.
   (b) Otherwise, the packet needs to be forwarded via a Mondrian TP.
2. The TP analyzes the packet, retrieving Z_S and Z_D based on the source and destination address of the packet, ensuring that the zone transition Z_S to Z_D is allowed.
   (a) If not, the packet is dropped.
   (b) If yes, the packet is forwarded towards the destination.
3. Next, based on the destination address, the TP evaluates if the packet is destined for an end host in the same branch site.
   (a) If yes, the TP forwards the packet towards the destination in the internal network.
   (b) In case the destination is in a different network across the inter-domain transit zone, the TP looks up the remote TP, creates a cryptographic authenticator, encrypts the original IP packet, and encapsulates the encrypted packet together with the Mondrian header in an outer Layer 3 header (see Fig. 5). The exact outer layer depends on the protocol used within the inter-domain transit zone. This packet is then forwarded to the remote TP.
4. Finally, the receiving TP decapsulates the payload, verifies the authenticator and, if all checks succeed, decrypts the payload back into the original IP packet which it then forwards to the destination inside the internal network.

5 A Flat Zoning Architecture for OT Networks

We now introduce TABLEAU, a zoning architecture for OT networks that leverages Mondrian in order to achieve flexible, future-proof network management.

Because Mondrian was originally designed for enterprise (i.e., IT) networks, we need to modify its deployment model before it can be used in an OT setting. In Sect. 5.1, we present this modified deployment model together with the remainder of the TABLEAU architecture using an example deployment. Then, we discuss additional TABLEAU features in Sects. 5.2, 5.3 and 5.4.

5.1 A TABLEAU Production Plant

In a standard Mondrian deployment, all the network zones at each site are connected to the same transition point (TP), which in turn is directly connected to the WAN (Fig. 3). Doing so results in a flat zone structure, which is one of Mondrian's key features. In order to preserve this feature when using Mondrian in OT settings, it is necessary to map the inherently hierarchical structure of industrial processes to a flat layout. Further, the use of a single TP per site is not a well-suited approach for OT networks. The reason for this is twofold. First, using a central TP introduces a single point of failure to the data plane. Second, the physical structure of OT networks and the spatial separation between network zones make connecting each zone to the same TP impractical.

In order to flatten the structure of OT networks, we split the network into multiple host zones and a transit network that spans across all traditional network levels, as illustrated in Fig. 6. The separation between zones can either be physical (i.e., a zone takes the form of a dedicated physical network), or virtual (e.g., a zone consists of one or more VLANs). In either case, the introduction of a transit network ensures that no transit traffic flows through the host zones.

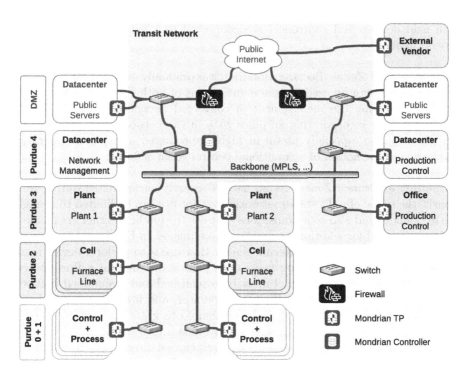

Fig. 6. The TABLEAU equivalent to the Purdue-based network shown in Fig. 2.

Next, we change the traditional Mondrian deployment model, and instead of connecting each zone to a central TP, we place a TP at the edge of each zone. Only when practical, zones share a TP (not shown in Fig. 4). Each TP is then directly connected to the transit network. When traffic leaves a zone, the TP encapsulates it in an encrypted and authenticated tunnel and forwards the traffic over the transit network to the destination zone, where it is decapsulated before being delivered to the final destination.

Many of the zones in Fig. 6 can be directly mapped to one of the hierarchical zones in Fig. 2 (we indicated the traditional Purdue level of each zone in Fig. 6), but there are a number of notable exceptions. We discuss these, together with other notable TABLEAU features, below.

Merging Purdue Levels 0 and 1. In today's industrial networks, field devices (i.e., sensors and actuators at Purdue level 0) are usually directly connected to their controllers (Purdue level 1) using a physically separated fieldbus network. Although in the future the functions of the fieldbusses might be taken over by a general-purpose network fabric, the close integration of field devices and controllers will remain critical, both for performance and safety reasons. Therefore, TABLEAU merges the lowest two Purdue levels and places field devices and controllers in the same zone. This captures both the traditional scenario using dedicated fieldbusses (as depicted in Fig. 2), as well as the future scenario where both field devices and controllers are connected to a general purpose (TSN) network fabric.

Integration of IT Zones. Because Mondrian was originally designed for enterprise IT networks, it can be used for the management of both IT and OT networks, greatly simplifying the management of converged networks. We demonstrate this in Fig. 6 by incorporating an office zone in the network map. Having this flexibility can be especially useful in highly automated or remotely operated plants, where the notion of a traditional control room is fading.

Integration of Remote Zones. As all data is securely encapsulated during zone transit, the scope of a TABLEAU network does not need to be limited to a single site or domain, and also zone transitions that use the public Internet are possible without the need for additional tunneling mechanisms. In Fig. 6 we demonstrate this with the use case of an external vendor that needs to perform device management or security monitoring tasks on a plant's network. In a Purdue network (Fig. 2), a dedicated tunnel must be established and maintained between the network of the vendor and the plant operator, and firewalls or jump hosts throughout the Purdue levels must be configured to grant the required access. Evidently, this leads to high management overhead. In contrast, in a TABLEAU network (Fig. 6) the external vendor's network can be directly integrated in the networks zone plan. We discuss further benefits of inter-domain zone bridging in Sect. 5.2.

Open Transit Network. By only allowing Mondrian encapsulated traffic to flow between network zones, TABLEAU largely eliminates the need for security enforcement within the transit network. We illustrate this in Fig. 6 by only placing classical firewalls on the Internet uplinks. An open transit network not only lowers the burden on the network administrators, but also increases the agility of the network.

Protection of Transit Traffic. Because of the hierarchical nature of Purdue networks, zones in a Purdue network need to handle both transit and local traffic. By mixing these two network functions, transit traffic is exposed to tampering by malicious devices in the network zones the traffic traverses. In contrast, TABLEAU splits the network into device zones and a transit network, separating local from transit traffic. Moreover, all inter-zone traffic is authenticated and encrypted while passing over the transit network. Both of these factors reduce the exposure of network traffic to tampering by malicious devices.

5.2 Inter-domain Zone Bridging

We have already shown how TABLEAU facilitates vendor access to OT networks. Not only can the same approach be used to allow remote workers to connect to the company network by running a local Mondrian instance on their laptop, but TABLEAU takes this one step further by splicing network zones across domains.

To make this more concrete, consider the network shown in Fig. 7a, the left side of which shows a plant network consisting of four network zones. For economic reasons, the plant operators use multiple cloud services to support the devices in the plant. Concretely, they use a digital twin for each of the turbines, a cloud HMI for remote management of the machine group, and a cloud-based data historian for the plant. These services span across all four network zones in the plant, so in order to maintain zone isolation, the zone structure from the plant is mirrored to the cloud. In today's networks, establishing connectivity from the zones of the plant to those in the cloud would either require bundling traffic from all zones together, or setting up separate tunnels between each pair of zones. Because the former approach breaks the isolation between zones and the later approach induces high management overhead, neither of them is desirable.

In contrast, TABLEAU makes it possible to extend network zones across domains. This means that the physically distant zones pairs (Fig. 7a), can be joined to form different subnets of the same logical zone (Fig. 7b), without creating additional management overhead. Moreover, because Mondrian uses different cryptographic keys for each zone, zone isolation is maintained across the network. Further, this approach is flexible and can be adapted to network operators' needs. For example, instead of extending the same logical zone across multiple domains, the subnets can also be made logically adjacent while remaining in separate zones. This allows for smooth communication to take place between the zones, while still allowing limitations to be placed on which traffic can flow between them.

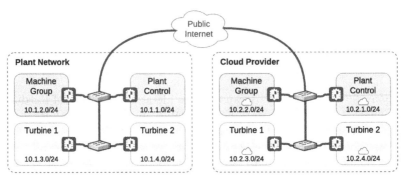

(a) Physical layout

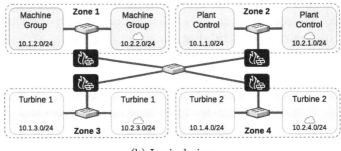

(b) Logical view

Fig. 7. Example TABLEAU topology for a hybrid plant-cloud network.

5.3 Decoupling TP from Logical Zone Connectivity

In a TABLEAU network, the logical connectivity between zones is decoupled from the underlying connectivity of the transition points. Besides simplifying the logical network topology, this also simplifies how redundancy and multihoming can be added to the network. For a concrete example, consider Fig. 8, which shows a minimal TABLEAU network consisting of a plant and a remote control room. In order to ensure availability, both the plant and control room are multihomed. To highlight the separation of the logical connectivity between zones and the underlying connectivity on the transit network, we use IPv4 addresses for the former, and IPv6 addresses for the later.

Because the devices inside of the TABLEAU zones are oblivious to the existence of the transit network, multihoming a zone only requires multihoming the zone's TPs. This stands in contrast to traditional multihoming, which directly affects each host in the network [2,16]. It also means that when the connectivity between two zones breaks (e.g., because of link failure), restoring connectivity between the zones (e.g., by falling back a secondary link) only requires intervention on the TPs, and is transparent to the hosts. Although similar properties can be achieved in a Purdue architecture using VPNs, VPNs generate additional administrative overhead, whereas TABLEAU provides these properties by default.

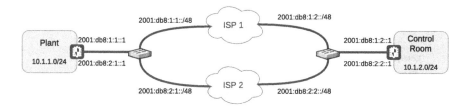

Fig. 8. Example of a TABLEAU deployment on multihomed networks.

5.4 Backwards Compatibility

In many cases, industrial networks are a brownfield environment. That is, any change to the network must be made while maintaining compatibility with existing devices and structures. To that end, TABLEAU offers two forms of backwards compatibility: partial deployment, and hierarchical overlay.

Partial Deployment. When it is not possible (or desirable) to convert the full network to a TABLEAU architecture, TABLEAU can be deployed on a subsection of the network instead. For example, when only a single cell in a plant is being updated, it can be desirable to deploy TABLEAU in this cell without changing the other parts of the plant's or organization's network. We demonstrate this scenario in Fig. 9, which shows the same network as Fig. 2, but in which one cell is converted to a TABLEAU architecture.

Although only a partial deployment, many of TABLEAU's advantages are retained. Most significantly, there is still full flexibility on how traffic can be routed across the TABLEAU zones. Moreover, assuming that the upstream firewalls are configured to allow TABLEAU traffic to pass through, inter-domain bridging remains possible. We illustrate this in Fig. 9 by including the external vendor in the TABLEAU deployment.

In order to facilitate direct communication between the TABLEAU-enabled cell and the plant's network, a dedicated *entry zone* is introduced. This zone acts as a gateway between the Purdue and TABLEAU worlds, giving it a similar function as a demilitarized zone (DMZ) in a Purdue network.

Hierarchical Overlay. A TABLEAU network provides full flexibility as to what traffic flows are permitted. This means that it is also possible to implement a policy that overlays a hierarchical network on top of TABLEAU. Doing so allows plants operators to convert their network to a TABLEAU architecture, without having to redraw all security and data-flow concepts at once. Instead, they can initially overlay the same hierarchical policies the network was operating on before, and gradually transition to new network policies and a new security concept from there.

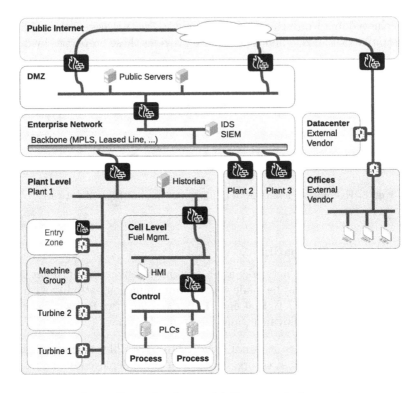

Fig. 9. Example of a partial TABLEAU deployment.

6 Security Aspects

By stepping away from the nested zone model used in today's OT networks, TABLEAU challenges a widespread design pattern in OT security. Next, we discuss the implications of this architectural change.

Hierarchical network zoning is often motivated by referring to the "defense in depth" security principle: the idea that by layering multiple defense mechanisms behind each other, the security of the system as whole is not compromised when individual defense mechanisms are found faulty. Although it is true that hierarchical network zoning can serve as a form of defense in depth, the true benefits from defense in depth cannot be obtained by using the same defense technique (i.e., firewalls) at multiple points within an organization. Instead, defense in depth requires several independent security mechanisms to be deployed throughout that organization (e.g., firewalls paired with physical security, personnel training, proper patch management, intrusion detection, etc.) [20]. In fact, past studies indicate that having complex, hard-to-maintain firewall structures in a network leads to poor policy management, and thus lowered security [1].

Moreover, as we discuss in Sect. 3, the threat model for OT networks is changing. Concretely, it is becoming increasingly more likely that attackers will not attack the network level-by-level from the top, but instead will enter the network immediately at one of the lower levels, e.g., after entering the network through a compromised software update [24]. Additionally, the centralized nature of new networking technologies (e.g., TSN and SDN) is reducing the robustness of distributed security enforcement [23]. Both these changes are further reducing the efficiency of hierarchical zoning as a defense in depth measure, and, in the medium to long term, will leave industry with a complex and hard to maintain security system, the security properties of which are based on assumptions that no longer hold.

In contrast, TABLEAU does not base its security properties on assumptions about the underlying system architecture, but instead simplifies and centralizes security management in order to facilitate the use of modern security tools. Concretely, by consolidating the security policy of a network into a single specification, TABLEAU facilitates policy simplification, fine-grained zoning, and automated network policy verification. We discuss each of these below.

Policy Simplification. Consolidating the network policy into a single specification removes much of the complexity currently encountered in firewall management. This makes policy administration less time-intensive and less error prone. Moreover, the policy becomes easier to audit.

Fine-Grained Zoning. As discussed in Sect. 3, an increasing number of devices in the network can function as attacker entry points. In order to limit the impact that a compromised device has on the network, it is desirable to reduce the size of each network zone, thus restricting the lateral movement of an attacker [21]. TABLEAU facilitates fine-grained zoning by lowering the administrative burden required to create and manage additional network zones.

Automated Network Verification. Not only does TABLEAU make it easier to manually audit network security policies, but aggregating the policy specification at the Mondrian controller also facilitates automated network verification [14]. Automated network verification refers to a set of techniques that make it possible to specify high-level policy goals the network should satisfy, and to automatically verify if a specific network policy satisfies these goals [14]. By doing so, network verification can provide strong guarantees on the correctness of the network policy. Moreover, when performed periodically or at every configuration change, automated network verification makes it possible to dynamically modify the network policy while maintaining a high level of confidence in the correctness of the network policies. This makes it easier and safer to update the network policy as the plant's network evolves.

We anticipate that in most networks, the advantages of trading the hierarchical network model for the flexibility and simplified policy management of a TABLEAU network will well outweigh the disadvantages, resulting in an improved level of security for the network. Nonetheless, in some environments the use of consolidated network policy enforcement may be considered undesirable. We address this issue by introducing *structured heterogeneity*, an approach that adds diversity and redundancy to a TABLEAU network, without interfering with TABLEAU's core features.

The principal idea behind structured heterogeneity is to standardize the interfaces between the various Mondrian components (i.e., transition point, controller, and policy), and to then add diversity to each of them. Concretely, diversity is added to each component as follows:

Transition Points: Different TP implementations (e.g., from different vendors) can be deployed in different zones. This limits the consequences of an implementation bug in a specific TP implementation to the zones in which this implementation is used.

Controller: Multiple controller implementations can be deployed in parallel. Each of these controllers connects to the same TPs, and uses the same policy specification. TPs are configured to only permit a zone transition if a threshold number of controllers approve it. This approach also improves network availability, as zone transitions remain possible if one of the controllers is unreachable.

Policy: In order not to increase policy administration overhead, a single policy specification is kept. Instead, we add diversity to the policy *verification*. By verifying the correctness of the policy using multiple methods (e.g., manual inspection combined with multiple automated network verifiers), this ensures that even if an individual verification tool fails, policy goal violations will be detected.

7   Related Work

Today's Standards and Models. The architecture and security concepts used in today's OT networks are heavily based on industrial standards and reference models. Although the Purdue Model is often presented as a security model, the original model only discusses information flow [26]. This information model is then used by other standards (i.e., the IEC 62443 [11] series) and architectures (i.e., Cisco and Rockwell Automation's Converged Plantwide Ethernet (CPwE) Architecture). Concrete networks, such as the one in Fig. 2 are then based on these derived standards and architectures.

Although TABLEAU represents a clear break from concrete traditional network architectures such as CPwE, it remains fundamentally compatible with IEC 62443. Concretely, IEC 62443-3-2 [10] does not prescribe a specific zoning model, but states "The organization shall group [control systems] and related assets into zones or conduits as determined by risk." (ZCR 3.1) and "[Control system] assets shall be grouped into zones that are logically or physically separated from business or enterprise system assets." (ZCR 3.2). TABLEAU provides the tool needed in order to implement these zones and conduits in modern networks. Specifically, zones in a TABLEAU network map directly to zones as intended by IEC 62443, and conduits are defined by the zone transition policy.

Future-Oriented Standards and Models. The most visible proposal for a future-proof OT architecture is the NAMUR Open Architecture (NOA) [19]. NOA places a secondary *monitoring and optimization* network in parallel to the existing *core* automation infrastructure. Data is fed from the core network into the secondary network through data diodes, where it can be analyzed. Control commands from the secondary network are transferred back to the core network through a request verification gateway. Although NOA has the advantage that it leaves the existing automation network largely untouched, the functionality of the secondary network stays limited to a supporting role. This means that NOA does not address how to handle changes to the core of the automation architecture, e.g., the introduction of virtual automation functions or the increasing prevalence of highly-autonomous remotely controlled facilities. In fact, the NOA approach is largely complementary to TABLEAU, as TABLEAU can be used to structure and secure the monitoring and optimization network of NOA deployment.

Another prominent standardization effort is the Reference Architectural Model for Industrie 4.0 (RAMI 4.0) [5], which was developed to support Industry 4.0 initiatives. However, RAMI 4.0 focuses on the representation and management of assets, and does not discuss network topologies.

8   Conclusion

The rise of the IIOT and the ongoing IT/OT convergence are challenging the ways in which we defend OT networks. If we ignore this reality, the security properties of our networks will slowly erode while administrative overhead will grow. Instead, we must reevaluate the security concepts used in the OT world, and adapt them to reflect the current—and future—state of the network.

In this paper, we introduced the Mondrian-based TABLEAU zoning architecture. TABLEAU provides the flexibility required by contemporary industrial workloads, lowers administrative overhead, is brownfield-compatible, and facilitates the use of modern security practices. Moreover, because Mondrian has its roots in IT networks, TABLEAU draws from the many years of experience the IT world has with managing the technologies that the IIoT and IT/OT convergence are introducing to our industrial networks.

References

1. Al-Shaer, E.S., Hamed, H.H.: Modeling and management of firewall policies. IEEE Trans. Netw. Serv. Manag. **1**(1), 2–10 (2004). https://doi.org/10.1109/tnsm.2004.4623689
2. Bates, T.J., Rekhter, Y.: Scalable support for multi-homed multi-provider connectivity. RFC 2260, January 1998. https://doi.org/10.17487/RFC2260, https://rfc-editor.org/rfc/rfc2260.txt
3. CISCO: IT/OT convergence (2018). https://www.cisco.com/c/dam/en_us/solutions/industries/manufacturing/ITOT-convergence-whitepaper.pdf

4. Cisco Systems and Rockwell Automation: Ethernet-to-the-factory 1.2 design and implementation guide, July 2008. https://www.cisco.com/c/en/us/td/docs/solutions/Verticals/EttF/EttFDIG.pdf

5. Deutsches Institut für Normung: DIN SPEC 91345:2016–04: Reference Architecture Model Industrie 4.0 (RAMI4.0). Technical Standard (2016)

6. Greenfield, D.: Is the Purdue Model still relevant? Automation World (2020). https://www.automationworld.com/factory/iiot/article/21132891/is-the-purdue-model-still-relevant

7. Hegrat, B., Langill, J., Peterson, D.: S4x19 panel discussion: is the Purdue Model dead? (2019). https://s4xevents.com/past-events-2/s4x19/

8. IEEE 802.1: Time-sensitive networking (TSN) task group (2020). https://1.ieee802.org/tsn/

9. IEEE 802.1, IEC SC65C/WG18: IEC/IEEE 60802 TSN profile for industrial automation (draft d1.2) (2020). https://1.ieee802.org/tsn/iec-ieee-60802/

10. International Electrotechnical Commission: IEC 62443 standard series: Industrial communication networks - IT security for networks and systems, Technical Standard

11. International Electrotechnical Commission: IEC 62443-3-2:2020 security for industrial automation and control systems - part 3–2: Security risk assessment for system design. Technical Standard (2020)

12. Koelemij, S.: The Purdue Reference Model outdated or up-to-date? (2020). https://otcybersecurity.blog/2020/06/08/the-purdue-reference-model-outdated-or-up-to-date/

13. Kwon, J., Hähni, C., Bamert, P., Perrig, A.: Mondrian: comprehensive inter-domain network zoning architecture. In: Proceedings of the Symposium on Network and Distributed System Security (NDSS) (2021). https://doi.org/10.14722/ndss.2021.24378

14. Li, Y., et al.: A survey on network verification and testing with formal methods: approaches and challenges. IEEE Commun. Surv. Tutorials **21**(1), 940–969 (2019). https://doi.org/10.1109/comst.2018.2868050

15. Lo Bello, L., Steiner, W.: A perspective on IEEE time-sensitive networking for industrial communication and automation systems. Proc. IEEE **107**(6), 1094–1120 (2019). https://doi.org/10.1109/jproc.2019.2905334

16. Matsumoto, A., Fujisaki, T., Hiromi, R., Kanayama, K.: Problem Statement for Default Address Selection in Multi-Prefix Environments: Operational Issues of RFC 3484 Default Rules. RFC 5220, July 2008. https://doi.org/10.17487/RFC5220, https://rfc-editor.org/rfc/rfc5220.txt

17. Miklovic, D.: IIoT will change our view of CIM; the Purdue Model is becoming dated. Industrial Transformation Blog (2015). https://blog.lnsresearch.com/iiot-will-change-our-view-of-cim-the-purdue-model-is-becoming-dated

18. Mission Secure: Is the Purdue Model relevant in a world of industrial Internet of Things (IIoT) and cloud services? (2021). https://www.missionsecure.com/blog/purdue-model-relevance-in-industrial-internet-of-things-iiot-cloud

19. NAMUR: NAMUR Recommendation NE 175: NAMUR Open Architecture - NOA Concept, Technical Standard (2020)

20. NSA: Defense in depth: A practical strategy for achieving information assurance in today's highly networked environments (2012)

21. Paloalto Networks: 2020 unit 42 IoT threat report (2020). https://unit42.paloaltonetworks.com/iot-threat-report-2020/

22. Sauter, T., Soucek, S., Kastner, W., Dietrich, D.: The evolution of factory and building automation. IEEE Ind. Electron. Mag. **5**(3), 35–48 (2011). https://doi.org/10.1109/mie.2011.942175
23. Scott-Hayward, S., Natarajan, S., Sezer, S.: A survey of security in software defined networks. IEEE Commun. Surv. Tutorials **18**(1), 623–654 (2016). https://doi.org/10.1109/comst.2015.2453114
24. Temple-Raston, D.: A 'worst nightmare' cyberattack: The untold story of the solarwinds hack (2021). https://www.npr.org/2021/04/16/985439655/a-worst-nightmare-cyberattack-the-untold-story-of-the-solarwinds-hack?t=1619951063586
25. VDI/VDE Gesellschaft Mess- und Automatisierugnstechnik: Cypber-physical systems: Chancen und nutzen aus sicht der automation. Technical report (2013)
26. Williams, T.J. (ed.): A Reference Model for Computer Integrated Manufacturing (CIM). Instrument Society of America (1989)
27. Wollschlaeger, M., Sauter, T., Jasperneite, J.: The future of industrial communication: automation networks in the era of the internet of things and industry 4.0. IEEE Ind. Electron. Mag. **11**(1), 17–27 (2017). https://doi.org/10.1109/mie.2017.2649104

Link Prediction for Cybersecurity Companies and Technologies: Towards a Survivability Score

Santiago Anton Moreno[1]([✉]), Anita Mezzetti[1], and William Lacube[2]

[1] EPFL, 1015 Lausanne, Switzerland
santiago.antonmoreno@epfl.ch
[2] Cyber Defence Campus, Armasuisse Science and Technology, 1015 Lausanne, Switzerland

Abstract. On the cybersecurity market, novel entities – technologies and companies – arise and disappear swiftly. In such a fast-paced context, assessing the survivability of those entities is crucial when it comes to make investment decisions for ensuring the security of critical infrastructures. In this paper, we present a framework for capturing the dynamic relationship between entities of the Swiss cybersecurity landscape. By using open data, we first model our dataset as a bipartite graph in which nodes are represented by technologies and companies involved in cybersecurity. Next, we use patents and job openings data to link the two entities. By extracting time series of such graphs, and by using link-prediction methods, we forecast the (dis)appearance of links. We apply several unsupervised learning similarity-based algorithms, a supervised learning method and finally we select the best model. Our preliminary results show good performance and promising validation of our survivability index. We suggest that our framework is useful for critical infrastructure operators, as a survivability index of entities can be extracted by using the outputs of our models.

Keywords: Technology monitoring · Network science · Link prediction · Time series · Supervised learning · Critical-infrastructure protection

1 Introduction

The fast-paced development of technologies reshapes the security of information systems [8]. Examples of technologies that redefine cyberdefense are numerous: e.g., quantum computing threatening cryptography protocols, adversarial machine learning, novel communication protocols, behaviour-based authentication of IDS, distributed ledgers. In such a complex technology-development context, both threats and opportunities emerge for actors of the cyberspace [3], including operators of critical infrastructures (CIs). Consequently, a race for a technological advantage takes place between attackers and defenders [7].

© Springer Nature Switzerland AG 2021
D. Percia David et al. (Eds.): CRITIS 2021, LNCS 13139, pp. 228–233, 2021.
https://doi.org/10.1007/978-3-030-93200-8_13

The assessment of the cybersecurity technological landscape has become a central activity when it comes to develop cyberdefense strategies [2], especially in the context of the recent supply chain attacks against CIs[1]. Such an assessment helps defenders to grab an edge in this technological race by developing threat-intelligence tools to reduce the information asymmetry between attackers and defenders [12]. In particular, it enables to foster cyberdefense by identifying the survival probabilities of entities – i.e., technologies and companies – involved in the cybersecurity technological landscape and, then investing in the most relevant ones. Especially, these aspects constitute strategic tools for procurement, one of the greatest challenges faced by governments and CI operators [5].

In this work, we aim to contribute to the technological landscape assessment effort by presenting a framework for capturing the relationship between entities of the Swiss cybersecurity technological landscape. By using a dataset coming from the *Technology & Market Monitoring* (TMM) platform, we first model the data as a bipartite graph in which nodes (i.e., entities) are represented by technologies and companies involved in cybersecurity. We then use patents and job openings to link entities. By extracting time series of such a graph, and by using link-prediction methods, we forecast the (des)appearance of links between entities. We apply several similarity-based algorithms and a supervised learning machine-learning model that uses outputs from the former. Next we select the best model based on perfomance measures. We suggest that our framework is useful for decision-makers involved in the security of CIs, as a survivability score of entities can be extracted by either using the similarity metrics or probability calculations from the supervised learning model.

The remainder of this paper is structured as follows: Sect. 2 present the related work; Sect. 3 presents the data and methods; Sect. 4 shows the preliminary results; Sect. 5 sets the agenda for future works and discusses limitations; while Sect. 6 concludes.

2   Related Work

Percolation theory has been previously used as a network-centrality measure – i.e., for determining the degree of influence of a node within a given network –, as well as for investigating the effects of a node disappearance on the overall network structure (e.g., [10]). In network science, such a percolation phenomenon can be investigated through link-prediction methods (e.g., [9]). By accounting for network structures and other available variables, link-prediction methods extract metrics accounting for the likelihood of edges (dis)appearances through time (e.g., [9]). In this respect, Kim et al. used link prediction to forecast technology convergence [4]. Additionally, Benchettara et al. [1] adapted link-prediction

---

[1] The 2020 Global Supply Chain Cyberattack is believed to have resulted through a supply chain attack targeting the IT infrastructure company SolarWinds, which counts many critical infrastructures among its clients. In order to fight against this type of attack, our framework may offer the possibility to identify less-secure elements in the supply chain.

metrics for bipartite networks. Moreover, Silva et al. [11] and Tylenda et al. [13] explored time dependant metrics to use with time series within link-prediction analysis. Finally, supervised learning has been applied to link-prediction investigations: Mohammad et al. [1] applied supervised learning to a co-authoring network for several classification algorithms.

However, to the best of our knowledge, link prediction as a method for assessing the dynamics of the cybersecurity technological landscape has not been explored yet. At least, we found no work focusing on predicting the survivability of entities composing the cybersecurity technological landscape. In this work, we present a network-analytics framework that employs link prediction and supervised learning to build a survivability score of entities composing the cybersecurity technological landscape.

3   Data and Methods

3.1   Data

We use the data collected by the TMM platform (ca. 1 TB) to create a bipartite network composed of technologies and companies of the Swiss cybersecurity technological landscape.[2] The TMM platform is an information system developed by armasuisse Science and Technology (S+T). TMM aims to exploit big data and open-source information in an automated way for intelligence purposes. The TMM system crawls and aggregates information from different online resources as patent offices (*Patentsview*), commercial registers (*Zefix*) and websites (*Wikipedia* and *Indeed*) to obtain a list of companies, patents and job openings based in Switzerland. By using the companies list, patents and job openings data, we link companies to technology, creating a bipartite network (2'996 nodes). We use predefined keywords of cybersecurity related technologies to compute word similarity with TMM technologies and select the most relevant. We verify the obtained list afterwards to delete any irrelevant technology and thus we obtain 69 keywords[3] from TMM. Data, available from March 2018 to December 2020 (34 time-series entries), are crawled from these platforms at different rates, and aggregated monthly. In the obtained graphs, we observe that the companies with most links are well established and long-lived tech companies like IBM but we can find all sorts of companies like the Swiss Post, Novartis and Ikea.

3.2   Methods

We define a network $G = (V, E)$, wherein V is any finite set called the vertex set and $E \subseteq V \times V$, called the edge set, corresponds to relation between elements of V. Let $x, y \in V$, such as:

- the neighborhood of x is $\Gamma(x) = \{y \in V \, s.t. \, (x, y) \in E\}$;

---

[2] https://tmm.dslab.ch//home.
[3] keyword list: https://tinyurl.com/jswtsmmn.

- the degree of x is $\delta_x = |\Gamma(x)|$;
- there is a path between x and y if there exists $(x_0, x_1, ..., x_n)$ such that $x_0 = x$ $x_n = y$ and $(x_i, x_{i+1}) \in E \ \forall \ 0 \leq i \leq n - 1$;
- a graph G is said to be bipartite if there exists $A, B \subset V$ such that if $(x, y) \in E$ then x and y are not in the same subset A, B.

In traditional link prediction, one computes the metrics for each possible edge in a frozen network. Then, if the metric is higher than a given threshold, the edge will appear in the next step. In our case, we compute specific metrics – listed below from ((1) to (3)) – for all graphs in the time series, except for the last entry. We use time series ARIMA modelling on each metrics to predict them for the final entry and use the last graph as a validation set to compute performance metrics presented here under.

As a next step, we apply a supervised learning framework in order to obtain the best results from the metrics computed. We use a Support Vector Machine (SVM) classifier that classifies each edge to a label 0 or 1, representing the existence or not of that edge in the network. This classifier needs feature for each edge to make a decision, so we use the three similarity metrics described here under as features [11]. We train the classifier on all but the last graph and obtain test performance on it.

Since the networks are sparse, the classification problem is highly imbalanced and thus we use the area under the receiver operating characteristic curve (AUC) as the main performance metric, which is widely used in link prediction frameworks [9]. We select and evaluate eight potential metrics from prior literature and adapt the best three ones to build the predictions:

(1) *Preferential Attachment Index* [9]: The mechanism of preferential attachment has been used to generate evolving scale-free networks, where the probability of a new link forming from x is proportional to δ_x. The corresponding similarity index can be defined as:

$$s_{xy}^{PA} = \delta_x \cdot \delta_y. \tag{1}$$

(2) *Katz Index* [9]: It is a global index based on the ensemble of all paths. It sums the number of paths of a given length between x and y multiplied by a damping coefficient. The mathematical expression reads:

$$s_{xy}^{Katz} = \sum_{l=1}^{\infty} \beta^l \cdot (A^l)_{xy}. \tag{2}$$

Wherein A is the adjacency matrix of the network and β is a free parameter that damps the influence of long paths.

(3) *Hyperbolic Sine Index* [6]: The exponential of the adjacency matrix is used as a metric in unipartite link prediction, but as we work with a bipartite graph, we can take the odd part of the exponential, which is the hyperbolic sine. It can be derived by the following sum:

$$S^{sinh} = sinh(\alpha A) = \sum_{i=0}^{\infty} \frac{\alpha^{1+2i}}{(1+2i)!} A^{1+2i}. \tag{3}$$

4   Preliminary Results

We apply the methodology and algorithms presented above and obtain the receiver operating characteristic curve (ROC) and AUC diagnostics in Fig. 1. As we can see the SVM highly improves the AUC of the link prediction by approximately 4% compared to the best unsupervised method. *Preferential Attachment Index* is worse than a random classifier which could be explained by the fact that link appearance probability in our graphs is poorly related to nodes degrees. Companies may prefer investing in emerging technology which are not linked to many entities, because they may seek exclusivity in the race for technological edge.

The AUC obtained for the top 3 methods assures the validity of our metrics as a building block for a survivability index. This would help decision-makers, involved in CI's security, to identify emerging technology and companies. Future algorithms optimization presented in Sect. 5 should increase performances and thus the validity of the survivability index.

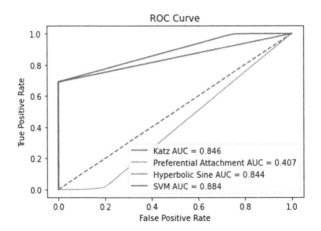

Fig. 1. ROC curves and AUC values for the 4 algorithms considered. Hyperbolic sine and Katz Index ROC curves are indistinguishable from one another. For those index β and α were set to 0.05. The dotted line represents the performance of a random classifier.

5   Further Steps

The next steps are to fine-tune the hyperparameters of our models and apply cross-validation to obtain a more robust performance measure. We want to explore other forecasting methods to have a wider view on the effect it has on performance. We will explore new features like the number of patents or job openings liking a company to a technology. Finally, we will use the best model to compute a survivability index for each entity in the network.

6   Conclusion

To the best of our knowledge, our framework is the first investigation that mimics the creative-destruction and the survival mechanisms of innovations within the cybersecurity technological landscape. By modelling percolation dynamics through link prediction, we path the way for further research aiming to compute a survivability score of different entities (i.e., technologies and companies) represented by nodes of a network (i.e., the graph representation of the Swiss cybersecurity technological landscape). We suggest that our framework is useful for decision-makers involved in the security of critical infrastructures, as a survivability score of entities can be extracted by either using the similarity metrics or probability calculations from the supervised learning method.

References

1. Benchettara, N., Kanawati, R., Rouveirol, C.: Supervised machine learning applied to link prediction in bipartite social networks. In: 2010 International Conference on Advances in Social Networks Analysis and Mining (2010)
2. Fleming, T.C., Qualkenbush, E.L., Chapa, A.M.: The Secret war against the United States: the top threat to national security and the American dream cyber and asymmetrical hybrid warfare an urgent call to action. Cyber Defense Rev. **2**(3) (2017)
3. Jang-Jaccard, J., Nepal, S.: A survey of emerging threats in cybersecurity. J. Comput. Syst. Sci. **80**(5) (2014)
4. Kim, J., Kim, S., Lee, C.: Anticipating technological convergence: link prediction using Wikipedia hyperlinks. Technovation **79**, 25–34 (2019)
5. Keupp, M.M.: Militärökonomie. Springer, Wiesbaden (2019). https://doi.org/10.1007/978-3-658-06147-0
6. Kunegis, J., De Luca, E.W., Albayrak, S.: The link prediction problem in bipartite networks. In: Hüllermeier, E., Kruse, R., Hoffmann, F. (eds.) IPMU 2010. LNCS (LNAI), vol. 6178, pp. 380–389. Springer, Heidelberg (2010). https://doi.org/10.1007/978-3-642-14049-5_39
7. Laube, S., Böhme, R.: Strategic aspects of cyber risk information sharing. ACM Comput. Surv. **50**(5), 1–36 (2017)
8. Lundstrom, M.: Applied physics: enhanced: Moore's law forever? Science **299**(5604), 210–211 (2003)
9. Lü, L., Zhou, T.: Link prediction in complex networks: a survey. Physica A Stat. Mech. Appl. **390**(6), 1150–1170 (2011)
10. Piraveenan, M., Prokopenko, M., Hossain, L.: Percolation centrality: quantifying graph-theoretic impact of nodes during percolation in networks. PLOS One **8**(1), e53095 (2013)
11. da Silva Soares, P.R., Prudêncio, R.B.C.: Time series based link prediction. In: The 2012 International Joint Conference on Neural Networks (IJCNN) (2012)
12. Qamar, S., Anwar, Z., Rahman, M.A., Al-Shaer, E., Chu, B.T.: Data-driven analytics for cyber-threat intelligence and information sharing. Comput. Secur. **67**, 35–58 (2017)
13. Tylenda, T., Angelova, R., Bedathur, S.: Towards time-aware link prediction in evolving social networks. In: Proceedings of the 3rd Workshop on Social Network Mining and Analysis. Association for Computing Machinery (2009)

Author Index

Printed in the United States
by Baker & Taylor Publisher Services